BLACK BRITISH
LITERATURE

BLACK BRITISH LITERATURE
Novels of Transformation

MARK STEIN

THE OHIO STATE UNIVERSITY PRESS • COLUMBUS

Copyright © 2004 by The Ohio State University
All rights reserved.

Library of Congress Cataloging-in-Publication Data
Stein, Mark, 1966–
    Black British literature : novels of transformation / Mark Stein.
        p. cm.
    Includes bibliographical references and index.
    ISBN 0-8142-0984-X (cloth : alk. paper) — ISBN 0-8142-5133-1 (pbk. : alk. paper) — ISBN 0-8142-9058-2 (cd-rom)
1. English fiction—Minority authors—History and criticism. 2. English fiction—Black authors—History and criticism. 3. Minorities—Great Britain—Intellectual life. 4. Blacks—Great Britain—Intellectual life. 5. Postcolonialism—Great Britain. 6. Postcolonialism in literature. 7. Ethnic groups in literature. 8. Minorities in literature. 9. Blacks in literature. I. Title.
    PR120.M55S74 2004
    823'.9109920693—dc22
                      2004011415

Cover and text design by Jennifer Shoffey Forsythe.
Type set in Adobe Palatino.

Contents

	ACKNOWLEDGMENTS	ix
	INTRODUCTION	xi

Part One

1. Black British Literature, Post-colonial Studies, and the Bildungsroman — 3
2. Performative Functions of the Black British Novel of Transformation — 36

Part Two

3. Crossing a Notion—The (Im)possibility of Returning — 57
4. Of Aunties and Elephants—Kureishi's Aesthetics of Postethnicity — 108
5. Amorphous Connections—Post-colonial Intertextuality — 143

CONCLUSION	170
NOTES ON WRITERS	185
FURTHER READING	199
NOTES	201
BIBLIOGRAPHY	217
INDEX	237

All that entire ideology of separation and exclusion and difference etc.—the task is to fight it.
 —(SAID 1992, 242)

What is interesting is always interconnection, not the primacy of this over that, which has never any meaning.
 —(FOUCAULT 1999, 141)

In a time when your 'belonging,' who you *really* are, is judged by the colour of your skin, the shape of your nose, the texture of your hair, the curve of your body—your perceived genetic and physical presence; to be black (not white), female and 'over here,' in Scotland, England or Wales, is to disrupt all the safe closed categories of what it means to be British: that is to be white and British.
 —(MIRZA 1997, 3)

Acknowledgments

As if to bear out the tenet of this study, the field of black British literature has been transformed enormously over the last ten years or so, while this book was in the making. And for myself, too, this has been a formative process. During this time I've been supported, challenged, and encouraged by more colleagues and friends than I can acknowledge here.

This book originated in a doctoral thesis which I completed at Johann Wolfgang Goethe Universität in 2000. My first thanks go to Dieter Riemenschneider (Frankfurt) and to Lyn Innes (Canterbury) for whose crucial and sympathetic ongoing support I am most grateful.

Draft sections of my work have been presented at Frankfurt's Postcolonial Studies AG and I'm indebted to many extended and heated debates we had in this forum: my thanks go especially to Frank Schulze-Engler, and to Gesa Mackenthun, Markus Heide, Mita Banerjee, Christine Matzke, Katja Sarkowsky, Bernhard Klein, Susanne Mühleisen, Susanne Opfermann and Angie Koeth. Similary, Lyn Innes's colloquium at UKC and the combined intellectual rigor of Furrukh Khan, Michelle Keown, Paul Delaney, Maggie Awadalla, and Rana Dayoub was an important stimulant and resource. Yet ultimately I can date back my interest in Black British literature to a seminar by Marlies Glaser-Tucker, many years ago; and to the support and encouragement at Warwick University by David Dabydeen, Benita Parry and Rolf Lass.

My first steps into the academy were taken at conferences by the Association for the Study of the New Literatures in English and here I would like to thank in particular Liselotte Glage and Norbert Platz as well as Peter Stummer and Gordon Collier. Much of this book has been presented at academic conferences and I'm indebted for their encouragement and for invitations to Barbara Korte, Klaus-Peter Müller, Wolfgang Klooss, Monika Reif-Hülser, Klaus Hofmann, Gerhard Stilz, Bénédicte Ledent, Geoff Davies, Peter Drexler, Jürgen Kramer, Graham Huggan, and Joan Anim-Adoo. I have also drawn on materials published earlier (Stein 1995, 1996, 1998a, 1998b, 2000a, 2000b, 2001, 2002) and I'm grateful to *Acolit*, C. Winter, G. Narr, *Journal for the Study of British Culture*, *Kunapipi*, *Matatu*, and WVT for granting permission. I'm also grateful to the London Transport Museum for granting permission to reproduce the images by Ernest Dinkel and Christopher Corr.

Over the years, Caroline Rooney, Abdulrazak Gurnah, Louis James, and Bart Moore-Gilbert have been supportive of my work. I am also thankful to Susheila Nasta for being helpful during my stay at QMW, University of London, and also in the years that followed, and for reading parts of the manuscript at a crucial moment. To the late Anna Rutherford I am obliged for her attentive reading. My time at the University of the West Indies (UWI Mona) was most fruitful and enjoyable; I much appreciate the support of Eddie Baugh, Mervyn Morris, Nadi Edwards and Maureen Warner-Lewis. At UWI St. Augustine I enjoyed the support of Kenneth Ramchand, Gordon Rohrlehr, Funso Aiyejina, and Sharon Kowlessar—their help and their interest are much appreciated. The Kurt-Tucholsky-Stiftung, the Graduiertenförderung des Landes Hessen and the German Academic Exchange Service (DAAD) have enabled many of my travails and travels.

The committed and efficient staff of Ohio State University Press have been, without exception, a pleasure to work with, and I admire in particular the expertise and energy of Heather Lee Miller. Ohio State University Press's perspicacious and careful external readers have helped to make this a better book. I appreciate the ongoing support of my new colleagues at Potsdam University; and thanks for the careful assistance go to Brian David Aja and, especially for compiling the notes to authors, to Nilüfer Caglayan.

I'm much indebted to Tobias Döring's careful and constructive reading of several parts of this book at various stages. With Susanne Reichl, too, I have been in an ongoing exchange over several years from which I have profited much. Likewise Markus Heide, Karin Kilb, and Christian Schmitt-Kilb are not only good friends, they have also carefully read earlier versions of these chapters and helped me significantly. For their intellectual stimulation and friendship my thanks also go to Sabine Bröck, Sukhdev Sandhu and Tony Ilonah. Throughout, my parents have been sympathetic and supportive. To Yomi I owe a large intellectual debt and she has borne with me through several transformations. I dedicate this book to my parents and to Yomi.

Introduction

> This has been the century of strangers, brown, yellow and white. This has been the century of the great immigrant experiment. It is only this late in the day that you can walk into a playground and find Isaac Leung by the fish pond, Danny Rahman in the football cage, Quang O'Rourke bouncing a basketball, and Irie Jones humming a tune. Children with first and last names on a direct collision course. Names that secrete within them mass exodus, cramped boats and planes, cold arrivals, medical checks. . . . Yet, despite all the mixing up, despite the fact that we have finally slipped into each other's lives with reasonable comfort (like a man retuning to his lover's bed after a midnight walk), despite all this, it is still hard to admit that there is no one more English than the Indian, no one more Indian than the English. There are still young white men who are *angry* about that; who will roll out at closing time into the poorly lit streets with a kitchen knife wrapped in a tight fist.
> —(SMITH 2000, 281–82; ORIGINAL EMPHASIS)

Zadie Smith's novel *White Teeth*, which was widely hailed as the first black British novel of the new millennium, looks back to the twentieth century. It contends, following *The Tempest*, that "What is past is prologue" and takes an interest in how history is used and misused, how it can affect young people growing up, and how they deal with the desire to know their history and to be unfettered from it. With compelling lightness, *White Teeth* unfolds the stories of three British families across several generations and links them to India, Bangladesh, the Caribbean, and via the Second World War to Bulgaria and Italy. Though the affluent Chalfens are a well-established family and represent the white middle classes, Marcus Chalfen is himself part of the Jewish diaspora and his son is described as "a cross-pollination between a lapsed-Catholic horticulturalist feminist, and an intellectual Jew!" (Smith 2000, 267). His family's immigration to Britain took place earlier than that of the British Jamaican Joneses and the Bangladeshi Iqbals who stand at the center of *White Teeth*. All three families inhabit and make up a London of social and cultural admixture and ongoing change. They are *creating* a space in which "brown, yellow and white" are strangers alike, where conflicting first and last names reflect a jumble of history, culture, and religion. *White Teeth* celebrates a metropolis in which all are strangers and yet all can be at home, a world where different heritages can be juggled within the same neighborhood, within the same household, and within the same person. The novel helps us imagine a world where "Indian" and "English" do not refer back to an essentialized identity, but where, in fact, there is "no one more English than the Indian, no one more Indian than the English." Such cultural hybridity does not come without its tensions, tensions which energize *White Teeth* (and cultural production more generally), but which also stimulate racist violence, as the excerpt acknowledges. *White Teeth*, however, believes not only in the possibility of change, it also possesses a Utopian quality that suggests the multicultural clock cannot be turned back.[1]

Many of the book's concerns can be drawn from the paragraph quoted. The construction of a place to call home; access to and release from a history that is one's own merely in part; effects of migration and displacement onto subsequent generations; the combination of different aesthetic traditions and the interdependence of distinct cultural territories; the vexed issue of identity (personal, cultural, ethnic, national identity); phenomena of intermixture and cultural hybridity; cultural difference and the notorious problem of racism; the processes of cultural change, of creating new spaces, of transformation—these are all issues raised by the texts discussed in this book.

Black British literature (which is as multifarious as the cast of *White Teeth*) not only deals with the situation of those who came from former colonies and their descendants, but also with the society which they discovered and continue to shape—and with those societies left behind. This writing is related to Britain in many ways while being concurrently endowed with perspectives that are not manifest in all of Britain's literatures. Thus Hanif Kureishi's protagonist Karim Amir, on the opening page of *The Buddha of Suburbia* (1990), describes himself as "an Englishman born and bred, almost." Laconically tagging on "almost" emphasizes the condition of an ambivalent cultural attachment. It reveals the status of the *insider* who simultaneously knows the perspective of an *outsider*.

The Buddha of Suburbia depicts Karim's formation and can therefore be read as a novel of formation. Yet the text is not only about Karim growing up but also about the transformation of his environment. Capitalizing on its ambivalent cultural attachment, what I term the *novel of transformation* portrays *and* purveys the transformation, the reformation, the repeated "coming of age" of British cultures under the influence of "outsiders within." Like *The Buddha of Suburbia* and *White Teeth*, a large section of black British literature describes and entails subject formation under the influence of political, social, educational, familial, and other forces and thus resembles the *bildungsroman*. These novels of transformation, set in Britain, constitute the main textual basis for this study.

The selected texts work with and rework the prominent genre of the bildungsroman. Starting with earlier black British writers who anticipated (Olaudah Equiano) or were influenced by (Sam Selvon, Kamala Markandaya, and V. S. Naipaul) the bildungsroman-genre, the study proceeds to focus on the black British novel of transformation of the late twentieth century. It is argued that the novel of transformation is a dominant form in black British literature. By investigating crucial moments within black British literature, the study charts a genealogy of the literature of transformation which not only describes its protagonists' formation but also exerts textual agency and reveals the transformative potential held by the protagonists.

The black British novel of transformation, it is argued here, is about the *formation* of its protagonists—but, importantly, it is also about the *transformation* of British society and cultural institutions. At the center of this book, then, stands the examination of such transformative potentials inscribed in and induced by black British texts. It has been my aim to develop a framework for theorizing the field of black British fiction by engaging with post-colonial theory and black cultural studies. This framework constitutes an approach to a highly popular field of cultural production. Working with a mixture of well-established and emergent writers, the book provides a way of relating these texts not only to each other but also to ongoing debates in a society that seeks to come to terms with its increased cultural diversity.

Historically speaking, Britain has long been subject to such processes of cultural transformation, induced not only by immigration but also by being annexed as well as by having annexed foreign territory. Britain, therefore, cannot be considered an autochthonous society of *True-Born Englishmen*. But since the middle of the twentieth century, when Britain recruited workers from the Caribbean Isles and granted British citizenship to the inhabitants of its colonies and former colonies, the texture of British society has increasingly changed, a process to which migration from the former colonies on the Indian subcontinent, in Africa, and elsewhere has also contributed.[2] Britain has experienced major transformations during the second half of the twentieth century, among them the collapse of Empire, large-scale immigration from former colonies, and multiculturalism. Processes of cultural transformation are thus not new phenomena in Britain, but they have been more marked since the 1940s.

This chapter of recent British history is related to black British literature. The texts nurtured by this situation are marked by a degree of heterogeneity that almost resists definition. They are texts by male and female writers with African, South Asian, Indo-Caribbean, and African Caribbean backgrounds (backgrounds which could be further subdivided); writers who belong to different generations and social classes; and who are (or were) located in different geographical regions of Britain. This body of texts consists of different genres such as the novel, poetry, drama, film script, and essay; texts which are written in different varieties of English, varieties born out of the interaction between distinct linguistic communities in Britain and abroad.

Supported by a wide readership, this corpus of black British literature has grown remarkably since the middle of the twentieth century, and especially over the last two decades. It has been anthologized (e.g., Newland and Sesay, Procter, C. Phillips), put out on film and television (e.g., Syal, Kureishi, Zadie Smith) and as talking books (e.g., Rushdie, Kureishi, Syal). It has also been encouraged by existing awards (e.g., the Booker Prize) and new ones, such as the Saga Prize and the Caine Prize for African Fiction. Many black British writers have not only gained national as well as international recognition; some, like V. S. Naipaul, Salman Rushdie, and Caryl Phillips, have indeed received the highest honors and achieved a preeminent standing.[3]

Given the scope of the literature in question, this study will have to limit the ground it covers. While the bibliographer Prahbu Guptara argues that "it may be helpful to remember that books written by black Britons go back at least as far as the eighteenth century" (1986, 17), I will not focus very much on these early black British texts. Inquiring whether there exists an uninterrupted history of black British texts from its beginnings until today is a different project altogether, one which Lyn Innes has recently undertaken in her book *A History of Black and Asian Writing in Britain, 1700–2000*. My study concentrates upon novels published since 1985, considering other genres and earlier texts only occasionally.[4] And it focuses on texts whose outlook on Britain is multiply refracted and fractured, as embodied by *White Teeth* and *The Buddha of Suburbia*.

■ ■ ■

For a variety of reasons, terms such as *post-colonial literature*[5] or *black British literature* are often considered problematic. The heterogeneity of texts so labeled seems to defy the logic of these categories, which also applies to designations such as *English literature* or *British literature*. This raises the question whether a group of texts indeed has to be homogenous in order to be considered "a group of texts"—whether English, British, or black British. The question of categorization is always a political one, especially when we consider categories such as English Literature. The political implications of inclusion and exclusion remain. Grouping texts together as black texts, or as women's writing, or as post-colonial or gay, are acts in history, because such interventions condition the significance and the meaning that texts attain in any given reading.

Aiming to systematize black British novels *across* a range of cultures and ethnicities, the body of selected texts is marked by a high degree of heterogeneity. One important issue is therefore the concept of black British literature itself; it is historicized and developed further because it enables the comparative approach required here. This is not uncontroversial as there are those who would prefer to separate black and Asian British writers according to cultural or ethnic provenance. Yet Diran Adebayo recently remarked that his writing has been enabled by both Hanif Kureishi and Nick Hornby; and it is precisely such affiliative gestures and intertextual connections *across* cultural and ethnic enclosures which remain concealed unless a range of authors and texts is studied within a comparative framework. The call for differentiating "black" in the phrase *black British literature* sounds ever louder. (The second constituent, "British," is under scrutiny less.) Nevertheless, it continues to be used in its narrow definition as well as in the wider sense employed here.[6]

Syncretism, ambivalence, mimicry, hybridity, and other paradigms put forth by post-colonial theory rest on the assumption that the intense interactions between British culture on the one hand and indigenous and post-colonial cultures on the other are negotiated outside the metropolis. But with respect to the location of its "contact zone" (Pratt 1992, 6–7), black Britain is distinct from other post-colonial cultures: It lays claim to post-colonial and to British cultures *in Britain,* creating in the process "a new kind of space at the centre" (Hall 1987, 44). Therefore this book aims to change the way in which we conceptualize black British literature.

By relating black British literature to the bildungsroman-genre and by suggesting links to other post-colonial literatures, this study crosses disciplinary boundaries. But this literature is not only *related* to other post-colonial literatures—some of it may in fact intersect with these other bodies of literatures.[7] At the same time, black British literature is related to British literature. It may even be thought to transform British writing into being "post-colonial" in its entirety, making it a *new* New Literature in English, despite the misgivings of someone like A. S. Byatt. In her controversial introduction to the recent *Oxford Book of English Short Stories*, Byatt defends her editorial policy of including only "writers with pure English national credentials," a policy which invariably *excludes* black and Asian British writers (Byatt, xv). Chapter 1 addresses these questions of intersection and exclusion further.

■ ■ ■

Each of the five chapters is built around a debate and introduces a range of texts which bear upon this debate. There is a development from engaging with a wider selection of texts in the first part of the book to dealing with fewer texts in more detail in the second part. The first part of this book comprises two chapters. Chapter 1, "Black British Literature, Post-colonial Studies, and the Bildungsroman," starts with Paul Gilroy's concept of the Black Atlantic which connects Africa, the Americas, and Europe. Black British literature appears to be located on the European side of this structure, yet it has connections with other cultural territories, across the Black Atlantic and beyond. Some sociopolitical, historical, and cultural background to the study is provided when touching upon the early black presence in the British Isles, and a particular focus is given to the postwar writers and their descendants. The term *black British literature* is discussed with reference to its rival terms before the central concept of this study, the black British *novel of transformation*, is introduced.

Chapter 2, "Performative Functions of the Black British Novel of Transformation," argues that these texts are characterized by performative functions and that they reach beyond the text. The process of "coming of age" traditionally associated with the novel of formation is here understood in a double sense. On the thematic level, novels of formation depict the process of growing up. On other levels, a *performative function* can be ascribed to these fictions in that they are not only inscribed by the cultures they inhabit: the texts in turn mold these very cultures. Two distinct types of performative functions are differentiated here: the construction of new subject positions which in their inception become more readily available or conceivable to protagonists and, arguably, to readers. Secondly, we can speak of the novelistic transformation of Britain which is accomplished through the redefinition of Britishness, the modification of the image of Britain. The novel of transformation not only portrays changing Britain but, crucially, it is also partly responsible for bringing about change. This is accomplished by the symbolic transgression of space, by depicting racist phenomena, by redressing the iconography of Britain, and by the exertion of cultural power.

The second part of this book comprises three chapters. Chapter 3, "Crossing a Notion—The (Im)possibility of Returning," investigates the concepts of diaspora and generation in dealing with the theme of returning. While the bildungsroman is traditionally about generational conflict and social differentiations, in the *diasporic* novel of transformation generational conflict often signifies a concurrent *cultural* conflict between a parental generation who migrated and the generation born in Britain. The chapter concludes by making observations on authors' relationships to generation and diaspora.

Chapter 4, "Of Aunties and Elephants—Kureishi's Aesthetics of Postethnicity," reads several of Hanif Kureishi's novels and one of his films as postethnic literature. Kureishi's first two novels are taken as examples of self-consciously post-colonial novels of formation that parody the post-colonial and ironize ethnicity. In his third novel, *Intimacy*, however, both ethnicity and the novel of formation are seemingly bypassed. *Intimacy* attempts to go beyond colonial cultural and oedipal anxiety. The strategy of postethnicity is also in evidence in the film *London Kills Me*, a strategy which works towards stalling what Sara Suleri calls the "otherness machine."

Chapter 5, "Amorphous Connections—Post-colonial Intertextuality," reads David Dabydeen's novel *The Intended*. Sepulchred in a library, the narrator has fulfilled his ambition of becoming a writer by the time the novel closes. However, interred in the "heart of whiteness" he has, simultaneously, almost forsaken his "dark self" (Dabydeen 1991a, 196). Paradoxically, his intertextual narrative confines him to textuality while it releases him by permitting self-expression. The narrator self-consciously inquires what it may mean to write a "post-colonial" narrative and the novel plays with the expectations of post-colonial criticism.

The conclusion suggests that the construction of a voice is a central element of the black British novel of transformation, a voice permitting expression, negotiation, and transformation. Returning to Zadie Smith (and her enormous success), the book closes with a comment on the modes of marketing black British fiction, modes that have so radically changed in recent years. This transformation signals not only the present popularity of black British fiction, it also bespeaks the marginalization of texts (and entire genres) that do not stand at the hub of the hype.

PART ONE

1

Black British Literature, Post-colonial Studies, and the Bildungsroman

Paul Gilroy's concept of the Black Atlantic in theory connects Africa, the Americas, Europe, and the Jewish diaspora. According to him,

> the contemporary black English, like the Anglo-Africans of earlier generations and perhaps, like all blacks in the West, stand between (at least) two great cultural assemblages, both of which have mutated through the course of the modern world that formed them and assumed new configurations . . . —black and white.
>
> (Gilroy 1993b, 1)

This positioning of black people in the West amid a divergent relationship entails Gilroy's premise that striving "to be both European and black requires some specific forms of double consciousness" (1993b, 1). However, in the face of racism, nationalism, and ethnic absolutism, "occupying the space between" is a provocative and also dangerous practice (1993b, 1). Nevertheless, Gilroy is convinced of "the inescapable hybridity and intermixture of ideas" (1993b, xi), and hence defines the Black Atlantic as the space of "the stereophonic, bilingual, or bifocal cultural form" (1993b, 3). His work seeks to critique cultural nationalism, "ethnic absolutism," and "overintegrated conceptions of culture" (1993b, 2), and lodges against these positions "the theorisation of creolisation, métissage, mestizaje, and hybridity" (1993b, 2). The black British novel of transformation is poised correspondingly and it is marked by the connections with other cultural territories to which some of Gilroy's work points, a situation which is relevant to this study and which will be explored in this chapter.

I. FROM THAT DAY TO THIS: BRITAIN'S BLACK SETTLERS AFTER 1950—CONTINUITIES AND NEW BEGINNINGS

"From that day to this, there has been a continuous black presence in Britain," Peter Fryer argues in *Staying Power* (1984, 12); he notes that there "were Africans in Britain before the English came here. They were soldiers in the Roman imperial army that occupied the southern part of our island for three and a half centuries" (1984, 1).[1] Moreover, from the middle of the sixteenth century onward, and particularly in the following two centuries (in the course of British expansionism and the so-called triangular trade), Africans were captured, enslaved, and transported across the Atlantic to the Americas. But millions of Africans were not only transported to the New World; some Africans and their descendants reached Europe and the literary testimonies to this are well known. For example, Ukawsaw Gronniosaw (1770), Ignatius Sancho (1782), and Olaudah Equiano (1789) in the eighteenth century, and the autobiographies of Mary Prince (1831) and Mary Seacole (1857) in the nineteenth century.[2]

What these narratives have in common with those texts under scrutiny in the main part of this study is that the authors record both a confrontation between their protagonists and Britain, its institutions, its people, and some of the strategies that were employed in this situation. These early examples of black British literature share with the literature written after the arrival of the SS *Empire Windrush* in 1948 (discussed below) the experience that their authors were born elsewhere and migrated to Britain.[3] The "*Windrush* generation" includes those who migrated from the West Indies to Britain, such as V. S. Naipaul, Sam Selvon, Beryl Gilroy, Wilson Harris, and George Lamming; at about the same time authors from Asia and Africa like Kamala Markandaya, Attia Hosain, Wole Soyinka, H. S. Bhabra (who publishes as A. M. Kabal), Ambalavaner Sivanandan, and later, in 1962, Buchi Emecheta arrived.[4]

After World War II Britain was in need of workers; this facilitated immigration from its colonial possessions, and starting in the 1960s, Britain actively recruited labor in the West Indies for the National Health Service, London Transport, and factories in the North. In the wake of the *Windrush*, which carried Jamaican, Guyanese, and Trinidadian migrants, half a million migrants arrived in Britain.[5] Although the arrival of the *Windrush* is crucial in that it marks the start of large-scale postwar migration, there had obviously been an influx of migrants in the years before then. Abdulrazak Gurnah's novel *Dottie* (1990) is a highly successful example of the complex telling of such a story. The Sierra Leonean-born Ernest Marke came to Britain in 1917 as a stowaway and has recorded his experiences in his autobiography *In Troubled Waters: Memoirs of Seventy Years in England!* (1975).[6]

During World War II—before the independence of Britain's West Indian colonies—there had been West Indian soldiers in the British army. But with the end of the war, and the influx of larger numbers of migrants, these migrants became less and less welcome—despite their British passports, and despite their record of fighting for Britain. This population movement was initially viewed as a "Return to the Mother Country" by migrants and British people alike. Soon this changed, however, as xenophobic responses were matched by the passing of increasingly restrictive immigration laws, to the point where immigration for black Commonwealth citizens has become nearly impossible. As the recently published oral history of this period, *Windrush: The Irresistible Rise of Multi-Racial Britain* indicates, the "Windrushers" were asked time and again: "When are you going back to your own country?"[7]

The literature from this period of postwar reconstruction and interracial hostility is distinct from the later writings of the so-called second generation (i.e., authors who started writing in the 1970s and 1980s, a period also marked by racial hostility), and also from writers of the third generation who started writing in the 1990s. It is the texts of the second and third generation which I will focus upon in this book. However, the term *generation* needs to be problematized; like the term *literary history*, it suggests neat separations and an idea of organic growth which does not accurately describe the literary texts in question. Between the passing of the Nationality Act in 1948 (which created a composite UK citizenship for UK and colonial citizens) and the Immigration Act of 1971 (which virtually ended all primary immigration), *more* than one generation arrived. And the new arrivals, while mostly in their twenties and thirties, did indeed vary in age.[8]

This section contrasts various generations of black British writers and thereby draws out important aspects of black British literary history. What constitutes a generation of black British writers? Do they share a similar age, i.e., birth within the same decade or two decades? Or is it instead their arrival in Britain that constitutes a birth (or rebirth) of sorts, forging a generation comprising *different* age groups?[9] In other words, is C. L. R. James (born in 1901, arrival in Britain in 1932) of the same generation as Ernest Marke (born in 1902, arrival in Britain in 1917) and Jean Rhys (born in 1890, arrival in Britain 1907), whose *Voyage in the Dark* (1934) is of relevance here? If they are of the same generation, what does this mean? Is Beryl Gilroy (b. 1942) of the same generation as the ten-years-older V. S. Naipaul (b. 1932) because they arrived in Britain around the same time (1951 and 1950, respectively)? Many writers born in the 1920s arrived in the 1950s and thus could be seen as one generation on both counts. But some came later, or were younger, or came later *and* were younger. Or some came earlier and were older, such as Sudhindra Nath Ghose, who lived in Britain from 1940 to 1957 but was born in 1899.

I'm problematizing the term *generation* because writers and texts cannot be readily taxonomized according to their age or the date of the authors' (or their parents' or grandparents') arrival in their country of residence. The point being made here is that it does indeed impact on a text whether its author is a migrant writer, passing through Britain, or staying there, or whether she was in fact born there, or whether the family has been in residence there for several generations. It is also true that a writer can often be seen as a "product" of her times and hence age makes a difference too. Yet with migrant writers particularly, these two points, arrival and age, do not correspond in the same way for all writers. The writer may be a "product" of her times—but she may have, metaphorically, brought her times with her, and may be partly out of synchrony with those around her as a result.

At the same time, the *Windrush* writers worked in very specific contexts and it is these writers who have often either returned to the West Indies (as George Lamming) or moved on (as the late Sam Selvon).[10] The term *generation* suggests an organic connection between the literature of different writers who may or may not stand in a *relationship of entailment*. The concept of the generation implies grouping certain writers as one (one body of texts, one generation), and a group of younger writers is also fused in this way; a generation can thereby be said to be "othered," while the concept concurrently suggests that one generation brings forth the next. A second generation, however, is not only influenced by the preceding one, but also by the political climate *they* are born into, and by the cultures they inherit from various sources.[11]

There exists an *affiliative* relationship between David Dabydeen and V. S. Naipaul, two writers with Asian Caribbean connections, which emphasizes the degree of *choice* in such affinities.[12] In *The World, the Text, and the Critic*, the late Edward Said (1983) differentiates between filial relationships and affiliative ones in order to stress the worldliness of texts and their relationships to each other: "To recreate the affiliative network is therefore to make visible, to give materiality back to, the strands holding the text to society, author, and culture" (Said 1983, 175). The young black British writer Joanna Traynor, author of *Sister Josephine* (1997) and *Divine* (1998), for example, seems more influenced by Jeanette Winterson, Virginia Woolf, and Margaret Atwood than positioning of her in a filial, generational framework restricted only to black British writers would allow.

Without entirely denying the usefulness of differentiation according to distinct generations, I am not convinced that the *linearity* it implies is helpful. Intertextual relations are not easily expressed in family terms. Lest I be misunderstood, it would be incautious not to take onboard the references, influences, and continuities which do exist between writers when perceived in a generational framework. However, this system of cultural kinship is not sufficient to situate the novels of interest here: "It ain't where you're from, it's where you're at," as Paul Gilroy concludes in *Small Acts* (1993a, 120), quoting the rap band Gang Starr.

■ ■ ■

The post-*Windrush* novelists on which this study is focused, who did not migrate to Britain as adults but arrived as young persons or were indeed born in Britain, find themselves in a particular situation. Their attachment to Britain is not only symbolized by the British passport they often hold; their birthplace is Britain, or at least much of their youth was spent there. British culture was therefore of greater import during their formative years.

The homelands left behind by their parents are less "available" to this group of writers. Most importantly, there are no direct memories, excepting those of journeys to these countries. The parents' homeland may be present through the parents' accounts and memories; these places may be visited, and these places may in fact be represented within Britain in neighborhoods, venues, cultural products, through teachers, political initiatives, and the like. But the connection with such an "origin" can be quite tenuous. Yet the attachment to Britain may also not be unbroken—hence Karim Amir's "almost."

II. USES OF THE TERM *BLACK BRITISH LITERATURE* AND ITS RIVAL TERMS

While all three parts—black, British, and literature—deserve interrogation, I will focus on the first two, black and British, that produce so fruitful a tension. This tension is a reciprocal one in that "blackness" redefines "Britishness" and "Britishness" redefines "blackness." In his notorious "Rivers of Blood" speech of April 1968, Enoch Powell voiced his opinion that while black immigrants might receive or have British citizenship they would never "truly" become British, let alone English.[13] It is the tension, then, between the two adjectives *black* and *British*—which contests Powell's exclusivist view—that is useful for our purposes.

But is Hanif Kureishi, for example, a "black" writer, and if so, what does this mean? In the British context, the adjective still frequently refers to a rather wider group than in the American context. According to the concept of *political* color, "black" refers to "people of color," people with an African, African Caribbean, or South Asian background. But the inclusion of South Asian writers under this heading is contested. In his bibliography of black British literature, Prahbu Guptara offered a straightforward definition in 1986:

> Being 'black' is a matter of visibility, with social and political consequences. . . . In my view, therefore, 'black Britons' are those people of non-European origin who are now, or were in the past, entitled to hold a British passport and displayed a substantial commitment to Britain. . . .
>
> (Guptara 1986, 14)

A somewhat more discriminating definition was proposed a year later by David Dabydeen and Nana Wilson-Tagoe (1987, 10): "'Black British' literature refers to that created and published in Britain, largely for a British audience, by black writers either born in Britain or who have spent a major portion of their lives in Britain." The authors go on to ask: "But what of the term 'black'? Does black denote colour of skin or quality of mind? If the former, what does skin colour have to do with the act of literary creation? If the latter, what is 'black' about black? And what are the literary forms peculiar to 'black' expression, what are the aesthetic structures that differentiate that expression from 'white' expression?" (1987, 10). The question of the character of the relationship between "blackness" and cultural production is raised here, and unease with an essentialist definition of "blackness" and "black literature" is palpable. Moreover, by stressing the *aesthetic* quality of texts, the authors insist on categorizing texts according to textual properties rather than by authors.

The term *black British literature* is accountable, then, in two ways: what holds the writing together, what are the shared features on the one hand, and what is it surrounded by, what is nonidentical with it, where does this body of writing stand in relation to other bodies of writing?

Differentiations of this sort are not uncontested; it is vital to consider, however, that differentiations need not be absolute. Categories always leak. Grouping "black" texts together, and defining what is meant by "black texts," is possible if it is conceded that the same texts could be grouped differently, according to distinct parameters such as gender or genre, theme or style. Grouping texts together as black texts, or women's writing, as post-colonial, or gay, is an act in history—an intervention—that conditions the significance and the meaning that texts will attain in a reading. It is therefore necessary to make unacknowledged categorizations explicit and to critically engage with them.

"What Is 'Black' about Black?"

In 1988 Alastair Niven presented a paper entitled "Black British Writing: The Struggle for Recognition" making his case that writing "produced in Britain by writers of non-European immigrant origin or descent, is being under-recognised both internationally and at home" (Niven 1990, 326). Like the above-mentioned commentators, Niven uses *black British* in its overarching sense. It is ironic that today—with black British writing eminently successful and indeed central to British cultural production—the terms of its reception still remain largely undefined. Today much more work on black British writing has been done, yet the field still requires more specific approaches which take into consideration on which terms black British literature exists.

Whereas the so-called New Literatures in English were initially considered part of English literature (e.g., the English language literatures from Australia, New Zealand, and Canada which originated in the last century), those literatures in English which developed in Africa, the Caribbean, Asia, and in the Pacific were categorized regionally or nationally (Riemenschneider 1983). Apart from studies of subnational groups (e.g., Maori writing), supernational regions (e.g., East-African writing, anglophone Caribbean writing), or superregional (Post-colonial literature or Black Women's writing), and comparative studies, there is research on individual (groups of) authors for which the questions of national, regional, and cultural contexts are obviously of import as well.

Into this context black British literature does not fit too neatly: it does not exclusively pertain to one geographical region or its own nation space. In that black British literature overlaps with British literature, it cannot easily be compared to the post-colonial literature of another state. Moreover, in contradistinction to the relationship between Maori and Pakeha literature of New Zealand, for example, in Britain there are widely distinct groups which make up black British literature, groups that hail from all over the globe.

In a sense, however, black British literature *does* have its own space, its own nation, even if it is an imaginary space, and, to echo Derek Walcott's Shabine, an "imagi-nation."[14] This is not a slight to the field: it is only through the imagination that the multilayered connections to numerous traditions of writing, to numerous cultures, to numerous histories, to numerous nation-states across the continents can be conceived and abstracted. Black British literature derives from its own *space*, yet this space is not homogenous in terms of time or culture or location, it is an imagined experiential field of overlapping territories.

■ ■ ■

An important debate between Fred D'Aguiar and David Dabydeen takes us further into the problematization of the term *black British literature*. A paper presented by Dabydeen at the same conference at which Niven spoke in 1988 caused the novelist and poet D'Aguiar to write a rejoinder. Dabydeen had asserted that he feels sufficiently different for him "to want to contemplate that which is other in [him], that which owes its life to particular rituals of ancestry" (1989b, 134). Dabydeen here speaks of *rituals* of ancestry, i.e., connections that are forged through practice. They are thus neither essentialist (and thus beyond control), nor are they purely constructed (and thus arbitrary): "blackness" is then something in between these two extremes for Dabydeen. He accuses positions like D'Aguiar's of aspiring to universalism and stresses that he himself is unwilling to drop the epithet "black" in order to be considered a writer (Dabydeen 1989b, 134).

In this debate D'Aguiar argues "there is no Black British literature, there is only literature with its usual variants of class, sex, race, time and place" (1989, 106). The term is criticized for falsely suggesting homogeneity in that it may trigger the assumption that all black British literature be similar rather than variegated. D'Aguiar adds that a text "by a black author in Britain is no more black than a similar product by a white author is white" (1989, 106). To this one could respond that a black British text is no *less* black than a text by a white writer is white. The experiences of authors and their structural position do influence their texts, whether the authors be black or white. It would be fallacious, however, to assume that the experience of a white person in a predominantly white society be strictly analogous to that of a person of a minority background within the same society. It would be equally fallacious to conclude that the experiences of people with a minority background do not differ widely.[15] Therefore, D'Aguiar's argument would seem to underestimate structural inequalities which impact on "black" and "white" writing and its reception.

Arguably the experience of exclusion and deracination constitutes links between writers of distinct backgrounds. The term *black British* does *not* signify a *homogenous* social group that shares a common ethnic, cultural, regional, or national background. It can rather be understood as a collective term as the cultural critic Stuart Hall argues in "New Ethnicities" (1988).[16] Although the designation *black British* refers to a heterogeneous group, the members of this group, according to Hall, share the experiences of marginalization, experiences which induce a process of "diasporization." Not only the sense "dispersal" is called to the fore here, but also quite the opposite, a process of consolidation in view of the threat or the experience of dispersal. Thus the social position as an immigrant or a descendant of an immigrant entails commonalities without purveying cultural or ethnic homogeneity.[17]

This position is in opposition to that of Fred D'Aguiar, who elaborates his point of view as follows:

> Colour as a main indicator has come about by racism and the response to it.
>
> It seems an anathema to give blackness special status in the imagination when the basis for its stress is racially motivated . . . creativity is not confined to experience alone. . . . Blackness, at the level of the vexed and overrated question of identity, must be evaluated independently of assaults from racists.
>
> (D'Aguiar 1989, 110)

D'Aguiar here makes clear that it is possible to speak of black experience(s) and black language(s) in Britain which corresponds to Dabydeen's notion of rituals of ancestry. He rightly points out that this is so partly in view of an underlying racism, in view of social differentiation and discrimination between people on the grounds of phenotypical differences. These discriminations amount to partly distinct experiences that are related to phenotype and hence shape people partly according to phenotype. The underlying complex processes, however, do not lead to singular, homogenous results; they don't amount to *one* black experience but a plurality of experiences. Nevertheless, it is possible to mark out particular features and themes of ethnic minority discourse (JanMohamed and Lloyd 1987; Lloyd 1994), and hence label texts as "black texts." This attribute is thus not derived directly (and ludicrously) from authorial phenotypes; it is rather an indirect derivation, via the notion of experience in a particular context.

But D'Aguiar's point is that what he calls a "black experience" comes about in a racist or at least a racialist society; for him, labeling texts as "black" is a response to a racist society. In this (dialectical) sense, he argues, labeling texts as "black" (or, by extension, black British) is embroiled in racism or racialism and its effects.

Societies in which phenotype is of no relevance are conceivable; speaking of black texts or white texts would not make sense in such a society. However, if we are to group texts, to compare texts, whether as novels or dramas, whether as women's literature or men's literature, or whether as black or white texts, there is no escape from being enmeshed in ongoing debates, in being imbricated in social practices (such as racism, sexism, ageism, and the like).[18] But *imbrication* is not the same as a *perpetuation* of social practices; rather, the critic is, like the author, the reader, or the publisher, inescapably imbricated. This does of course not bar him or her from attempting to critically engage social practices and discourses.

New Ethnicities

The term *black British* is older than my references to Niven, D'Aguiar, and Dabydeen would suggest. It was deployed by the Caribbean Artists Movement in the late 1960s, a movement which, in the words of its chronicler Anne Walmsley, "bridged the transformation of Britain's West Indian Community from one of exiles and immigrants to black British" (Walmsley 1992, xviii). At its inception, then, *black British* was used in an overarching sense, referring to distinct groups of West Indian migrants from Trinidad, Jamaica, Guyana, and Barbados, etc., with distinct backgrounds. It thus included African Guyanese, Indo-Guyanese, and Sino-Guyanese people, for example. Later the concept was used to include migrant groups from other parts of the world.

The term *black* was coined, Stuart Hall has noted, "as a way of referencing the common experience of racism and marginalisation in

Britain." Hall tries to account for the shift in the terminology, its widened scope, by speaking of two phases. In the first phase the concept implies, politically speaking, that "'the Black experience,' as a singular and unifying framework . . . became 'hegemonic' over other ethnic/racial identities" (Hall 1988, 27). It is this assumed hegemony of "the Black experience" (in the narrower sense) which poses a significant threat to the feasibility of an overarching concept of a "black British identity."

This first phase of black British cultural politics has seen an ongoing shift toward "engag[ing] rather than suppress[ing] difference" (Hall 1988, 29). These two phases account for the process of contesting and dissolving the hegemonic ethnicity of "Englishness" by its confrontation with an ideally unified black British counter-ethnicity *giving way to the construction of new ethnic identities.* This process involves "the splitting of the notion of ethnicity between, on the one hand, the dominant notion which connects it to nation and 'race' and on the other hand what I think is the beginning of a positive conception of the ethnicity of the margins, of the periphery" (Hall 1988, 29). Explaining what he terms the second phase, Hall here suggests an understanding of ethnicity that is not tied to nation, "race" (or culturalism, one might add), but to a positive understanding of the margin as a space of productive negotiation, productive of centeredness, and of cultural, social, and political change. To counter Englishness these pluralist spaces feed on their diversity (instead of a self-inflicted homogeneity) and it is from this that they derive their energy. What Hall refers to as the "politics of ethnicity predic[a]ted on difference and diversity" (1988, 29) is a move toward *strengthening* the political concept of black British identities in the plural, precisely by *weakening* its boundaries, by making it a more pluralist concept.

What is at issue here too is the question *which* of the new British groups come into representation and gain corresponding recognition through the category *black British*.[19] This seems to be foremost a political question, one that cannot be addressed primarily in terms of literary artifacts. If the term *black British* implies only the experience of people with a Caribbean or, more narrowly still, an African Caribbean background, it will rightly be considered hegemonic by those groups with a dissimilar background. If, however, heterogeneity and difference become recognized features of black British identities, more of the different groups' experiences can be considered part of a variegated black British experience.

Coming to Terms

Ashwani Sharma and others recently argued that in "the 1990s, it has become protocol to distinguish 'black' (that is, African Caribbean) and 'Asian' groupings in Britain" (Sharma et al. 1996, 11). I take this quotation as emblematic of a moment in British cultures where alliances between distinct black British groups have become more difficult and where diversity is emphasized, partly in the light of emphases on Sikh and Islamic identities. If the term *black British literature* rests on a political understanding of "blackness," the concept of political color, then questioning the possibility of alliances also entails having to rethink the category *black British literature*.

The citation stems from the study *Dis-Orienting Rhythms* which responds to a growing presence and commodification of "Asian" musical production in Britain such as bhangra, Southall beat, northern rock bhangra, and house bhangra. This increased visibility of a British Asian cultural presence is true for the arts generally. Think of the success of the sculptor Anish Kapoor's work; think not only of writers such as Salman Rushdie or Hanif Kureishi, but also Monica Ali, Hari Kunzru, or actress, novelist, and scriptwriter Meera Syal. Parminder Nagra, who played Jess Bhamra in Gurinder Chadha's film *Bend It Like Beckham* (2002), is well received on both sides of the Atlantic. There are not only the fields of fashion or food, but also TV productions and soaps such as *Goodness Gracious Me*, *The Kumars at No. 42*, or *Second Generation*. Although I am limiting my inquiry to the field of writing, the larger question of the politics of British Asian cultural production vis-à-vis the older and overarching denomination black British is at issue here.

In broad terms, the denomination *black British* has been used to forge political alliances between culturally distinct groups from Asia, Africa, and the Caribbean in order to stress commonalities faced in Britain, as was seen above. In its broadness and strategic inaccuracy the term has received criticism from the start. But it is not without scruples that the editors of *Dis-Orienting Rhythms* stress the need in the 1990s to distinguish between black British groups. The editors ultimately concede the "valency of 'Black' as a political positionality that strategically unites disparate groups against increasingly organized and vicious manifestations of Euro-racism" (Sharma et al. 1996, 7). What they refer to as the "autochthonous naming of an Asian identity that takes account of the cultural specificities" indeed constitutes a prerequisite for a remaking of political alliances (1996, 7); however, it may unfortunately also constitute an entryway into essentialist ethnic identity politics.

The collective category of black British literature is also undermined by the recently launched Saga Prize "for the best unpublished novel by a writer born in Great Britain or The Republic of Ireland having a black African ancestor."[20] Problematically, the prize bases entry into the competition on certain geographical and biological data which allow submission of a manuscript. The prize was founded by the actress and writer Marsha Hunt, who claimed that "[t]here is no black British fiction" and conceived of the prize as a remedy (Kellaway 1995, 6). However, the prize was under fire before being set up. Hunt explains: "The Commission for Racial Equality didn't want it to happen. They told me I might be subject to prosecution if I went ahead; the Society of Authors withdrew support" (Kellaway 1995, 6). The fact that Saga, a travel and insurance firm catering for the aged, sees a literary prize as a fit means of drawing attention to its business gives testimony to the wide interest now directed toward black British literature.[21] However, the exclusive conditions of the prize—barring, for example, people with an Asian or Asian Caribbean background—confirm once more the unsettled nature as to what constitutes black British literature.

The Asian Women Writers' Collective,[22] whose founders drew up precise boundaries as to who is eligible for group membership, is of interest in a discussion of the concept of black British literature. The group, which supported writers between 1984 and about 1997, was not only constructed around a gendered and cultural background; the collective opened itself up to writers beyond the South Asian diaspora "whose ancestry, part or whole, is from West Asia, South Asia and East Asia, spanning the regions from Turkey to Japan and the diasporas" (Ahmad and Gupta 1994, vii). While cooperation with black women's groups was welcome, black group members were not, it seems. The stated aim was "to explore our common identities as Asian women and as black women, but without making invisible the differences in our experiences and cultures" (Ahmad and Gupta 1994, vii). Here, subtly, the fear of being culturally erased if non-Asian women were to be included, is manifest. Unfortunately this fear entails an exclusive politics.[23] The implicit assumption that the cultural proximity between Turkish and Chinese women be necessarily greater than, for example, between women of African Caribbean and Asian Caribbean backgrounds would appear specious.

There is certainly room for these more specialized collectives of creative work and debate. Yet, following the politics of their logic of demarcation, one could aim for even more specific groups, for example, collectives of British-based Guyanese or Jamaican or Pakistani writers respectively, which in turn could be subdivided further into Indo-Guyanese, Sino-Guyanese, and African Guyanese groups. There are certainly reasons for such bonding in particular political and historical circumstances on the side of *production;* cultural practice needs its own space—and in some instances a protective space—in order to flourish. But practicability would seem to go against fundamental ethnic particularism as far as the *reception* of literature is concerned. The danger of writers being pigeonholed looms large, and it could be added that a divide and rule policy cannot be countered in this way.[24]

Most importantly, we cannot assume that writers from a particular place by default situate their writing in an aesthetic tradition that derives foremost from their own or their parents' or their grandparents' birthplaces. Ultimately we have to be wary of attempts at neatly categorizing writing according to one or two ready parameters. It may once have seemed less problematical to see Sam Selvon merely as a Caribbean, Buchi Emecheta as a West-African, and Salman Rushdie as an Indian writer—although seeing them as Trinidadian, Nigerian, and as Pakistani writers, respectively, would have then been equally possible. However, it is imperative to consider the *various* affiliations and connections that mark contemporary writing.

In *The Location of Culture,* Homi Bhabha has observed that the "very concepts of homogenous national cultures, the consensual or contiguous transmission of historical traditions, or 'organic' ethnic communities—*as the grounds of cultural comparativism*—are in a profound process of redefinition" (Bhabha 1994, 5). This is a reference to *transnational* interconnections, that is, correlations across nations and disjunctions within them, which throw into relief the notion of the homogeneity of national cultures and nation-states. Given these disjunctions within and correlations of national culture beyond the nation-state, its function as procuring (or stabilizing) homogeneity is weakened. The Swedish anthropologist Ulf Hannerz notes that "transnational connections are becoming increasingly varied and pervasive, with large or small implications for human life and culture" (Hannerz 1996, 4).[25] There is therefore a tendency toward viewing cultural production in international or transnational or transcultural terms.[26] John Thieme, for example, includes a section of "trans-cultural" writing alongside chapters of material organized by region in his *Anthology of Post-Colonial Literatures in English.* Some writers even appear in both the "regional" and "Trans-cultural" sections while Thieme concedes that the texts anthologized "are *all* ultimately trans-cultural" (Thieme 1996, 4).

Thieme's organization of his anthology indicates the diminishing import of culture conceived on *national* terms (which the prominence of terms such as *transnational* or *transcultural* seems to corroborate).[27] While this emphasis may at present still be more appropriate for film and music than for writing, it cannot be ignored that literature increasingly transcends national boundaries too, be it in themes,[28] production, reception, or the blending of aesthetic traditions.

Seen from a different angle, however, one could object that the label *black British literature* is too divisive—rather than too inclusive—in differentiating between different writers of Britain.[29] The argument put forth by my book is for a sufficiently wide conception of a body of writing, wide enough to accommodate a variety of black British literary forms, and to cut across the bounds of cultural identity, ethnicity, race, class, generation, and gender. The category *black British literature* does not tend to reify nationalist categorizations since the second adjective is kept in check by the first, and because of its references to cross-cultural and transnational cultural contexts. The writing, moreover, is not necessarily confined to one category, for I would argue for a model of plural alliances whereby, for example, Samuel Selvon can be and ought to be read in West Indian and Canadian, as well as black British, contexts.[30]

One of the values of the term *black British literature* lies precisely in its reference to Britain and Britishness and its implied proposition that these concepts are subject to redress. While the insistence on "black British-ness" was initially provocative in that it meant "we're here to stay," the term is now provocative in a different way: it is about redefining where one is staying, about claiming one's space, and about reshaping that space. The younger writers speak and write from a much more empowered position than the *Windrush* veterans. As novelist Andrea Levy put it: "If Englishness doesn't define me, then redefine Englishness."[31] There is not only a strong and clear element of rejection in Levy's statement—the rejection of a traditional, an exclusive, an unattainable Englishness—but also one of attachment, however tenuous and circumspect. Writers like Hanif Kureishi, Diran Adebayo, or Patience Agbabi have been brought up in Britain and their texts are British, but they are so in a specific way. It is this intricate attachment to Britain that is written out if we insist on categorizing texts according to authors' (or authors' parents') cultural origins.

The term *black British literature* does not necessarily claim to represent a singular experience. Rather, I use it as a collective term that covers an imagined experiential field of overlapping territories. While at its narrowest it merely refers to writers with an African Caribbean background, at its widest it can include writing that takes recourse to domains such as Africa, Asia, or the Caribbean, and attendant cultural and aesthetic traditions. Britain, then, is being constructed as a part of, say, the Caribbean, if and when a writer chooses to fashion such an alliance, and the text draws on these distinct cultural traditions, thereby forging a new imaginary space.[32] This new space denoted by the label *black British literature* is far from homogenous; on the contrary, its heterogeneity is one of its defining features.

Fusing Culture: *Some Kind of Black*

Following on from discussing the concept of the term *black British literature* and the complexities it contains, by discussing *Some Kind of Black* this section considers how these complexities are reflected in a literary text. While the text is not examined in detail, this section illustrates some of the methodological problems involved in reading black British writing. It then links up with a discussion of the novel of transformation. Diran Adebayo, born in 1968, has landed quite a success with his début *Some Kind of Black* (1996a): he was the first recipient of the Saga Prize in 1995 for his unpublished manuscript. A year later he was the first living man the major feminist publisher Virago knowingly published, to much acclaim. Since then he has published a second novel, *My Once Upon a Time* (2000). *Some Kind of Black* is about the black male student Dele, who graduates in law from Oxford and to maturity in the course of the text. He has to come to terms with the incidents surrounding a racist police attack on his sister Dapo, a sickle-cell sufferer, which leaves her in a coma for most of the story.

Dele describes himself as "a Londoner yet to set foot in his home country" and feels "nostalgia without memory" for the Nigeria he misses without ever having visited (Adebayo 1996a, 29, 169). At the same time, "Nigeria" is revealed to be an unstable signifier, as even in London we need to differentiate between "Nigerians resident off the Jubilee Line" and "Nigerians coming like Yardmen in Hackney" (Adebayo 1996a, 180).[33] What is significant is that the novel is solidly based in the south of England but this setting is described as constantly in flux. It is *this* context and its fluidity which frames the novel. Not unlike the hybrid dance music Sharma et al. discuss (above), Adebayo's London is marked by a welcome irreverence for ethnic and cultural purity and a delight in play and fusion.

The novel's protagonist, Dele, moves between Oxford and his hometown, London. In the different areas of his life he self-consciously performs several different rôles, thereby illustrating the concept of the performative character of identity. As a sickle-cell sufferer, a disorder which only affects people of African origin, his sister Dapo inserts into the text a reminder of the constructedness of identity and the limits of *performativity:* Dapo's illness is dependent on her genetic makeup. In growing up Dele not only negotiates the conservative expectations of his parents, who came to London in the 1960s and who constantly remind him of what life in Nigeria would have been like, but he is also pressured by streetwise friends in London into "acting Jamaican" and wearing "rudebwoy gear" (Adebayo 1996a, 47, 27). Dele thus bridges his parental Nigerian background with West Indian diasporic cultural forms, and thereby illustrates that this fusion is not as incongruous as it might seem.

It is in keeping with the novel's interest in divisions, and its concurrent dislike of absolutist identity politics, that Dele's London is fragmented according to a North-South divide, as well as along the lines of distinct diasporic communities: "Nowhere in London gave him that feeling of crossing a border the way Brixton did" (1996a, 131). These divisions are borne out by the linguistic varieties and vernaculars Dele employs, and by his self-conscious dress sense. He faces a "mini clothes-crisis" when inclined to don a patterned agbada (a Nigerian traditional dress) while feeling a strong desire to disassociate himself from the "cult-nats in similar attire" (Adebayo 1996a, 216). Dele does not want to rub shoulders with the cultural nationalists, and is wary of their desire for Africa, which to him is a mere nostalgic entity, a composite of "hoary myths of the integrity of strong African cultures" (1996a, 21).

The multiplicity of divisions described in *Some Kind of Black* disallows any clear identification with *one* locality, *one* identity, or *one* positionality. If anything, movement itself—between localities, identities, and positionalities—is characteristic of Dele. As he tells his sister Dapo: "'roots this' and 'roots that.' I am more worried about my branches, you know. It's the branches that bear fruit and tilt for the sky" (1996a, 9).

Some Kind of Black plays with the idea of spaces, such as the dance hall, where social divisions can apparently be temporarily suspended—yet the novel's tragic plot throws this very tenet into relief. As "the fusion of elements of south Asian culture and the rituals of the reggae dance hall" characterize much of modern Asian dance music, Dele inhabits spaces where "social collectivities [are] producing cultures of interbeing and mutual identification" (Back 1995–96, 133–34). These spaces can simply not be accounted for in terms like *African British literature, West Indian literature,* or *British Asian literature;* these spaces feed on the blending and, crucially, the *heterogeneity* suggested by the category *black British literature and culture*.

What is most pertinent here is the fact that the protagonist navigates not only from one social rôle to the next; he at once bridges gaps between different communities whether he is with "African-Africans"—who not without irony are tagged as "hyphenated"—whether he is "acting Jamaican" (Adebayo 1996a, 47), or whether he contemplates pleading to a policeman "of colour" when being attacked by the law. It is this navigation across a continuum of black British identities which calls for the novel's appropriate contextualization.

Perceiving the literature written by Britain's black and Asian writers predominantly in terms of the cultural spaces from which their authors "derive" is problematical in that these interpretative contexts point to spaces and attendant cultural practices that were left behind by the writers in question—if not already by their parents or grandparents. The connection, then, to these "origins" is not unbroken and has to be considered as *mediated*. This mediation, its processes and achievements, has been under scrutiny in a number of disciplines. Older (anthropological) models analyzing the contact of cultures, and assuming unilateral processes of integration, acculturation, or assimilation, have been surpassed with the realization of the complexity of the processes involved. The settlement of new social, political, and creative spaces that are distinct from both the points of departure and of destination, the settlement of a third space, is reflected in the theorizations of creolization, métissage, mestizaje, and hybridity (Gilroy 1993b, 2). Since there has been an increased awareness of Britain's ethnic diversity in the twentieth century, and a steady influx of black settlers into Britain, the existence of a body of writing (and film, music, and fine art) reflecting these changes deserves our particular attention. This body of literature not only tells the story of the proliferation and change of British cultures. Beyond the thematic level, these changes are reflected—and indeed brought about—by the very production, circulation, and reception of cultural artifacts, along with artifacts and practices not under consideration here. The texts about which I speak, then, *are* a significant part of a newly invigorated British culture.

III. THE BLACK BRITISH NOVEL OF TRANSFORMATION: PERPETUATION AND REFRACTION

> Contamination is the wrong word to use here, but some notion of literature and indeed all culture as hybrid (in Homi Bhabha's complex sense of that word)

> and encumbered, or entangled and overlapping with what used to be regarded as extraneous elements—this strikes me as *the* essential idea for the revolutionary realities today, in which the contests of the secular world so provocatively inform the texts we both read and write.
> —(SAID 1993, 384)

> It is the British, the white British, who have to learn that being British isn't what it was. Now it is a more complex thing, involving new elements. So there must be a fresh way of seeing Britain and the choices it faces: and a new way of being British after all this time.
> —(KUREISHI 1986, 38)

> Now that, in the postmodern age, you all feel so dispersed, I become centred. What I've thought of as dispersed and fragmented comes, paradoxically, to be *the* representative modern experience! This is 'coming home' with a vengeance! . . .
> I've been puzzled by the fact that young black people in London today are marginalized, fragmented, unenfranchised, disadvantaged and dispersed. And yet, they look as if they own the territory. Somehow, they too, in spite of everything, are centred, in place: without much material support, it's true, but nevertheless *they occupy a new kind of space at the centre*.
> —(HALL 1987, 44; SECOND ITALICS MINE)

All three quotations speak of a transformation of culture, and the latter two indicate the transformation of Britain specifically. The effects of what is often referred to as globalization on our understanding of culture, on the notion of Britishness, and on the question of black British identity are also thematized. Writing in *Culture and Imperialism,* Said's understanding of "all culture as hybrid" problematizes the notion of a *British* national culture and literature; Hanif Kureishi's claim to inclusion voiced in his essay "The Rainbow Sign" implies and demonstrates that cultures are constantly being made and remade, and therefore permit the insertion of new elements; Stuart Hall, addressing a conference on identity at the Institute of Contemporary Arts (ICA) in 1986, focuses on the "coming home" with a vengeance of young black Britishers who like himself find a new space at the center. It is this latter angle specifically, the newness and what brings about the change, that interests me here.

Angie Jacobs, Aladele alias Dele, Hari-Jan, Karim Amir, Shahid Hasan, Dottie Badoura Fatma Balfour, Angie, Meena Kumar, Hyacinth, and Pupatee—these are the names of the protagonists of recent black British novels.[34] It is no accident that these novels can all be read as novels of transformation. This mode describes and entails subject formation under the influence of social, educational, familial, and other forces. The black British novel of transformation, as I understand it, has a dual function: it is about the formation of its protagonists as well as the transformation of British society and cultural institutions.

The black British novel of transformation commences with those writers born in Britain. In the texts by *Windrush* writers there is a peculiar romance with London, an attraction to the metropolis which is maybe best embodied in Selvon's short story "My Girl and the City" (1957); and romance, of course, brings with it a fair amount of volatility. The younger writers are more adamant as to where they belong, as the quotations by Hanif Kureishi (in the epigraph) and Andrea Levy (above) indicate. The post-*Windrush* writers pursue the project of their inscription into a literary tradition and of rewriting Britain, a project to which the novel of transformation is eminently suited.

Precursors: The Bildungsroman and Equiano's *Interesting Narrative*

> Bildungsroman . . . a kind of novel that follows the development of the hero or heroine from childhood or adolescence into adulthood, through a troubled quest for identity.
> —(BALDICK 1990, 24)

> The subject of [the bildungsroman] is the development of the protagonist's mind and character, in the passage from childhood through varied experiences—and often through a spiritual crisis—into maturity and the recognition of his or her identity and role in the world.
> —(ABRAMS 1993, 132)

> [The bildungsroman] describes the youthful development of the central character. . . . In the contemporary novel, the *bildungsroman* form has often been adopted by feminist writers, as a narrative of emancipation or growing consciousness.
> —(WYNNE-DAVIES 1995, 63)

The bildungsroman has a curious prominence in literary studies; to some a rather outmoded, almost dusty term, it is still at the center of many contemporary studies.[35] And one cannot help but be reminded of the genre when reading much contemporary literature. At the same time, it is not entirely settled what constitutes a bildungsroman. The above citations suggest it to be a novel of education for life through life, broadly speaking; its focus is an individual protagonist undergoing the process of character formation which takes him or her out of familial or educational institutions (and possibly society at large) and through a crisis, before, and this is crucial, a return to the fold. In the process, the complex relationships between individual and community are scrutinized, hardship and evil are laid bare and (often) overcome, and the individual heads for or assumes a recognized position. In view of this return, and despite its critical potential (i.e., despite its history of pointing to social inequalities), the genre is ultimately marked by a conservative bend.

If, however, as Abrams suggests, the bildungsroman depicts the "recognition" of the protagonist's "identity and role in the world," then this genre's performative potential is acknowledged, a position I will develop below. Wynn-Davies's definition of the bildungsroman as "a narrative of emancipation" concords with this understanding as well; her definition further suggests that the genre has been strategically "adopted" for a particular purpose by feminist writers and she thereby confirms one of the bildungsroman's makeovers in the course of its career.

However, the bildungsroman had for a long time been thought of as the novel of formation of a young, white man, and is sometimes traced back to Wieland's *Agathon* but more regularly to Goethe's *Wilhelm Meister's Apprenticeship*. Despite this late eighteenth-century ancestry, the bildungsroman is very much a nineteenth-century phenomenon, and in English literature it calls forth titles such as *Great Expectations, David Copperfield*, and also, with a female heroine, *Jane Eyre*. However, the actual term *bildungsroman* dates back only to the early twentieth century when popularized by Dilthey's *Experience and Poetry* (1906).[36] Hence Marc Redfield, in *Phantom Formations* (1996), speaks of the bildungsroman as a "pseudo genre" which can be proven to exist and not to exist at the same time. He concludes that the "*Bildungsroman* exemplifies the ideological construction of literature by criticism" (1996, vii).

Why bother with a genre that may not exist? Why speak of adaptations of this "phantom formation"[37] in black British literature? And why run the risk of inflicting yet another Eurocentric body of thought onto post-colonial texts? Such questions are not easily dealt with. As will be seen below, the novel of formation allows for formalizing a large number of black British novels; moreover, it will be argued, their ideological contents, their symbolic potential, their potential not only to portray but also to induce change or to bring about "newness" can be gauged when employing the concept of the novel of transformation.

When the definition of a genre like the novel of formation is under investigation, numerous questions are thrown up. When did the bildungsroman as a generic form come into existence? When will it or has it ceased to exist? What are its precursors? Moreover, what *is* a bildungsroman? What is the relationship between the bildungsroman and theorizations of the bildungsroman? What is the relationship between the bildungsroman, attendant theorizations, and concepts of *Bildung* (education)? Is the bildungsroman characterized by certain contents—the story of a young person growing up?[38] Could the bildungsroman instead be characterized by formal criteria: the auctorial or narrative intent not only to depict a process of education but also to educate the reader; an ironic distance between narrator and protagonist; a teleological structure? Or is the bildungsroman identified by a mixture of formal elements and contents? In which literatures is the bildungsroman to be found? Is it a phenomenon of German-language literature or can it be found in literatures written in other languages?[39]

Since all of the above questions have engaged scores of scholars over the last two centuries, I can only suggest a suitable understanding of the black British novel of transformation. W. Witte has warned that "[a]ny generalisation about the 'Bildungsroman' as a genre is apt to be bedevilled by the variant meanings of the word 'Bildung' in German" (Witte 1979, 91). Narrower definitions of the term *bildungsroman,* tied to a humanist concept of formation/education (*Bildung*) as current during Goethe's lifetime, prove problematical in that, then as today, not a single and homogenous understanding of *Bildung* was in circulation. Moreover, to limit the bildungsroman genre to particular ideological concepts of education is bound to exclude texts on ideological grounds.

In an influential definition Jerome Buckley opts for defining the bildungsroman via its contents:

> A child of some sensibility grows up in the country or in a provincial town, where he finds constraints, social and intellectual, placed upon the free imagination. His family, especially his father, proves doggedly hostile to his creative instincts or flights of fancy, antagonistic to his ambitions, and quite impervious to the new ideas he has gained from unprescribed reading. His first schooling, even if not totally inadequate, may be frustrating insofar as it may suggest options not available to him in his present setting. He therefore, sometimes at a quite early age, leaves the repressive atmosphere of home (and also the relative innocence), to make his way independently in the city (in the

English novels usually London). There his real 'education' begins, not only his preparation for a career but also—and often more importantly—his direct experience of urban life. . . . By the time he has decided, after painful soul-searching, the sort of accommodation to the modern world he can honestly make, he has left his adolescence behind and entered upon his maturity.

(Buckley 1974, 17–18)

The black British novel of transformation is not necessarily marked by the move from country to city and back which is suggested here. While David Dabydeen's *The Intended* features a protagonist who comes to London from the country, albeit from Guyana (see chapter 5), in Andrea Levy's third novel, *Fruit of the Lemon,* the protagonist, Faith, travels from the metropolis to Jamaica as part of her maturation (see chapter 3). However, although many black British novels take place within London, there is sometimes a movement from suburbia into the center. Although Meera Syal's *Anita and Me* is set in the provincial Tollington, and in the course of the novel Meena does not (yet) move on to the metropolis, her first romance occurs in the somewhat more metropolitan hospital (see chapter 2). Hanif Kureishi's *Buddha of Suburbia* comprises two parts, "In the Suburbs" and "In the City," a shift which can also be found in his second novel, *The Black Album* (see chapter 4). Buckley's notion of the protagonist making his or her journey can thus, with alterations, be found in the black British novel of transformation.

The family situation may again not correspond exactly to Buckley's scheme. The modern family does not necessarily have both a mother and a father, but there can also be an extended family which leads to different constellations.[40] Nevertheless, the conflict of generations is part and parcel of the novel of transformation, and it is of particular importance in that different generations correspond to different cultural and social affiliations; chapter 3 deals with this nexus.

Likewise alienation and relations to the larger society are often dealt with, through the protagonists' experiences in school, for example, or the way they feel (mis)represented in the media or by politicians. Many novels of transformation can also be charted as a quest for an outlook on life which accommodates the protagonists' own identity, and which is shaped by a struggle with the parental generations, and one's peers and society at large.

However, Buckley's set of criteria will not all at once be found in a single text. "No single novel," he himself concedes, "precisely follows this pattern" (1974, 18). But Buckley is adamant that "none that ignores more than two or three of its principal elements . . . answers the requirements of the Bildungsroman" (1974, 18).[41]

The criterion of certain narrative contents certainly conjoins a large amount of texts written in various languages; however, by themselves, contents do not allow differentiating the bildungsroman from the picaresque novel, the *testimonio*, or the autobiography. While many novels of formation—black British or otherwise—are autobiographical, autobiographies cannot be considered novels of formation by the same token.

Ideally, then, formal criteria would set off the novel of formation from other genres. Given the thematic concerns of the novel of formation, it is mostly constructed around one central character (although there is the dual bildungsroman also); while the central character is developing, his or her depiction is often marked by an ironic or distanced narration; the plot often approaches a happy ending, which in many cases is not achieved without some misgivings.

D. F. Mahoney has suggested that we should define *bildungsromane* not according to the story but via the "intended influence on the reader" (Mahoney in Jacobs and Krause 1989, 34). A related notion is the thesis that it is not a picaresque hero but the educated narrator who is at the narrative's center (Selbmann 1988, 36). *The Black Album* features a protagonist who develops from Picaro at the novel's opening to a more educated narrator at its close. Ultimately it may be useful to stress the openness of the term *bildungsroman*; this openness (which does not amount to vagueness) is the "condition of its hermeneutic applicability," according to one critic (Köhn in Selbmann 1988, 30).

Opinions differ as to whether the term *bildungsroman* should be used for texts other than German-language literatures. In practice, however, the term is widely used in various literatures; moreover, contemporary literatures are characterized by cross-fertilization rather than by confinement to national borders, which is why the term is used in the context of this study.

■ ■ ■

If the novel of formation is defined as the narrative of a white male, it is an inept tool for my purposes here. Ellen Morgan was among the first critics to discuss *female bildungsromane*. The ambiguity of the phrase *female bildungsroman* is noteworthy; it remains unclear whether these are texts about women, or written by women, written for women, or any combination of the above. Notably a structurally similar ambiguity marks the term *black British novel of transformation*. According to Ellen Morgan, the genre is "the most salient form for literature influenced by neo-feminism" (1972, 183). A few years later, in 1980, Margaret Butcher argued that the history of the "Commonwealth novel" is very much a history of female bildungsromane. This study argues that the novel of transformation is a central genre in black British literature. A question that follows from this is *how* the bildungsroman genre is used and in which ways the genre is changed in its appropriation by black British literature.

In a different area, comparing African Caribbean with African American novels of formation, the Jamaican scholar Geta LeSeur has done work on what she terms the "Black bildungsroman." LeSeur looks at novels which show the experiences of "growing up black" (1986, 3). To her, bildungsromane are "autobiographical novels of education, tracing the growth of the hero from childhood to adulthood" (1986, 4). With special emphasis on gender, her study looks at six African American and six African Caribbean writers in terms of the bildungsroman genre. LeSeur sees the "Black bildungsroman" as antagonistic, as a mode of protest. She argues:

> Within the canon of African American literature, the bildungsroman has no distinct prototype equivalent to that created by white European writers. . . . In early Black literature, the form had as its precursors early autobiographies like Olaudah Equiano's . . . (1789) and Frederick Douglass's . . . (1845).
>
> The term *Black bildungsroman* is being used here to suggest a difference between those stories written by white (that is, American or European) writers and those written by African, African American, and African West Indian writers.
>
> (LeSeur 1995, 18–19)

Here LeSeur apparently rejects European ancestors for the "Black bildungsroman" and insists that within African American literature this genre has no clear exemplar either. Her terminology serves to set off novels by black authors from those by white authors. But it seems contradictory to use the term *bildungsroman* (which insinuates some connection to European texts of that genre) when stressing two things, a fundamental difference between these texts, *and* the absence of shared pretexts. In the situation envisaged by LeSeur, overlappings with the European genre of the bildungsroman are mere accidents and a term other than *bildungsroman* would seem more appropriate.

Compared to the West Indian texts she considers, LeSeur observes that the African American bildungsroman is less determined by generic conventions of the bildungsroman, and that even the connections of early African American *bildungsromane* to the early black writers she mentions are loose. I agree with this estimation in that Equiano and Douglass's texts are mostly and aptly read under the rubric of slave narratives (although this is changing fast with the rise of Equiano Studies). But the texts by Wright (1945) and Brown (1965) are also autobiographies, and therefore only indirect precursors of the African American bildungsroman. The novels by Hughes (1930) and Brooks (1953) indeed constitute early twentieth-century examples of the genre. I would argue that a novel is foremost a work of fiction, although it may be autobiographical, while the slave narratives and autobiographies LeSeur mentions are mainly autobiographical narratives or *testimonios,* even if some of the contents are of a fictional nature and obey the rhetorical modes prescribed for such narratives at the time.

Equiano was an influential and articulate black Briton and also an eminent translator of "black identity into literary text" (Thomas 1999, 5). However, since Equiano's *Interesting Narrative* actually predates Goethe's *Wilhelm Meister,* which was moreover not translated into English by Carlyle until well into the nineteenth century, LeSeur's suggestion of Equiano's ancestorship of the bildungsroman is more far-reaching than she seems to acknowledge. If Equiano's *Interesting Narrative* was to be considered an early "Black bildungsroman," then the genealogy of the bildungsroman would have to be rewritten quite substantially, with Goethe's role being complemented by that of Equiano.

However, as I indicate above, in this reading the boundaries between autobiography/*testimonio* and bildungsroman are rendered all too blurred, and LeSeur herself does not want to follow through the implications of her own suggestion. As autobiographies, the early narratives she has in mind share the function of a "subject-writing-him-or-herself-into-existence" by way of the bildungsroman without, however, constituting a distinct bildungsroman as such. In his book, Equiano narrates his and his sister's West African childhood before they were snatched away and enslaved; his *Interesting Narrative* takes the reader from there all the way to his adult years. Hence also in terms of subject matter, the *Interesting Narrative* is comparable to the novel of formation; and with this genre it shares the picaresque element. Yet it cannot formally be considered a novel.

When developing a model for reading the black British novel of transformation it is, however, very tempting to claim Equiano, who can be counted as one of the early black British writers, as the founding father of the bildungsroman; yet it seems more appropriate to see in his narrative *one* of the formative influences on the novel of transformation—a forerunner and ancestor—rather than considering it the first instance of a black British novel of transformation.

Another ancestor figure is the early black British writer Sake Dean Mahomet (1794). Prahbu Guptara considers his two-volume *Travels of Dean Mahomet* the first instance of a writer of Indian origin publishing a book in English; however, the *Travels* were written and published in Cork, Ireland, albeit for a British audience, and the text is hence not part of my present considerations.

I see no harm in the assumption that the black British novel of transformation also has European ancestors; unlike LeSeur I fail to see the need for considering it wholly separate from the European tradition. In fact, Ignatius Sancho, Equiano, Mary Prince, and Mary Seacole, all of these early black British writers of the eighteenth and nineteenth centuries, were influenced in different ways by the books they read, by teachers, and by people they corresponded with, so that their texts are partly a product of their place of residence. This holds true for black British writers generally, and for the novel of transformation. Obviously European tradition was but one of many influences for the writers thus labeled.

The Novel of Transformation: Definition and Examples

The novel of transformation implies radical generational conflict; in many cases this is a conflict between a generation that migrated to Britain and one that was born there.[42] In *Some Kind of Black*, the central character, Dele, can lead neither his parents' life nor the one they have in mind for him; this is partly due to cultural differences between the two generations. At the same time, the path he is to take growing up is less clear than that of his white peers.[43] In contradistinction to them, growing away from his parents entails distancing himself from one of his cultural backgrounds as well. This is not an easy choice in the face of an inhospitable society. As is typical of the novel of transformation, Diran Adebayo's Dele has no predetermined route to choose but is required to chart his journey himself. This blending of what could vaguely be referred to as generational and cultural conflicts, then, also accounts for the state of flux, i.e., the transformations and cultural developments which are brought about by Dele charting his journey, and by others doing the same. As Dele finds out how to be "some kind of black," Britain is being reconfigured.

The feature of finding a voice and the relationship between the individual and a larger group is, in my view, the main distinction from the traditional bildungsroman, and can of course also be related to the *burden of representation*, about which I will say more below. This is not to say that the protagonist is by necessity silenced at the beginning of the novel. For example, in the case of Andrea Levy's first novel, *Every Light in the House Burnin'*, the central character Angela is quite articulate. This, however, has to be seen from within the context of the protagonist's parents, who are not. Having partly internalized the host society's notion that as Jamaican immigrants they should not really reside in Britain, they tried to "blend in" and remain silent (Levy 1994, 88). In opposition to that, Angela is *of* Britain and she is determined to stand the ground beneath her feet.

Apart from coming to terms with the protagonist's identity, the genre is about the *voicing* of this identity; the very voice becomes manifest through the novel. Thus the black British novel of transformation does not predominantly feature the privatist *formation* of an individual: instead, the text constitutes a symbolic act of carving out space, of creating a public sphere. The genre, therefore, is in the midst of the debates which surround "black representation," about which Kobena Mercer has said:

> Precisely on account of its semantic ambiguity, which turns on the tension between representation as a cultural or artistic practice of depiction, and representation as a political or legal process of delegation, this key phrase linked together two strategic axes of contestation: struggles for access to material resources (that is, funding), and debates over aesthetic paradigms and priorities (that is, film language).
>
> (Mercer 1994, 18)

Irrespective of whether it is appropriate to stress the epitaph *black* in the black British novel of transformation, or whether this constitutes an undue limitation to the readings of these texts, the genre is uniquely suitable for the process of the redefining of Britishness. For, through the process of subject formation, the bildungsroman negotiates the formation of its protagonist or protagonists within the social world that is encountered and shaped. While the individual, then, struggles with family, education, and the expectations of society at large, this struggle is significantly not without consequence for the cultures within which it takes place. Rather it is projected outward, beyond the text, as will be seen in the next chapter.

The Postwar Writers: Rite de Passage or Bildungsroman?

This section discusses postwar black British writing vis-à-vis the bildungsroman genre; the discussion leads up to the form of the novel of transformation. There are continuities and distinctions between the texts on which this book focuses and their precursors. The postwar writers (migrants from the Caribbean, India, Pakistan, and Bangladesh; African and Asian migrants from Africa; and migrants from other parts or former parts of the commonwealth) on the whole did not write novels of formation located in Britain. Moreover, to this day, Roy Heath, for example, has not written a novel set in Britain, and for V. S. Naipaul, too, novels set in Britain are a rarity.[44] Many of these writers did locate (some of) their stories in Britain, such as Sam Selvon, Beryl Gilroy, and E. R. Braithwaite. But, significantly, the novels of formation by writers who migrated after the war are mostly located elsewhere, e.g., in Barbados and Trinidad, respectively, for George Lamming's *In the Castle of My Skin* and C. L. R. James's *Minty Alley*. Into this pattern fit Sudhindra Nath Ghose's *And Gazelles Leaping* (1949) and the late Attia Hosain's *Sunlight on a Broken Column* (1961), which can both be considered novels of formation depicting childhood, adolescence, and adulthood in India.

Both Samuel Selvon, with *The Lonely Londoners,* and V. S. Naipaul, with *The Enigma of Arrival,* have written *rite de passage* novels which script the passage from empire to mother country. Again, Kamala Markandaya's *Nowhere Man* (1972) fits into this pattern, as does *A Triangular View* by Dilip Hiro (1969). Mahmood Mamdani, the South Asian writer who came to Britain from East Africa, can also be considered within this context, with his *From Citizen to Refugee* (1973).

Charting the growth of its central character, Moses Aloetta, from immigrant to settler, *The Lonely Londoners* by Samuel Selvon (1956) depicts a paradigmatic development. In his essay on Selvon's novel, Kenneth Ramchand shows that the narrating voice gradually "becomes a person" (Ramchand 1985, 11); the opening pages of the novel are characterized by a palpable difference between the narrator and the central character, but by the end of the novel "there is a significant identification" between the two (1985, 17). This development mirrors the development that Moses goes through in the course of Selvon's text: the process of "Moses's individuation, and his emergence as a thinking creature" (1985, 18).

Moses, who has come to London ten years before Galahad, recalls through the younger initiate his sense of romance with the metropolis, a feeling which he takes to have left behind: "Galahad say when the sweetness of summer get in him he say he would never leave the old Brit'n as long as he live and Moses sigh a long sigh like a man who live life and see nothing at all in it" (Selvon 1956, 109–10). Between Galahad and Moses, then, we see the ground that Moses has covered. Galahad is excited by toponyms like "Charing Cross" or "Piccadilly Circus": when he is near these places "he feel like a new man" (1956, 84). But Moses says offhandedly: "Ah, in you I see myself, how I was when I was new to London. All them places is like nothing to me now" (1956, 85). It is the development from feeling the magnetic attraction of the metropolis before it is reached to taking the metropolis for granted (without forsaking the attraction entirely, as is indicated by Moses' studied disillusionment as conveyed to Galahad). It is this development that is typical of many *Windrush* writers.

V. S. Naipaul's novel *The Enigma of Arrival*, published some thirty years after Selvon's *The Lonely Londoners*, can also be read as a *rite de passage* in various ways. It covers a greater distance (in terms of time), and is about a writer rather than the migrant workers portrayed by Selvon. Naipaul's autobiographical novel narrates the story of a young writer coming from Trinidad to England and tells how, in the process, he "arrives." The text features a narrator "on the move," staging a migratory, fluid identity. His journeying is representative of his quest for identity, which involves leaving his home(land) for England, and compels the protagonist to question the ground he inhabits and the very structures which reflect and symbolically house his identities. But his is an inquiry into "Englishness" as much as into his own identity, the two being connected. Rejecting the role of the "colonial subject," the "black man," and the "immigrant," while also resisting wholesale assimilation into white England, he comes to question the barriers drawn by and for English culture by questioning the boundaries and landmarks he encounters.

It is in keeping with the novel's conciliatory gesture that in Naipaul's narrator merge the disruption of the relationship of place and identity of the displaced "colonial subject" who has *chosen* migration (linking him also to those in forced exile), and that of the "citoyen metropolitain" who feels the force of globalization, new technologies, and the resulting "time-space-compression" to similar effects. This is despite the narrator's withdrawn lifestyle in the countryside; he also bounces between different parts of the world (Naipaul 1987, 309–11).

"But then gradually the failure, the withdrawal at the centre, began to show" (1987, 79): in the metropolitan center the narrator finds withdrawn individuals, patriots, narrow-mindedness, decay, and death. He encounters nervous illnesses and "madness." There is Alan, the suicidal writer, the landlord's accidia which "had turned him into a recluse" (1987, 53), and Ray's inexplicable tears that can only be stopped by psychopharmaca.

The Enigma of Arrival makes use of a narrator whose perception is inflected by his particular cultural and historical background. Coming to England, where he is confronted with an iconography of landscape and architecture, and an intellectual topography which are at once familiar and alien, his distinct sensibility allows him to perceive the post-Edenic landscape and architecture as an *inscenation,* a theatrical representation. Moreover, he perceives the people he encounters as inscenations, or rather as continuously inscenating themselves. His own identity, too, is construed in this manner. Naipaul's narrator regards picturesque English villages as "fraudulent" (1987, 49), the charming farmhouse as "artificial" (49), and he exposes his landlord's imperial grandeur and his very own idea of England as a "fantasy" (177 and 120).

In his efforts to map his position in the English context, Naipaul's narrator explores the countryside. He tries to retrieve the histories of people with whom he comes into contact and he also explores their external surroundings. The narrator finds the country curiously marked by "those oddly-placed rolled-up plastic sacks" (1987, 28), which Jack's father-in-law had placed, thereby creating "padded passing-places," over the barbed wire (1987, 27). The old man has thus left visible traces of his daily walk which counter a newer pattern etched on the land with barbed wire. As he encounters one "order" superimposed onto another, he realizes that a "whole life, a whole enduring personality, was expressed in that 'run'" (1987, 28). This kind of "mapping" mediates between imposing one's own marks and reading/utilizing those which others have left. While it has allowed the late father-in-law to inscribe himself onto the land, it also provides the narrator with a model for accommodating himself to his new environment. It can be argued, then, that the narrator's "arrival" is facilitated by a similar act of reading and inscription: "My own presence . . . another kind of change" (1987, 34). The narrator's arrival is achieved as he comes to self-consciously gauge the impact of his presence; he can see himself from the outside, as it were, while being concurrently inside, constituting the very change he perceives. It is in this respect that *The Enigma of Arrival* anticipates the novel of transformation as developed by younger writers.

The narrator-protagonist of David Dabydeen's novel of transformation *The Intended* fashions his self-conscious "arrival" in related acts of reading and inscription (as will be seen in chapter 5). Like Naipaul, Anita Desai's novel *Bye-Bye Blackbird* also leads up to the black British novel of transformation, for it charts an unforeseen development of the two protagonists, Adit and Dev, as they "exchange the garments of visitor and exile":

> It was Adit who had found himself a pleasant groove to fit into, with his English wife and the education that had . . . brought him up to love and understand England. Why, then, was it Adit who was leaving while he stayed on? . . . England's green and gold fingers had let go of Adit and clutched at Dev instead. . . . Walking out of Waterloo Station, he walked out of the diffidence and uncertainty of his old existence in London and into the groove already cut and warmed for him by Adit.
>
> (Desai 1985, 228–29)

As Adit loses his love for England, Dev warms to his friend's place in society and unexpectedly stays on. Adit has made his mark and leaves it up to Dev to be his successor. Again, an arrival is achieved, though it is counterbalanced by a departure. Again, an inscription is made, a groove is cut, and marks are thus reread and modified.

In summation, the self-consciousness acquired by Naipaul's narrator; the sense of romance that impelled Selvon's "Lonely Londoners," and enabled its development into a more realistic appraisal of the metropolis; the process of superimposition and inscription, seeing London, England, Britain with other eyes; speaking its toponyms in tongues; and, finally, transforming them: all of these characteristics mark the writing which leads up to the novel of transformation.

These three novels by Desai, Selvon, and Naipaul, although written at different times, all have in common the protagonist's journeys, and their sense of arrival in (and departure from) England. These journeys require their protagonists to find their place, to cut their groove, to superimpose their map. The texts by the younger writers, on which this study focuses, feature protagonists who also need to find their place in a Britain which is not theirs in any straightforward way. But they pick up from where Dev and Adit, Moses and Galahad, and Naipaul's unnamed narrator left off; when Karim Amir or Dele or Angela[45] chart their journey, they find footsteps in the snow which they follow—or pass over.

2

Performative Functions of the Black British Novel of Transformation

> [L]iterature unceasingly "produces" *subjects,* on display for everyone. So paradoxically using the same schema we can say: literature endlessly transforms (concrete) individuals into subjects and endows them with a quasi-real hallucinatory individuality.
> —(BALIBAR AND MACHEREY 1978, 10; ORIGINAL EMPHASIS)

I do not endorse Etienne Balibar and Pierre Macherey's heavy textualism; and it seems difficult to establish the impact of literary discourse on other discourses, on individuals, on individuality, and on subjectivity. Nevertheless, both the notion of a *performative function* and the concept of the black British novel of transformation ascribe agency to texts, but, significantly, this is done without denying the agency of subjects. The previous chapter concluded by arguing that the black British novel of transformation reaches out beyond the text, and labeled this characteristic a *performative function*. This means that the process of "coming of age," which is associated with the novel of formation, is here understood in a double sense. On the one hand, on the thematic level, novels of transformation depict the process of growing up. On the other hand, these fictions are not only inscribed by the cultures they inhabit, they in turn mold those very cultures.[1] Novels of transformation do not only deal with the protagonists' coming of age. They at once describe and purvey the transformation, the reformation, the repeated coming of age of British cultures under the influence of what I call "outsiders within."[2] This chapter is divided into two sections which outline two distinct types of performative functions.

I. THE CONSTRUCTION OF NEW SUBJECT POSITIONS

Meera Syal is a well-known actress, scriptwriter, and novelist. In her successful first novel, *Anita and Me,* Meena, the daughter of Indian immigrants to Britain, is the first local child in "a whole decade" (Syal 1996, 136), as it is put hyperbolically, to pass the Eleven-plus exam. This makes her the only pupil from the fictitious Midland village of Tollington allowed to go on to grammar school. In Meena's case, upward social mobility is facilitated through education. It is striking that this path is not open to any of Meena's white, working-class peers whose "elevation" would conform to a classic motif. Rather, Meena is singled out in the novel to take a path closed to her peers. This depiction of a social climber serves to illustrate a potential path for readers of the novel who choose to identify with Meena; I say *choose* to identify in order to suggest that such identification is possible for readers with an Asian background as well as for those of other ethnicities.

Along similar lines a mock-gothic streak of the novel is resolved. Toward the close of the text it becomes clear that the "Big House" is inhabited by a Punjabi man and his French wife, rather than the witch, whom Tollington lore had planted there, and who had made the mansion so mysterious to the local children. Referring to a stately home as the "Big House" is reminiscent of a time when a plantation owner might reside in such a building. But the term also denotes, in American slang, a jail. On one level, then, history seems to have come full circle in view of the present residents, assuming that the Big House may have been originally financed by African slave and South Asian indentured labor in the Caribbean. On another level, though, the present residents would seem to be locked up in their mansion as much as they are by a society which is biased against both French and Indians. Meena, therefore, is confused when she finally meets up with the landlord:

> He must have been the former mine owner, he must have owned a lot of something. . . . [I]n his shovel-sized hands he held the lead of a jumping spaniel. But all of this became secondary when he finally spoke. "Chup Kar Kure, Thahar Jao Ik Minut!"
>
> . . . My miracle was complete. The Big House boss was an Indian man, as Indian as my father, and he spoke Punjabi with a village twang to his dog. . . ."Namaste, chick," he said as he passed, patting me clumsily.
>
> (Syal 1996, 317)

A scene that shows off Syal's talent for comic drama has Meena shell-shocked. It is obvious Meena felt that ownership of large property, if not wealth in general, could only be associated with white Britons. The sudden recognition that this need not be so, as she sees someone resembling her father in a position of wealth, entails and suggests a host of future options for the protagonist. These possibilities become *conceivable* upon seeing someone with whom the protagonist can identify, someone who is in a position which had previously seemed out of reach. Crucially, such an expansion of scope arguably has repercussions *outside* the novel also, where more subject positions can become conceivable. This estimation rests upon the presupposition that the effect of the mine owner's speech on Meena is analogous to the effect of the novelistic discourse on its readership. By representing the unusual and the new, and by voicing the unheard, both entail a widening of scope and a furthering of subject positions.

■ ■ ■

Similar scenes can be cited from many novels of transformation. Diran Adebayo's *Some Kind of Black* was already referred to. This text is irreverent toward ethnic or cultural purity and is delightful with play, parody, and fusion of "disparate elements" (a gesture of refusal). The very notion of disparate elements is questioned by the programmatic blending which *Some Kind of Black* parades.

> Now Jonathan was about the only person around who had had anything like a similar background to Dele's own—West African descent, inner city (albeit Liverpool), elevated post-GCSEs to a state grammar school—and Dele was keen for them to get better acquainted. (Adebayo 1996a, 20)

The sociological accuracy of the narrator's observations ironizes Dele's concern with the parameters listed. The passage stresses the uniqueness of the protagonist, and acknowledges his difficulties of identification and role-modeling. But the law student does not restrict himself to finding people whose background is exactly equivalent. His incessant reinvention of himself demonstrates an independence from his background(s), or more precisely, it suggests the desire for such autonomy.

Dele is portrayed in manifold ways, is very adaptable, and seems to cope well with the diversity of people he regularly encounters in Oxford and London. Charting his path across a continuum of distinct identities, "acting Jamaican," offering what he calls the "romance of the real nigga," and meeting "renegade UK Africans," the protagonist contemplates whether to "drop the dress of his Queen's grammar and go for pure ragga blather? Or maybe go for the vulnerable, Woody Allen, mildly tortured tip?" (Adebayo 1996a, 47, 20, 13, 38–39). He self-consciously chooses a way of being almost in the way he dons different outfits when going out.

Despite (and to a point, because of) this assumption of a variety of identities and the resolute emphasis of self-conscious choice, the protagonist is not free from external ascriptions. The range of identities from which he chooses is limited in part by the options a race-conscious society permits; but Dele's conduct constantly questions and renegotiates the limitation of those options. The text reveals that the range of options open to Dele depend upon ethnicity, race, social station, geographic location, and so forth. Still, Dele realizes—given the police attack on him and his sister—that despite being an "Oxbridge man," his "mere papers counted for little" (Adebayo 1996a, 185). Toward the end of the didactic novel he concludes: "He couldn't square the circle. He had always been some kind of black" (1996a, 190). Dele is no cultural nationalist, but what the novel does show is that the protagonist needs to carve out specific spaces, such as at Oxford, in his relationships of love, and within his family. The novel of transformation is an apt genre for demonstrating these processes of carving out and claiming space, and of creating such spaces.

The text problematizes Dele's sense of unbelonging which becomes manifest in his constant geographical, interpersonal, and identity shifts. At a party Dele feels that hardly anyone present is "truly sorted," and that they are rather "unreconciled either to their families or to their role here" (1996a, 21). Two recurring and significant features, the relationship to the family and to Britain, are here noted in passing. The novel dramatizes how its protagonist tries to come to terms with his family, especially his father, and how to be at once black and British. Dele himself has an ambivalent relationship to Britain: "he wanted to fuck English history, like some horn of Africa" (1996a, 38), and marvels how "greys clad in Levis that their flat-jack backsides could not properly fill out" had been able to "build an empire?" (1996a, 22). On the one hand, Dele imagines his interaction with English history as a sexual encounter in which he is affiliated with Africa, which is reminiscent of Dabydeen's first novel (see chapter 5). In scoffing at the physiognomy of "greys," white Englishmen, and in aligning physiognomy with the ability to exert political control, Dele seeks to address and reverse constricting conceptions of black male physiognomy which are designed to circumscribe black men. The novel thus exemplifies an important thematic concern of black British literature, the protagonist coming to terms with being black in an often hostile and predominantly white society.

Yet Dele is not only victimized as a young black male, he in turn has a distinctly misogynistic way of treating white women, whom he distinguishes along a spectrum from "home-maker" to "butt-shaker," and from "easy European pickings" to "trashy 'Black Man Whore' types" (1996a, 50, 176, 141). In a tour de force, *Some Kind of Black* constructs a large number of behavioral patterns and identities. Many of these sketchy types are tainted by the adolescent narrator's often superficial perceptions. But it is significant that the text concurrently communicates its impatience with the sort of particularism (with respect to physiognomy, racial identity, and gender) evidenced by the above quotations. With reference to Dele's father, then, such a narrow mind-set is censured as a "simmering stew of comparative anthropology" (Adebayo 1996a, 88). Given the text's critique of restricted conceptions of identity and its display of Dele's ethnic charades, *Some Kind of Black* does not merely make subject positions conceivable: it also problematizes their enforced stability while it laments their fluidity. It is in this sense that the text exemplifies the importance of literature in the reflection and construction of subject positions within and without the text.

Syal's and Adebayo's text differ in many respects. Syal's rural 1960s setting contrasts with Adebayo's 1980s London; the protagonists also differ with respect to their ethnicity and age, and with Meena being at the onset of her secondary education while Dele finishes his university course when the novels close. Yet both come from very strict families, with parents expecting them to do well and to pay respect to the parental, minoritarian cultural background. Adebayo's text offers a more intricate site for the construction of a wide array of subject positions than Syal's novel provides. While the example of *Anita and Me* has shown how Meena's discovery adds to the scope of options she beholds, *Some Kind of Black* illustrates that despite carving out space and negotiating options, Dele's freedom is ultimately curtailed in ways that he can only partly control. But Meena also learns that in a white community her acceptance and her friendships remain circumscribed by the fact that she is a young woman with Asian origins. Coming upon these realizations at the end of their novels of transformation, both protagonists enter a more mature stage.

■ ■ ■

Dottie Balfour, the central character of Abdulrazak Gurnah's novel *Dottie*, is orphaned and has to take care of her younger sister and their brother. To further her own education—when she is not "wandering aimlessly among the shelves, sheltering from the desert winds" (Gurnah 1990, 60)—she regularly reads in the local library. Here she sees two black men and is particularly intrigued by one whom she considers "her true fantasy of a grandfather" (1990, 61). Dr. Murray, who is always seen reading newspapers, follows the Algerian struggle for independence (1954–62); this means nothing (yet) to Dottie. The novel, which is concerned with the history of black people in Britain, particularly in the twentieth century, shows Dottie reconstructing her own family history and becoming interested in black history. In the face of being left to fend for herself and without much knowledge of her parents and family, Murray can be seen as a catalyst for Dottie, triggering her interest in history.

While her mother tried to escape from her own family and the stories of ancestors, Dottie realizes toward the end of the novel that she needs these memories in order to make sense of her existence and in order to feel at home. Although she understands that her mother rejected the stories told to her because they tied her to her father whom she had sought to reject, Dottie regrets that her late mother did not provide her with a clearer sense of family and family history.

The unexpected death of Dr. Murray saddens Dottie and her grief is partly due to the fact that he dies before she has met him properly. Losing Murray reminds Dottie of her grandfather's loss of his itinerant daughter and makes her feel guilty toward the latter; moreover, she mourns for her late mother's relatives whom she has never met (Gurnah 1990, 62). Although Murray is no relative of Dottie's, he is the vehicle of her reconstructed family history. The image of Murray provides Dottie with the option of visualizing her grandfather's grief. Feeling close to Murray, he functions as a matrix on which to project her feelings about lost family bonds.

Dottie is as surprised as her social worker to learn that Murray was an eminent man. The women are astonished to find out that he was a medical doctor with a successful practice in well-to-do Wimbledon as well as the owner of a large house overlooking Clapham Common. Dottie was not only "intrigued by the thought of a black doctor living on the edges of Clapham Common," but also by him having "found enough patients for a practice forty years or so before, during England's dark ages [i.e., the 1920s]" (Gurnah 1990, 63). Murray is of a different generation and social position, yet Dottie is not only drawn to him but also identifies with him to a point. She comes to realize that despite his success, now, after his death, he will be forgotten and left without a trace—the newspapers don't even print an obituary.

The remark of a librarian (1990, 62) teaches Dottie that the omitted obituary is not only an oversight, but a significant political act. The novel shows how Dottie and her siblings are continually treated as foreigners, as interlopers in the land of their birth, even though their maternal family has lived in Britain for a few generations. Since black people in *Dottie*'s Britain are persistently relegated to the status of newcomers and immigrants, despite a historic presence of black British residents and citizens, Dottie's family history is not respected and the history of black people in Britain is ignored and obliterated. It fits into this picture that Murray passes into oblivion when he is officially disremembered.

Unearthing Murray's personal history, then, points to Dottie's ill-reception, to gaps in black British historiography, and to the necessity of countering these features. Telling the *British* history of several generations of Dottie's family through a series of flashbacks, Gurnah's novel acknowledges, addresses, and contests these gaps, and (symbolically) tries to fill one of them.[3]

The friendship between Murray and Dottie—signified only through silent acknowledgments of each other—is an essential step on the protagonist's path to perceiving the need for community, for family, and for history. In its concern with history and politics, with migration, colonialism, empire, and the situation of the Jewish diaspora in Europe, the novel disseminates the need for a knowledge of history, a position which is corroborated by Dottie's developing interest in her own past. The subtle didacticism of *Dottie* is thus an example of a novel of transformation reaching out, and of the construction of new subject positions.

II. THE NOVELISTIC TRANSFORMATION OF BRITAIN

The redefinition of Britishness and the modification of the image of Britain is accomplished by using, if not hijacking, the novel as a machine of cultural representation and reproduction. This section demonstrates that the novel of transformation not only portrays change in British society and culture, but, significantly, is also partly responsible for bringing about change. The second performative function to be discerned concerns the redefinition of Britishness and the modification of the image of Britain by way of the novel. This could be seen as a crucial "literary stocktaking" from different perspectives. There is obviously a lot of scope for this, so there are several, quite diverse examples.

This feature is not limited to the novel of transformation and can be found in the greater part of black British literature. The view previously cast on the colonies in colonial literature is refracted, transposed, and applied to situations in contemporary Britain. The former objects of the anthropological view become themselves acting and narrating subjects, and focus on situations of interest to them. Thus, not only is the English language spoken with an accent and appropriated in the process, but once more the country and the city are taken literary stock of. In other words, when Dickens's London is contrasted with the London of Sam Selvon, a *rewriting* of central topoi occurs.

Transgression of Space

One such redress is the transgression of space, a transgression that leads to the erosion of the notion of borders. Being steadily crisscrossed, these borders become increasingly irrelevant. In David Dabydeen's novel *Disappearance* (1993), the crumbling coast of Hastings suffers from erosion—the coastline is decaying as a result of the onslaught of the sea. This process is supposed to be stopped by the Guyanese engineer at the center of the novel. The villagers are intent on saving the coast in order to save their village which rests on it. In that sense they are resistant to the notion of eroding borders. At the end of the novel, however, the engineer leaves Britain, convinced that his task cannot be fulfilled. While his frustrated retreat indicates that borders have not yet become irrelevant, his conviction that a seawall cannot save the coastline predicts the ultimate fall of clear borders. It is of course ironic that the likely destruction of the Hastings coastline entails destruction in the novel's diegesis (it echoes the Norman invasion), rather than a Utopia without borders. The narrator returns to his native Guyana, a country with large parts below sea level, and which owes its very existence to the seawalls built by Dutch colonial engineers. Post-colonial Guyana and "post-colonial" Britain thus appear to face a similar predicament of exposure to the change they seek to resist.

Chaudhuri's novel *Afternoon Raag* is a case in point where the narrative shifts back and forth between India and Oxford.[4] These places, however, do not stand in a relationship of center and periphery. Rather, they are two centers which are connected by virtue of the narrator's living circumstances. The transgression of national boundaries as a matter of course—for which there are many examples in black British literature—entails a relativization of Britain with its fiction revolving around other territories in equal measure. Selvon's short stories in *Ways of Sunlight* (1957), falling into two sections, "Trinidad" and "London"; or Rushdie's collection, *East West* (1994), with three sections ("East," "West," and "East West"), are examples where this transgression is not yet integrated (except perhaps in the third section of Rushdie's collection). In contradistinction to that, there are novels like Chaudhuri's *Afternoon Raag* (1993), Rushdie's *Satanic Verses* (1988), Dhondy's *Bombay Duck,* or Kamila Shamsie's *Salt and Saffron* (2000) which seesaw more easily between the subcontinent and Britain. Demonstrating an even higher degree of amalgamation, Pauline Melville's short story "The truth is in the clothes" from her first collection *Shape-Shifter* (1990) features a London which constitutes an annex to a Jamaica which is accessible through a hidden door. Black British literature, then, is not just "love letter[s] to London," as Sukhdev Sandhu (2003, xxvi) has recently put it in his wide-ranging study *London Calling;* black and Asian writers have also composed love letters to Bombay, Kingston, and Port of Spain.

Redressing Iconography: The Case of Britain

Britain's image is also modified by the novelistic depiction of racist phenomena. Instances of racism ranging from stereotypes to verbal and physical abuse are common to most black British texts. Consider this example from *Some Kind of Black*.[5]

Dele and his girlfriend Andria [sic] visit a tiny Kentish village, a "place [that] was the living advert for an age he thought had done":

> The little roads were dotted with old-school butchers' shops, passed by women in fitted blouses, white minis and white stilettos. Elsewhere, clutches of young white adults, lank of hair and limb, stalked the streets. (Adebayo 1996a, 151)

Out of the blue, this idyllic scene is disrupted when the mixed-race couple is attacked by a group of racist thugs. The couple escape in their car, leaving behind them the illusion of an intact "little England." The violent juxtaposition of racism with the pastoral idyll of the garden of England interrupts notions of a liberal society. It also indicates the asynchronous development of country and city with respect to cultural pluralism and tolerance.

While such depictions of racism would seem to indirectly redress the image of Britain, there are instances of a more direct rewriting of Britain and its icons. In V. S. Naipaul's *The Enigma of Arrival*, a tinned milk label becomes an icon of English country life. The Wiltshire landscape reminds the narrator of a milk label from his Trinidadian childhood, "where cows as handsome as those were not to be seen" (38).[6] It is with cutting irony that Naipaul has his middle-aged narrator comment: "I was in the original of that condensed-milk label drawing" (1987, 297). The irony is heightened by two accounts of mutated English cattle which, though "healthy, big . . . [and] beaut[iful]," were numbered and without "sanctity" (1987, 81). The cattle betoken failures of "assisted insemination" and genetic engineering, because they have an "extra bit of flesh and hair (with the black and white Frisian pattern) hanging down their middle, as of cow-material that had leaked through the two halves of the cow-mould" (1987, 81). The deterioration and decay of Britain and its culture, as perceived by the narrator, is set into relief by Naipaul's mutated bucolics and its detached representation. By appealing to the icon of the healthy, larger-than-life cow, whose very proliferations are covered in Frisian pattern, cultural deformation and its dimension—however disguised—are debunked. At the same time, Naipaul sends up his narrator's and his own misguided expectations hedged toward the erstwhile colonial center, subtly mocking both the attention paid to a brand label and the projections tied to it.

Another example in which the image of the nurturing "Mother Country" is redressed can be found in Andrea Levy's first novel. Levy is a London-based writer, born in 1956, whose novel *Every Light in the House Burnin'* is about an underprivileged family with a Jamaican background. In this text, Britain is portrayed as a rather sad affair. Central institutions such as the National Health Service (which in the 1960s attracted nurses from the West Indies) are hardly functioning; the physician's office, representative of Britain, "looked just a few repairs away from derelict" (Levy 1994, 88). In a bargain shop, Mr. Jacobs purchases for his wife what he thinks is a reading light. The narrator's father mistakes this "replica of somewhere" (1994, 99), a light modeled on the Vatican, with a tacky representation of Buckingham Palace, and he thus mistakes the pope for the queen of England. His wife tries "read[ing] by the light of the Vatican" but the revolving pope figure "got stuck peek-a-booing" and with a burning smell "its light was extinguished for ever" (1994, 100). This barren fixture renders one symbol of order and stability as empty and hackneyed as another.

The narrator and central character, Ange, is gifted and, again, a social climber. Not unlike Syal's Meena, she acquires a language which allows her access to vital information and to social circles that would have otherwise remained out of reach. She retains a "fear of authority" but grows more confident "through the years of grammar school and college education . . . gradually losing [her] cockney twang; of eating lunch instead of dinner and supper instead of tea" (1994, 88). The narrator's observations point to and critique the importance of sociolects in British society as entryways to positions of relative power. Although she is in awe of the doctor's expertise, Ange's own growing knowledge boosts her influence and power; after all, it is the young woman rather than her parents who deals with the hospital and other figures of authority.

The importance of sociolects and cultural knowledge here stressed by Ange's story reminds the reader that black British identity is also determined by social factors that apply to the white population as well: namely, the constraints imposed by class.[7]

Ange brings in a further reason for her better chances:

> I knew this society better than my parents [whose] strategy was to keep as quiet as possible in the hope that no one would know that they had sneaked into this country. . . . But I had grown up in its English ways. I could confront it, rail against it, fight it, because it was mine—a birthright. (Levy 1994, 88)

Here a deep generational conflict evolves in terms of gender roles, class expectations, and cultural bonding. Ange is confronted with her parents' self-defeating conviction that "[p]eople like us don't get famous" (1994, 192), and that her plan of becoming an actress is out of reach for her as a working-class, black Briton. But she is more confident about belonging than her parents, and is consequently better equipped to challenge the personal and social forces that hold her back. This not only includes challenging her parents' well-meaning but stifling advice; it is also revealed that Ange's background is not equivalent to that of her parents. She has grown up in a fusion of "English ways" and parental ways. Likewise her class context is only partly determined by her parents and is modified by her own achievements.

Ange realizes that to achieve her own aims she needs different strategies than those of her parents; this generational conflict is fused with Ange's different relationship to the country of her birth. Her affinity to Britain (signified by her "birthright") differentiates her from her migrant parents. She is distinct from them not only in terms of generation and class but also in terms of cultural bonding.

Thus language, access to higher education, and "birthrights" mutually reinforce each other to allow for Ange's upward social mobility. The protagonist is better equipped to survive and succeed in a racist society than her parents because she has grown up (however precariously) as a part of that society, is conversant with its workings, and is ready to assert her claim to a place in it.

Hanif Kureishi's Karim makes this connection explicit when explaining that the "easy talk of art, theatre, architecture, travel; the languages, the vocabulary, knowing the way round a whole culture" constitutes "invaluable and irreplaceable capital" (Kureishi 1990, 177). Ange and Karim's example show that social ascent and accent (or *sociolect*) are intimately linked. In the case of these particular protagonists their accent is tied more to their class background than to their parents' ethnic position.

As far as Ange is concerned, however, there is an additional aspect which facilitates her social mobility: it is the phenomenon of passing.[8] On account of her light skin color, Ange is not necessarily perceived as black; her teacher Mrs. Kromer, for example, who supports Ange throughout, thinks her either Italian or Jewish, and thus white. Ange herself feels "pale" when with black people but "black among the pasty-faced English" (Levy 1994, 166). In addition to the above, therefore, phenotype also impacts on the accessibility of social positions. Significantly, Ange's three siblings, whose complexions are darker, pursue a distinctly different path from that of the protagonist. They all move away from England to Wales, New Zealand, or Africa. In view of this, *Every Light in the House Burnin'* has to be considered a multiple[9] bildungsroman, following the development of a foil to the protagonist. As in David Dabydeen's novel *The Intended*, it is the light-skinned character who is more successful than her peers. By introducing the phenomenon of passing, Levy renders her protagonist's upward social mobility more complex than at first apparent, and moreover exposes British society as color-conscious.

Ange's success story is set off against her father who dies of lung cancer at the end of the novel. The long story of his illnesses allows the novel to critically engage with the NHS (the state-run health service), which seems more interested in its internal struggles than in the welfare of its patients. In a macabre case of "passing," Mr. Jacob gets the "wrong treatment" not only before but also after his death: the nurses call a rabbi since, on account of his complexion and name, they assumed he was Jewish.

It is quite unusual for the male body to take the brunt, to signify the sufferings of the migrant generation. Mr. Jacob's twin brother faces the same cancer condition which indicates that metaphorically their predicament is less an individual one than a concern of the entire *Windrush* generation. At the same time, the text makes it quite clear that Mr. Jacobs had been too complacent in not fighting against his predicament until he was on his deathbed: "The first rail against injustice. Why now?" (Levy 1994, 243). The text not only differentiates between two distinct generations; it appears outright didactic by contrasting an accepting and passive Mr. Jacobs with a determined and therefore successful Ange.

A good example of the iconography of Britain being redressed can be taken from the title-giving sequence of Levy's novel. During the visit of relatives from Jamaica, the whole family is sitting together. Having been scrubbed clean, the entire house is sparkling down to every nook and cranny. When the guests arrive, every light in the house is burning. The eponymous house providing comfort and shelter on one level is representative of the expectations the Jacobses may have had when coming to Britain on the SS *Empire Windrush*.

Asked about her life in Britain, Angela's mother asserts: "Well, I have everything I need just here" (Levy 1994, 126). Ironically, just as Mrs. Jacobs claims being well provided for, the money in the light meter runs out and the power is cut. With everybody left in the dark, Mrs Jacobs's appreciation of Britain is counteracted by the cloak of darkness. The images of provision and shelter are negated, and the expectations toward the house and by extension Britain are frustrated; these expectations in fact seem to have been directed at symbols as delusive as the Vatican/Buckingham Palace light discussed above.

The harsh regime of a coin meter is reminiscent of the early days of post–World Word II migration and of Selvon's *The Lonely Londoners* (1956):

> Always every Sunday they coming to Moses, like if is confession, sitting down on the bed, on the floor, on the chairs . . . the gas going low, why you don't put another shilling, who have shilling, anybody have change? And everybody turning out their pockets for this shilling that would mean the difference between shivering and feeling warm, and nobody having any shilling, until conscious [sic] hit one of them and he say: "Aps! Look I have a shilling, it was right down in the bottom of my trousers pocket, and I didn't feel it." (Selvon 1956, 138)

If Moses is the high priest of this group, he is also a father figure who holds the congregation together. The ritual of recounting stories establishes a symbolic family, comforting individual members in response to a cold city where "the boys" always stand out and have to fight for jobs. Their experience of rejection is mirrored by the image of the cold; this diasporic community keeps itself warm by listening to each other, by helping each other out, and by—albeit grudgingly—sharing the cost of the gas meter.

Levy's novel cites this tradition, thereby establishing a form of continuity. While for the depicted family it might not be a matter of money as such, but of loose change, the power cut is real enough and evokes a history of hardship. The ease with which the festive mood of a dinner party is aborted points to the continued vicissitudes that affect even established immigrant communities.

The darkness could be cast off but the parents don't have the requisite coins for the meter and as a result ask their daughter to get some out of her piggy bank. Therefore, by drawing upon their child's savings, the parents are shown as compromised. However, it is finally the Jamaican relatives who help out, returning the light to Britain. The implication of this final twist is not only that the *Windrush* generation's possibly exaggerated expectations toward Britain have been frustrated, for as the relatives decide to leave a handful of shillings behind, it is the visitors who support their Britain-based family and not vice versa. The novel can thus be seen as transforming the image of the sustaining "Mother Country" to one whose support is contingent upon being fed coins.

Exertion of Cultural Power

Another way of redressing the image of Britain is the representation, exertion, and normalization of black British cultural power by way of the novel. In order to articulate this more complex process of redress of Britishness, the work of Stuart Hall is helpful. With reference to the colonial encounter in the West Indies and the attendant processes of interpellation of the subject, Hall says:

> The ways in which black people, black experiences, were positioned and subject-ed in the dominant regimes of representation were the effects of a critical exercise of cultural power and normalisation. Not only, in Said's "Orientalist" sense, were we constructed as different

and other within the categories of knowledge of the West by those regimes. They had the power to make us see and experience *ourselves* as "Other." (Hall 1990, 225)

Hall is here drawing upon the work of the Martiniquais psychiatrist and anticolonial intellectual Frantz Fanon, in whose 1952 study *Black Skin, White Masks* the effects of a young white boy saying about the author "Look, a Negro!" are followed up (1952, 112). The white boy's remark has what Stuart Hall has defined as "the power to make [black people] see and experience [*themselves*] as 'Other'" and, in Fanon's words, to induce a "third-person consciousness" (Fanon 1952, 110).[10]

The processes described by Hall and Fanon, the othering and the seeing oneself as other, can frequently be observed in black British literature. However, and this is what interests me here, sometimes these processes can also be found in their reversed form in black British literature. This is not only indicative of black British cultural power but, more importantly, of the normalization of this power. With this at the back of our minds, let me briefly turn to Syal's novel *Anita and Me,* with which this chapter opened.

The protagonist, Meena, has always admired the rough and neglected Anita and her gang as well as the skinhead Sam Lowbridge. For a while she actually succeeds in becoming a gang member and Anita's close associate. Later in the novel, however, there is an episode in which Sam is verbally abusive of Indian people, which hurts and embarrasses Meena. In the last chapter, Meena confronts Sam in a most unusual way, a scene which bears quoting at length:

> "Those things you said at the spring fete, what were you trying to do?" . . .
>
> "I wanted to make people listen," he said finally.
>
> "You wanted to hurt people, you mean!" I yelled at him. "How could you say it, in front of me? My dad? To anyone? How can you believe that shit?" . . .
>
> "When I said them," he rasped, "I never meant you, Meena! It was all the others not yow!"
>
> " . . . I *am* the others, Sam. You did mean me."
>
> Sam gripped my wrists tighter for support. "Yow've always been the best wench in Tollington. Anywhere! Dead funny. . . . But yow wos never gonna look at me, yow won't be stayin will ya? You can move on. How come? How come I can't?" And then he kissed me like I thought he would, and I let him, feeling mighty and huge, knowing I

had won and that every time he saw another Meena on a street corner he would remember this and feel totally powerless.

(Syal 1996, 313–14)

It appears that Meena has won a power game. She is not disenfranchised but centered, in Hall's diction. Despite his perennial motorbike, it is Sam who is going nowhere. Instead, Meena has an ever increasing number of options given her results at school and her family's support. Sam is aware of the fact that, like many others of his white working-class peers in his village, he is stranded in the demising Tollington without a fair chance of finding employment. As a social outcast, there is no useful place for Sam in the society that has rejected him. Given his racist opinions, he feels betrayed in view of the opportunities in store for Meena. These feelings are of course augmented by Meena playing with his attraction to her, whereby she underscores her position of relative power.

Sam brings people under his sway by bullying them. This strategy, however, would spoil his romantic intentions in this encounter with Meena. Calling her over he is at pains to stress "I ain't gonna hurt yow, promise!" (Syal 1996, 312), and his status is therefore further curtailed when Meena is not overtly intimidated by him. Being subjected to her criticism further diminishes Sam, while it positions Meena as empowered. After all, she dares to single-handedly confront the man whom she suspects of having seriously wounded an Indian man. Having realized that Sam feels inferior to her, she seizes her opportunity. Permitting this scene of intimacy without losing control over the situation ("I let him" kiss me), Meena establishes her superiority over Sam, and, assuming that he will always be reminded of this when seeing another woman like her, she succeeds in turning Sam's stereotypical view of Indians against himself.

In this reading, Meena's complex strategy seizes on Sam's pariah status in order to position herself as superior. Irrespective of whether her attempt at acting as a representative for any other "Meena on a street" is successful, she can be seen to exert cultural power. Judging Sam within *her* categories of knowledge, Sam is induced to experience himself as "other."

My further point here is not only that the normalization of cultural power is depicted in this scene, but that it is notably purveyed *by* novelistic discourse. This, for instance, is achieved by Meena's family successfully disentangling itself from Tollington and moving on, whereas the other Midland villagers are left behind to face a brutal predicament.

Meena's fantasy of subduing and seducing a white skinhead is related to similar fantasies in Hanif Kureishi's *My Beautiful Laundrette* (the relationship between Omar and Johnny) and in Atima Srivastava's *Transmission* (Angie's relationship to the former skinhead Lol). Significantly, in all three cases, the protagonists act on their fantasy. This pattern suggests that negotiation with and "approval" by someone who is structurally, politically, and socially radically opposed exerts a high degree of attraction. Meena's "victory" over Sam provides her with the belief (and the experience) that she can tackle future instances of discrimination and racism. In contrast, meeting the Punjabi man in residence at the "Big House," her other significant encounter, provides Meena with confidence in her potential for success because she can identify with this man resembling her father. Significantly, however, the Big House, with its dual promise of accommodation and achievement, serves only as a temporary shelter from the world of Sam and Anita which Meena has just escaped. It is her triumph over Sam which gives Meena a sense of confidence, which the meeting at the "Big House" in and by itself does not provide.

Since Meena comes to position herself as a British girl with a Punjabi background in the course of the text, my reading relies on situating Meena as a British Asian girl. My understanding is therefore in disagreement with Berthold Schoene-Harwood's interpretation of Syal's text. He also reads *Anita and Me* as a bildungsroman; but according to him "hybridity is experienced as an onerous ordeal" and "seems like a curse" to Meena (Schoene-Harwood 1999, 161; 163). The girl does not cherish "the intrinsic hybridity and colourfulness of her exotic self" (1999, 161) but is rendered "whitened," which leads Schoene-Harwood to conclude: "Her identity has moved on . . . is moving . . . beyond (t)race" (1999, 167; ellipses in original).

While it is accurate that *Anita and Me* is decidedly *not* an uncritical celebration of "hybridity," of "syncretism," and of "in-betweenness," it seems incautious to assume that Meena can transcend "race" beyond "trace" in a society where race remains highly significant and racism deeply entrenched. Meena learns to survive in such a society, and her lessons are crucial precisely because of her phenotype and the heightened visibility it entails. It is indeed interesting to speculate upon how far phenotypic determination can be negotiated, a question that I will pursue when reading some of Hanif Kureishi's works (see chapter 4). But such a negotiation can neither start from denial nor end with erasure, but rather presupposes an acknowledgment of how one is perceived, as Meena's confrontation with Sam indicates.

This chapter so far has argued that the black British novel of transformation is not only about the character formation of its protagonists, it is at once about the transformation and reformation of British cultures. These processes of transformation and reformation are not only represented *in* the texts; they are at once purveyed *by* them. The texts are, in other words, part of the processes they deal with. This can be accounted for by the performative functions of the novel of transformation, which involve the construction of new subject positions, the reimagination and redress of the images of Britain including the transgression of national boundaries, the depiction of racism, and, most importantly, the representation, exertion, and normalization of black British cultural power.

More needs to be said, however, about the above, especially in view of the "burden of representation." The cultural critic Kobena Mercer indicates that minoritarian cultural practitioners such as writers are perceived differently than their majoritarian colleagues in that they are often taken to speak as "representatives." Mercer describes this structural problematics as resulting from the widely held expectation that minoritarian practitioners are able to "'speak for' the marginalized communities from which they come" (Mercer 1994, 235). This can severely restrict the choice of subject matter, language, and style available to practitioners who have to expect their work to be received in view of "their" community.[11] In one of his early essays, Homi Bhabha rereads V. S. Naipaul's *A House for Mr. Biswas,* criticizing previous readings that had cast it as a realist, Dickensian novel. Bhabha's thesis is that post-colonial texts resist being subsumed to the realist paradigm even when they appear to partake of it. Instead they are part of a "colonial fantasy [which] sets itself up as an uncanny 'double'" (1984, 119–20) in order to subvert the mode of realism.[12] The kind of theorizing exemplified by Bhabha's essay is potentially complicit with producing a composite, homogenized image of post-colonial literature or third world literature or the novel of formation. Such a penchant for totalization is widespread in post-colonial studies. (See also, for example, Fredric Jameson's thesis that "Third World Literature" can typically be read as "National Allegory.")[13]

In light of these criticisms by Bhabha and Jameson, one of the problems of assigning the genre "novel of transformation" to black British literature and arguing that there is a special twist to it is the implicit assumption that these novels of formation are nearer to the "testimonio" than others. If the "unifying feature of a testimony novel is its consciousness of a collective objective beyond the individual person" (Lima 1993, 44) then one would have to account for why this should be so. While it is good and well to find this consciousness in a text, ascribing it to the text, burdening the text—and its author—with the "consciousness of a collective objective " constitutes a severe limitation. The author qua his or her perceived belonging to a minority group is burdened with certain responsibilities that can curtail his or her work. Why should there be, by default, any collective objective, and why an awareness of it in a black or Asian British author of a bildungsroman?

Maria Helena Lima has done work on Michelle Cliff's *No Telephone to Heaven* and Merle Collins's *Angel* using and developing the framework of the bildungsroman in the West Indies. These "novels of development" are fundamental to "nation-building" according to her, because post-colonial writing functions to "turn a population characterized by differences of language, ethnicity, and religion, into a national unit, to achieve some form of wholeness out of fragmentation" (Lima 1993, 53). Although I have also been demonstrating with different examples the ways in which the bildungsroman describes *and* induces cultural change in Britain, I would be hesitant to subscribe to Lima's more prescriptive understanding of the genre. Working in the context of younger nations such as Grenada and Jamaica, she creates the impression that a writer can hardly escape the processes she describes and is, by definition, conscripted to nation-building, to forming "wholeness out of fragmentation." As has been emphasized, I don't see the black British novel of transformation as inducing that kind of homogeneity. In the context of Britain it instead disrupts homogeneity. It inserts and reinforces heterogeneity, and, crucially, engenders acceptance for constituents of this heterogeneity through representation.

PART TWO

3

Crossing a Notion
—The (Im)possibility of Returning

> . . . how choose
> Between this Africa and the English tongue I love?
> Betray them both, or give back what they give?
> How can I face such slaughter and be cool?
> How can I turn from Africa and live?
> —"A FAR CRY FROM AFRICA" (WALCOTT 1986, 18)

> I think that kind of "us analysing our traditions" is of the utmost importance. It's the most urgent thing we can do, and we understand how traditions are live and not passive things stuck in a closet but they are—and I go back to Vico—made by human beings and that they are recollections, they are customary practices, collective memory . . . but they are certainly not the simple pure thing to which people return and get comfort in.
> —(SAID 1998, 96)

"Return" is a prevalent theme in post-colonial literature.[1] It often takes the form of actual, physical returning, but spiritual, notional, and intellectual returns are also prominent. Returning is related to seeking an earlier state or position, to giving in to nostalgia and a yearning for home. It is encumbered by the weight of tradition; yet the absence of a tradition, its inaccessibility, can be as weighty and return inducing. But if tradition is always a motivated reinvention of the past to serve the requirements of the present, then returns signify agency and are geared toward the production of agency. Returning, in this sense, is an act of participating in the weaving of collective memory, in the *making* and remaking of tradition, rather than merely a comfort-seeking activity.

Although the bildungsroman resembles the picaresque novel, since both follow a simple basic pattern of departure, growth, and return, as David H. Miles (1974) and others have shown, there are crucial differences which the novels at the center of this chapter, *Lara* and *Fruit of the*

Lemon, render clear. The chapter is concerned with departures and returns, a pattern which can be found in many black British novels and which marks the literature as a diasporic one—one that has more than one home, or none. I have suggested in chapter 1 that black British writing is, with respect to its form, *multilocated,* and that it is characterized by connections to a variety of traditions and geographies. This is often also true of the protagonists and their stories, so that black British novels can also be considered multilocated with respect to their themes, as this chapter will show.

Since British-born black and Asian writers are often included in the concept of "diaspora,"[2] generational conflict, which is paradigmatic for the bildungsroman, must be concurrently formalized as a cultural conflict between distinct generations. The desire to return "home" from the diaspora is inflected differently for different generations. The interpellation of the subject caught between parental migrant culture and black youth cultures, the processes and results of growing up in between cultures, and their thematic rendition in the black British novel of transformation concern me here.

This chapter pursues the concepts of diaspora and generation in relation to the theme of returning. In its final section, the chapter makes observations on authors' relationships to generation and diaspora. The chapter is framed by a reading of Grace Nichols's paradigmatic poem, "epilogue," which speaks to the diasporic situation. The concept of the diaspora is examined next. The theme of return is then reviewed through *Fruit of the Lemon* by Andrea Levy and *Lara* by Bernardine Evaristo. After dealing with these fictional texts, I will look at how Caryl Phillips and George Lamming have considered returns, and whether they can be seen as part of distinct generations of authors. In keeping with Evaristo's syncretic text, a dramatic novel in verse, this chapter closes with a brief discussion of a further poetic text. Reading John Agard's "Remember the Ship" will allow me to tie the image of imperial expansion to contemporary negotiations (and navigations) of memory and identity.

I. VOYAGES AND INTERSECTIONS: GRACE NICHOLS'S "EPILOGUE"

> I have crossed an ocean
> I have lost my tongue
> from the root of the old one

a new one has sprung
"epilogue"
—(NICHOLS 1983, 87)

On its own, if not contextualized within Grace Nichols's work and black British or Caribbean literature, the poem "epilogue," taken from the collection *i is a long-memoried woman*, does not provide any clear reference points regarding temporal or geographical location, or concerning the identity or gender of the dramatic persona. In that sense, it speaks of migration and its consequences in an almost universalist fashion. While it would be overstating the case to claim that the dramatic persona passes for an "archetypal migrant," it is important to note that the poem, in its inspecificity, speaks to the experience of a vast number of people in this "Age of Migration."[3] The image of migration, of journeying, is not only central to this poem but is a prime motif in Nichols's poetry and in black British literature more generally.

The concise "epilogue," reproduced in two of Nichols's collections of her poetry, invites multiple readings. Both, "tongue" and "ocean," evoke the history of the linguistic and geographic displacement of enslaved African peoples and their progeny; the injustice and psychical and physical violence of the Middle Passage is intensified by the mutilation mentioned in line two, the image of the "lost tongue." However, it is not specifically the *Atlantic* Ocean which is mentioned, and the indefinite article is used. The metaphor of "an ocean" thus evokes the traumatic experience of the Middle Passage, but its vastness and depth also bespeak a wider predicament which this literal displacement entailed. The mutilated tongue refers to actual physical injuries (inflicted before and during the Middle Passage, and during slavery) while it also conjures up linguistic and cultural displacements of oceanic dimensions.[4] Slavocracy aimed at silencing its slave population to preclude unrest and rebellion by impeding communication.[5] The "lost tongue" then refers to barbaric punishments and the severing of cultural and linguistic ties with various West African cultures, a consequence of the systematic mingling of peoples from different backgrounds which entailed, amongst other things, alienation from home cultures, and ultimately the development of Creole cultures and cultural hybridity. This is, of course, not to posit the notion that the "original" cultures were not also "hybrid," a point crucially ignored or overlooked by Helen Tiffin when she asserts that a "pre-colonial cultural purity can never be fully recovered" (Tiffin 1987, 17).

The journey across the Atlantic is as much a crossing of an ocean of tears as it is the metaphoric attempt to leave behind the blemishes of a past of humiliation. Developing new languages (*new tongues*) is not only a sign of resistance but also a means of such resistance. Nichols acknowledges these acts of resistance, and celebrates them, but, crucially, her poetry also reenacts these instances of resistance.

The second half[6] of the poem therefore adds a strong optimistic and conciliatory tone—geographic and linguistic displacements are reconciled, vast distances overcome. Cultural "roots" have been partly retained and have given birth to novel cultural and linguistic identifications. The adjective *new* indicates that not a mere reproduction but genuinely new identifications are conceived. The verb *spring* connotes a suddenness, possibly an unexpectedness which enhances the optimistic tone; yet at the same time it corroborates the poem's organicist overtones, conjuring up biological processes like germination, flowering, and, by extension of this cyclical image, decline.

The crossing of the ocean can also be read in a slightly wider context, that of the Atlantic Triangle, the inclusion and commodification of enslaved Africans into an economic cycle between Europe, Africa, and the Caribbean, a triangle which—to further broaden the scope of reference—to this day also stands for the bonds and yearnings of migrants and sometimes their descendants to "imaginary homelands" in the Caribbean, Africa, and India. The "cross[ing of] an ocean," then, also alludes to the migration to Britain from the Caribbean and elsewhere since the late 1940s and 1950s.

The first collection, *i is a long memoried woman*, I contend, is primarily the vindication and inscription of a marginalized history, and thus a supplement to an incomplete history which is in turn supplemented by the poem "epilogue," which again acts on a preamble to the following three collections. I use the term *supplement* advisedly. It indicates that the cycle is not the attempt of writing a "final chapter," to close the historiography of a section of British society or to inflict closure on that history. Instead, the collection partakes in a sequence of writings opened up by Mary Prince and Mary Seacole between the 1830s and 1850s.[7] A supplement seeks to complete by adding to what has already been written; but in so doing it in turn participates in—and changes—that which it seeks to record, thus creating the need for a further supplement. This characterizes the relationship of the "epilogue" to the collection *i is a long memoried woman*, as well as the relationship of the entire collection to the stories it sets out to tell. This open-endedness of historiography, the continued need for a supplement volume, is expressed in the poem's syntactic structure: it consists of one sentence only, exemplifying the continuity of the endeavor of which it is a part. The sentence does not bear a full stop, is open-ended, and thus behaves very much like its subject.[8]

The pivotal position of "epilogue" allows us to read it as a meta-comment on what precedes and follows. As the title would suggest, the poem is placed at the end of *i is a long memoried woman*, after a narration of the history of slavery from women's perspectives. Retrospectively, the poem describes, serves as, and marks a catharsis,[9] clearing the way for greater contemporaneity in the following three collections by Nichols. It stresses the presence of "root[s]," of cultural origins, and at once the need for the development of new idioms and new cultures of belonging. Marked by a tension between its violent historical background on the one hand, and its soothing anapestic meter and simple language on the other, the poem's optimistic tone is far from revanchist. Its function is highly mnemonic (the simple and regular rhythm and structure committing the few lines to memory almost automatically), so that "epilogue" *enacts* what it conveys: the retrieval, recording, telling, and knowing of history. The soothing rhythm seems to belie the pain the poem speaks of, yet this is in keeping with the position and the function of the poem: it comes "after"; it looks to the future. While concerned with history, a vision of the future is presented, a future of new beginnings, new expression, and new visions. In Nichols's version, such beginnings can only be attained by acknowledging one's history—the future will "spring" only "from the root of the old one." While many poems in her first collection predominantly look back to the past, "epilogue" provides a view of the future in view of that past. Hence it serves as a preamble to her following three collections of poetry which can also be characterized as more forward-looking.

While *i is a long memoried woman* can be read as an allegorical reversal of the attempted[10] systematic disarticulation of African peoples under slavery, and while this project of reversal is summarized in the final poem through the metaphor of the "lost tongue" and the "new one," the poem also allows for an alternate reading. "[E]pilogue" speaks not only of "cross[ing] an ocean" but, homophonously, of *crossing a notion*—the notion of return. In this reading the impossibility of a return to a pre-Columbian age, to "authentic" Caribbean, African, or Indian roots, despite the nostalgia the collection expresses in part, is acknowledged. The poem displays a certain tenaciousness about the notion of a return but at length it is "crossed" out.

The "tongue," which is "new" and which grows from a "root," homophonously again, may also point to a *route*, to historical trajectories which do not unambiguously predetermine identifications but enable resistance, new idioms, new cultural forms, and new identifications. These interpretations are warranted in that Nichols frequently performs her poetry, thereby gaining an oral/aural presence apart from the printed page. Admittedly, these interpretations may constitute what Gayatri Spivak has called a "scrupulous and plausible misreading" (1987, 116). In other words, my reading of these homophones may conflict with other readings of the poem but it is justifiable within the structure of the poem. This maneuver allows me to underscore the tension between addressing a contemporary situation as well as an earlier condition or location; it also allows me to stress the tension between a determinist and a more open conception of history.

Reading Nichols's poem has brought forth the theme of return and the related area of memory and its negotiation. The tension between longing, belonging, looking back, and looking forward has been touched upon, with a view to organicism, and with the possibility of new languages and cultures evolving. These concerns will have bearing on the readings of *Fruit of the Lemon* and *Lara* in Section III. Before that, certain theorizations of diaspora are explored.

II. WRITING DIASPORA

One person's homeland is another person's diaspora. The question of "home," what it stands for, to whom it is available, how it changes, whether it exists at all, and if so, where, is of course a common preoccupation in many post-colonial novels, indeed in most novels that deal with cultural or geographic displacement. In her study *The Politics of Home*, Rosemary Marangoly George even goes as far as to conclude that "all fiction is homesickness." The notion of being at home can be contrasted with that of belonging to a diaspora. How does this condition relate to home, *heimat*, being at home? And where is home for those who are part of a diaspora? Diaspora is not a place to be circumscribed geographically; it is a relational term, pointing elsewhere, "always elsewhere," as Fred D'Aguiar concludes in one of his poems.[11]

Nikos Papastergiadis has explored the concept of diaspora and diasporic culture, which according to him "cannot be seen in organicist terms, as if it were a seed that could be transported, and planted elsewhere" (1998, xi). Instead diasporic culture is "more about a sensibility" and about "trajectories of belonging" (1998, xi). The novels that will be discussed here start on a different note. *Lara* in fact opens with an image of a seedling of a Baobab tree dropped by a bird (see below, "Webs of Attachment" section); *Fruit of the Lemon* opens with a seedling of a family tree (see below, "England" section). And yet they are texts which uncover and follow a particular sensibility; they pursue and develop trajectories of belonging.

In his inaugural lecture *Between Camps: Race and Culture in Post-modernity,* Paul Gilroy suggests that the concept of diaspora "introduces the possibility of an historical and experiential rift between the location of residence and the location of belonging" (1997, 10). In Gilroy's diction, *home* relates to "the location of belonging" from which *residence* is distinct. But how does the "historical and experiential rift" come about; what constitutes it? The experience of diaspora involves dispersal and the displacement to foreign lands, a traumatic experience that lies at the basis of such a rift and the sensibility ascribed to it.

According to Salman Rushdie the homeland, the location of belonging, becomes *imaginary* when it does not coincide with the place of residence (Rushdie 1991). The designation "imaginary" also implies that the *actual* connections, the ongoing exchange between home and residence, are mediated, and channeled through letters and telephone calls, or, in digital times, via e-mail and Chat.

■ ■ ■

How long does the experience of belonging to a diaspora remain formative; how long does it remain intact; how long does the rift of which Gilroy speaks remain open, unhealed? In its early, biblical meaning, diaspora refers to the exilic condition of the Jewish people.[12] Here, precisely, it is not necessarily personal memory of displacement but a communal memory and awareness of dispersal which marks the condition of diaspora, and is one of the decisive features of communal identification. Arguably, then, there is no end to the diaspora condition, since the rupture of displacement may be remembered forever. So the condition of diaspora can not only be *realized* in and through memory, but memory also *delimits* the diaspora condition.

In this view, however, the diaspora condition can comprise many generations. "Diaspora" can be inherited since its memory can be passed on. Only the first and possibly second generations have a direct memory of being exiled. However, without the direct experience of exile or displacement the rift between belonging and residence is culturally mediated, communally remembered, and potentially reconstructed from one generation to the next. In this sense, the diaspora condition is a historicized phenomenon that changes over time. There is a difference between one's own memories, the experiences of one's own generation, and those inherited from the preceding generations. In other words, the memory of the subcontinent, of Africa, of the West Indies is cast differently in the different generations of black British settlers.

One's *culture* is only "present," as far as it can be *made* present, is represented. Therefore, culture needs to be "remembered and remade" as Gilroy put it. This sliding from remembering to remaking is significant. The implication is that through such refashioning—and memory is seen here not as faithful but as creative—*change* becomes part of memory, memory becomes part of change. While memory is significant, *what* is being remembered is subject to redefinition.

Stuart Hall distinguishes between two distinct definitions of diaspora, between "the old, the imperialising, the hegemonising, form" that he calls a "backward-looking conception" which he contrasts with an experience of diaspora "defined, not by essence or purity, but by the recognition of a necessary heterogeneity and diversity; by a conception of 'identity' which lives with and through, not despite difference; by *hybridity*." He therefore describes diaspora identities as

> those which are constantly producing and reproducing themselves anew, through transformation and difference. . . . Young black cultural practitioners and critics in Britain are increasingly coming to acknowledge and explore in their work this "diaspora aesthetic" and its formations in the post-colonial experience. (Hall 1990, 235–36)

Here Hall suggests a definition of diaspora which stresses praxis over essence and recognizes heterogeneity as a precondition. Diasporic identities, in his view, thrive on difference and are marked not by constancy but by ongoing self-transformation. This understanding is useful in appreciating the novels which stand at the center of this chapter. As will be seen, particularly in *Lara*, the protagonist develops a "Diaspora identity" by the end of the text, one that is "constantly producing and reproducing" itself anew. Hall's definition, then, is useful in coming to terms with the texts' diasporia aesthetics.

If diaspora, and the memory that nourishes it, can be compared to an open wound, then the particular "injury" may not be constantly kept at the level of consciousness; nevertheless, the condition of "woundedness" necessitates attempts at healing, at sealing, at remaking. Literary texts participate in this healing and remaking process, and they partake of the construction of memory. Paradoxically, however, collective memory and literary texts can be seen as attempts at healing while they at once keep open the wound they are dressing.

"[T]he black diaspora culture currently being articulated in postcolonial Britain is concerned to struggle for different ways to be 'British,'" according to the anthropologist James Clifford, namely,

> to be British and *something else* complexly related to Africa and the Americas, to shared histories of enslavement, racist subordination, cultural survival, hybridization, resistance, and political rebellion.
> (Clifford 1997, 251–52; original emphasis)

Clifford's definition of the term *diaspora* emphasizes the political nature of diaspora positionalities and stresses the tension between "transnational" connections on the one hand and "struggles to define the local" on the other hand. The diaspora experience cannot be delimited by a single national space, be it Britain, or, say, the Americas; diaspora experience is *multilocated* and transcends the nation space. The two *multilocated* novels which I am about to discuss bear out such transnational affiliations, especially *Lara*, which has its protagonist draw upon and actively weave a complex web of attachments. And they seek to address a "local" situation, that of black Britain, with a wish to redress it.

III. WEBS OF ATTACHMENT

> A desperate foolishness. The crops failed. I sold my children. . . .
> I soiled my hands with cold goods in exchange for their warm flesh. . . .
> And soon after, the chorus of a common memory began to haunt me.
> —(PHILLIPS 1994, 1)

The previous chapter argued that the novel of transformation is characterized by performative functions, by a certain efficacy. The process of *formation* brings about the construction of a position from which to speak and hence, following Stuart Hall, the construction of an identity. The efficacy of the novel of transformation, then, is directed inward, at the protagonists of the texts. However, as part of their narrative, the two protagonists distance themselves from their hometown of London and make it seem distant and strange. It is to such a "strange" London that they later return, when they are able to make it their own. These *alienation effects* allow the protagonists to claim London, to make it their own. However, this process impacts upon the reader too, whose perception of London is interrogated and possibly changed. Inasmuch as the reader is thus affected, the performativity of these texts is also directed outward, beyond the text. Furthermore, in different ways, Lara and Faith, the two protagonists, can be adopted as models, or guides by readers, which also enhances performativity beyond the text.

The novel of formation is characterized by generational tension between the protagonist and their family or guardians. Jane Eyre, for example, is up against her oppressive aunt, Mrs. Reed, then the schoolmaster Bocklehurst, and later against her employers. Exceptions would be the more dystopian novels of the *Lord of the Flies*—type which are marked by a formation process outside society or rather in a separate society. In the case of the black British novel of transformation, the generational conflict which is central to the novel of formation can be concurrently formalized as a *cultural* conflict between distinct generations.

Since memory constitutes the basis for the diaspora condition, and at once delimits that very condition (as has been suggested in the previous section), it is not surprising that the uses of memory are thematized regularly in black British literature. Caryl Phillips's haunting novel *Crossing the River* starts with a chilling acknowledgment of guilt (see epigraph). An unnamed father admits to selling his children into slavery, an opening that conveys lifelong remorse—and memory.

The memorable "return" of the Middle Passage, not only in this novel, or in *Lara* and *Fruit of the Lemon,* marks a number of black British, Caribbean, and African American texts. In Phillips's novel, however, memory predates the middle passage which sets his novel off, since it structurally resists a dichotic opposition of perpetrator and victim along the color line. *Lara* opens with a prologue relating the mythical return of Tolulope, a slave woman who turns into a bird and circles the plantation, dropping a baobab seed, and living in the growing tree, until she returns across the ocean, from Brazil to Nigeria. One hundred years later, Lara's ancestor "Baba" follows her, and in 1990, Lara herself "returns."

Given Tolulope's prologue, *Lara* is from the outset a journey of return fraught with complicated historical involvement rather than an attempt at a rosy restoration. In Levy's novel *Fruit of the Lemon*, it becomes clear that the school's history lessons on the Atlantic Triangle have a different meaning for the black protagonist than for her white peers: Faith Jackson, born to Jamaican parents in London, conflates the vessel her parents took to England from Jamaica in 1948 with a slave ship that probably transported her ancestors centuries earlier. Both protagonists can hear only the echoes of the choral memory which Phillips's fictional father possesses, but they are impelled to reconstruct memory, and to construct it.[13]

Both narrators are "on the move," staging a fluid, migratory identity. Their journeying, a theme with which both narratives are imbued, representative of their respective quests for identity which for them imply leaving England and turning to familial homelands, motivates the protagonists to question the ground on which they stand, the very structures that fail to reflect and symbolically house their identities. Their travels reinterpret the borders drawn for them and constitute an inquiry into "Englishness" as much as into their own identity, for the two are connected.

Fruit of the Lemon: Columbus Is My Middle Name

> Identity is formed at the unstable point where the "unspeakable" stories of subjectivity meet the narratives of history, of a culture. And since he/she is positioned in relation to cultured narratives which have been profoundly expropriated[,] the colonized subject is always "somewhere else": doubly marginalized, displaced, always *other* than where he or she is, or is able to speak from.
> —(HALL 1987, 44; ORIGINAL EMPHASIS)

Andrea Levy's third novel, *Fruit of the Lemon* (1999), tells the story of Faith Jackson. Beginning with the young woman finding her first job at the BBC, flashbacks cover her childhood. At work she is barred from promotion by prejudiced managers, as her white colleagues had already led her to believe she would be. Her immigrant parents, too, had always warned her not to aim "too high." When a love affair with a young white man fails, and Faith feels that her skin color had been decisive also in this case, she has a breakdown and retreats, unable to face the world. Her parents present her with the option of traveling to Jamaica when they learn of her predicament.

It is significant that Faith works for the *British* Broadcasting Corporation; like the NHS in Levy's previous work (see chapter 2), this is a *pars pro toto* figure. As a sphere where racism is played out, a national institution is chosen by the writer. By synecdoche these institutions are related to Britain as a whole.[14] In her novel *Looking for Maya*, Atima Srivastava makes such a connection explicit; one of her characters learns in school "that the Welfare State and the National Health were the jewels in the crown of Britain" (1999, 191).

"England"

Lemon tree very pretty,
And the lemon flower is sweet,
But the fruit of the poor lemon
Is impossible to eat.
—(LEVY 1999, EPIGRAPH)

In *Fruit of the Lemon*, Faith "discovers" her family history. The novel is interspersed with illustrations of the growing family tree. As has already been mentioned, it opens with a sapling (her London family) which grows until the novel closes with a mature family tree, after eight generations have finally been covered. It would be more correct to say that Faith "discovers" her family tree, as it merely *seems* to grow, and is therefore a measure of her growing awareness of her family history. The much-used tree metaphor is employed in this novel to indicate the nuances and imbrications of Faith's history. Like Nichols's collection *i is a long memoried woman* with its organicist emphasis on "roots," Levy's tree also reverberates with such roots. (Indeed, if the visual image of a tree is turned on its head, a network of roots becomes visible instead.)

The novel is propelled by Faith's quest for self-knowledge. Her mother had been reluctant to tell her daughter much about the family's history; when asked such questions she is either evasive or short. This makes it difficult for Faith to counter the stories she comes up against. At school, for example, Faith is taunted by boys who bully her. "Faith is a darkie and her mum and dad came on a banana boat," we read in the prologue (Levy 1999, 3). When Faith later learns that her parents did in fact come on a liner which shipped passengers on one deck and bananas on another, she is quite shocked that the "little white boys were right" after all (Levy 1999, 3). In the course of the novel, Faith's self-knowledge grows. Growing up, for Faith, means collecting fragments "until I had a story that seemed to make sense" (1999, 5).

Faith's middle name, Columbine, was given to her in memory of a goat her mother much loved. But given the journey to Jamaica undertaken more than five hundred years after her near namesake, Columbus, Faith's travels are also a voyage of discovery.[15] Faith's explorations, however, are not so much driven by her own inquisitiveness. She leaves for Jamaica at the request of her parents and the book does not indicate that Faith actually goes out of her way to obtain the fragments of her family history. It seems that her relatives simply confront her with these stories, and this leaves Faith as a fairly passive "agent" in the story.[16]

The Jacksons have been saving cardboard boxes in England for as long as their daughter can remember. This had been taken by their daughter Faith as a parental quirk, rather than as a serious pointer to a possible return (Levy 1999, 44 et passim). But when Wade and Mildred Jackson announce they are considering selling their North London house in order to go home, Faith is shocked since she cannot understand why her parents might want to move to Jamaica. The Jacksons' growing collection of cardboard boxes, carefully arranged and preserved in the basement, reveals not only that they were prepared to move on; it also suggests that their time in England was but a temporary—if extended—*stay*.[17] This contrasts starkly with Faith's position in the land of her birth. While her parents, relatives, and visitors alike have talked of Jamaica as "back home," to her it is a place of the imagination, at best an abstract point of origin rather than a home country to which she might literally return.

Paul Gilroy has differentiated between the location of residence and the location of belonging (above). This distinction is of relevance to Faith's parents. House and home are not the same for Wade and Mildred; and their English house, as their previous council flat, may have been a mere habitation or a temporary home for them. But for Faith, her parents' house is her home. When they first mention "moving back," Faith initially mistakes them for wanting to return to the previous council flat. Faith's shock at her parents' plans suggests a fundamental rift running through the family, with Wade and Mildred being Jamaican, Carl and Faith being British. Faith is at home in London, at least more so than in Jamaica.

If the Jacksons' proposed return to Jamaica can be read in terms of homesickness, then this sentiment differs decidedly from Faith's *Heimweh*. Her feeling is sparked off not by geographical dislocation, by living elsewhere. Her "depressed state of mind and body caused by a longing for home"[18] is not stimulated by the *absence* from it. In *Fruit of the Lemon* the numerous rejections experienced by Faith mark her home as not-home. Home is put under erasure and Faith is signaled that she does not belong where she resides. Her location of belonging turns out to be a location of "unbelonging."

As with her parents, the location of residence and of belonging do not coincide for Faith, given her strong experience of "unbelonging" and rejection. However, in the course of the novel Faith finds out that she can choose to locate herself in London and to belong there. This is not dissimilar to Meena's prospects at the conclusion of *Anita and Me*, who has found the confidence to avail herself of belonging (Syal 1996).

Faith's situation comes to crisis when, within a short space of time, her parents consider leaving, her partner goes off with her best friend, and she experiences racism within the family and in a number of personal relationships, as well as on the job and in several other situations.[19] She is called "exotic" (Levy 1999, 125), in a job interview her attitude to work is maligned (1999, 106–7), and her brother and his girlfriend Ruth reprove her for living with white friends, claiming that she "doesn't really like black people" (1999, 143). Faith is subject to mounting pressure and feels assailed from all sides.

When Carl visits Faith in her shared house, she briefly perceives her own "brother as a stranger." She is struck not only by his "faded jeans" and "brown scuffed leather jacket" but also by him being a "black man with a round head of afro hair" (Levy 1999, 53). It is in the company of her white friends, that Faith is taken aback by her brother's appearance, as if setting eyes on him for the first time. Now she sees Carl with different eyes, is estranged from him, and sees him superficially: noting the color of his skin, his hair and physique, his clothes all leave her feeling menaced. She is able to *recall* his "sweet soprano voice" when her angelic brother sang in the church choir—but her racialized view now discerns the opposite: "[T]hey all thought he came to resemble the devil" (1999, 53), Faith remembers, effectively aligning herself with "them," her white peers.

In the previous chapter, reference was made to Hall and Frantz Fanon's work in order to analyze such a charged perception, a glance which amounts to the exertion of cultural power. In the present instance of othering, however, such an exertion of cultural power occurs between siblings, and this indicates that Faith has aligned herself with her white friends and sees her brother in the way that they might. This scene is but an overture to another one.

In the novel's first section entitled "England," Faith has a breakdown for the reasons given above and retreats from everybody to the comfort of her bed. When she glances at her mirror, Faith can see her own reflection, which is described as a "black girl lying in a bed" (Levy 1999, 160). At that moment, the first-person narrator speaks about herself in the third person. Faith now relies upon eyes no longer her own and comes to see herself like (and as) an outsider. Her ego is split; a rift runs right through her/self. Not wanting "to be black any more. I just wanted to live," Faith covers her mirror with a towel and "*Voilà!* I was no longer black" (1999, 160). In this moment of crisis, being black and living unencumbered appear to Faith as mutually exclusive entirely.

I would not want to cast a metaphysical status onto "blackness." It would therefore be incorrect to summarize the first half of the novel as Faith's development toward "disowning her blackness." But Faith loses a comprehensive sense of herself, one which comprises all aspects of her being. The various experiences she undergoes reinforce the rejection she has suffered in a color-conscious and racist society. She is not "black" enough for Ruth, she may not be "white" enough for her friends; she is "too black" for the BBC; she is not sufficiently independent in the eyes of her brother. Her art tutor praises her work that is allegedly marked by "an ethnicity which shines through" (Levy 1999, 31). It is in this state of a forsaken integration of the diverse aspects of her being that Faith "returns" to her parents' birthplace.

"Jamaica"

> And what's the worst thing? It is the emptiness of one's luggage. I'm speaking of invisible suitcases, not the physical, perhaps cardboard, variety containing a few meaning-drained mementoes. . . .
> —(RUSHDIE 1983, 86–87)

Her concerned parents' advice to visit Jamaica is heeded by Faith. Part 2 of the novel, entitled "Jamaica," opens with Faith waiting by the conveyor belt at Kingston Airport which does not, however, deliver her baggage. Faith appears denuded and faces a clean start. Instead of her luggage she is amazed to see the lounge "packed with black faces" (1999, 168), and is daunted to realize that she is struggling with Jamaican English. Leaving the terminal building unsure whether she'd recognize her relatives, Faith contemplates that any Jamaican family "could have claimed" her to find out "about my mum and dad and what had happened to them in the 'Mother Country'" (1999, 175). Her apprehension about a possible mix-up emphasizes that she does not feel attached to anyone in particular at her destination. However, when she meets her aunt and finds her talking and looking like her mother, a connection is forged and part 2 opens with a sort of birth of Faith's Jamaican self.

This "self" is nourished throughout the second part of the book so that when the novel reaches its conclusion, Faith is ready to go "home to England" (Levy 1999, 320). This constitutes a second return for Faith, who is now ready "to return to the rest of my life" (1999, 320). Her voyage of discovery has taught her that her history didn't start with the arrival of her parents in Britain (1999, 325), but that it extends further back in time and place than she had been conscious of. (What precisely has nourished her and how she has grown is not clear from the text, a point to which I will return later.)

> The country where I live, among people so unaware of our *shared past* that all they would see if they were staring at my aunt would be a black woman acting silly.
>
> Let those bully boys walk behind me in the playground.... I am the great-grandchild of Cecelia Hilton. I am descended form Katherine whose mother was a slave. I am the cousin of Africa.... Let them say what they like. Because I am the bastard child of Empire and I will have my day. (Levy 1999, 326–27; emphasis added)

This paragraph opens with Faith insisting on her awareness of a shared history (of colonialism) while reproaching her compatriots for their alleged ignorance of (colonial) history. Faith's explorations in family history have revealed numerous connections and have supplemented her historical knowledge. Before her visit to Jamaica, Faith herself had been unaware of some aspects of "our shared past." This ambiguous phrase refers to the shared past of her family and all Caribbean peoples; and the Caribbean history shared by white Britons is also intended. As history teaches and the protagonist's family tree records, the historical connections between the British and the Caribbean islanders were manifold and complex (cf. the Jacksons' Scottish and English ancestors, transportation across the Atlantic, the institution of chattel slavery). *Fruit of the Lemon* is interested in how these historical connections have repercussions on today's relations between black and white Britons. Its central character regularly hears echoes of a colonial history that involved not only her black and white ancestors but also the black and white people she deals with on a day-to-day basis. However, the impact of this shared history on distinct constituencies is quite varied (cf. below).

Faith had been afflicted by a reduced vision of herself and her brother before she left for Jamaica. Now this perspective has been expunged: "all they would see" is different to what *she* will see from now on. The rift she suffered has begun to heal; she has been purged from crippling self-perception, and is now intent on having her day, on fighting back against "the bullies."

Although it is in character with the protagonist, the strident ring of the last sentence quoted above ("I am the bastard child of Empire and I will have my day") is not untypical for Levy,[20] and it reveals the didactic nature of *Fruit of the Lemon*. In Jamaica, the protagonist uncovers what can be called an alternate history, stories that pertain to her in one way or another. In Jamaica, Faith finds herself—when she opens her aunt's photo album the first page is covered with images of herself, her brother, and her parents. "My family took up nearly half the album," Faith concludes (Levy 1999, 202). But apart from such manifest representations of herself, Faith is drawn into the stories that she "collects," stories reaching back many generations and told to her by various relatives. Faith has family members who were born slaves and who passed through apprenticeship into freedom, as well as a plantation owner who came to Jamaica from England, probably in the late eighteenth century. Her relatives are also of Scottish and Arawak or Indian descent, and some family members have lived in Cuba and in the United States.

Whereas her parents left for London, and Faith and Carl therefore grew up British, their cousins Pauline and Vincent remained in Jamaica while their parents earned a living in New York. Faith realizes how very easily she could have been in her cousins' position. Being thus confronted with how her life could also have turned out differently not only puts into perspective her existence in London, it also makes it easier for her to conceive of alternate histories—and alternate futures as well.

■ ■ ■

M. G. Vassanji's novel *The Gunny Sack* has "Memory" as its first word; its concerns are the play between baggage that is carried by hand, and that which the mind carries. *Fruit of the Lemon* plays with the image of cultural baggage:

> "You can't leave England and come all that way without losing some bit of you."
>
> But I was taking much more back from Jamaica than I could ever have brought with me.
>
> She was surprised at how little of my past had been carried on that banana boat to England. (Levy 1999, 185, 321, 333)

Initially Faith is not only without her luggage, she also loses a bit of herself. She is able to rid herself of her self-hatred and returns to England strengthened as has been seen in the previous section. She returns with stories of herself, of her family, and with a mind of her own.

In view of her extended and multinational family tree, Faith is able to situate herself as a "cousin of Africa" and a "child of the Empire," whereby she lays claim to a personal history that embraces Africa, the

Caribbean, and the British Isles. Faith's story ties her directly to both England and Jamaica, and bridges the British Empire's divide between colonizer and colonized. This also means that she has freed herself from relying solely on her parents' life story; she is beginning to author herself with the help of the narratives she can now recollect. Now she feels equipped to survive England in whose story she is firmly embedded long before her parents' arrival in the metropolis.

Part of the self-assurance, which her travels in Jamaica provide her, stems from the experience of not standing out. It gives Faith comfort that no one takes notice of her; the fact that no one stares or whispers triggers in her the feeling that she could "blend" in and "be anything" in Jamaica (Levy 1999, 293). Whereas in London she had stood apart as a black woman in a number of contexts, in Jamaica being black and inconspicuous is not mutually exclusive.

This is pointed out when Faith observes a poster showing "the people of Jamaica—Chinese, Indian, black with light skin, black with dark." The advertisement (eliding white Jamaicans) bears the caption: "Have you been nice to a tourist today?" (1999, 226). According to Faith's reading of this placard, she *belongs* because she is effortlessly represented in everyday life, as in this poster. The young woman feels she can be part of "the people" in the visualization. However, she also belongs to that other group represented in the poster, the visitors who are supposed to be treated nicely. And ironically Faith finds out later that her parents had tried to ensure just such a "nice treatment" at the hands of their relations. Not only the tourist authority's poster raises questions about the sincerity of geniality experienced by visitors in Jamaica; in Faith's case this is exacerbated by her parents' request of a special treatment.

In many ways, then, Faith *does* stand out as a visitor—certainly as soon as her North London accent becomes audible or her style of dressing is in sight. Shortly after experiencing "blending in," Faith is indeed confronted with stares and whispers; by wearing trousers to church she receives much unwanted attention, and the illusion of effortless belonging bursts (1999, 295).

This happens at a celebration, where Faith encounters her great-aunt Constance, who as a young woman had also returned to Jamaica after being educated in Britain. Her Jamaican mother and English father had sent her abroad for an education, but upon her return Constance rejected both her parents and her English education to live with a Rastafarian community. However, she was no longer accepted by that community when her son turned out to be almost as light-skinned as herself, and in consequence Constance left the group. Having been influenced by Marcus Garvey, Constance and her son, Kofi, "returned" to Sierra Leone. On this journey she experienced further rejections; the other group members "trac[ing] their ancestry" offended her by calling her "Bakkra" and "white." In a further attempt to connect symbolically with Africa, her chosen location of belonging, Constance adopted the name Afria when back in Jamaica.

This episode about the difficulty of belonging to a community which partly rejects one can be related to Faith's story. In London, she had not only been rejected by others but had ultimately rejected herself at the time of her breakdown. Constance/Afria rejected her family, her name, her education, and her community; she was rejected by the Rastafarian community to which she sought to belong, and by her family. In Jamaica, Faith does not stand out in terms of her skin color, which proves a valuable experience for her, but she stands out in other ways. This is mirrored by Constance/Afria's tragic story of one who could have belonged to an educated and light-skinned upper class but who futilely wanted to belong elsewhere. Constance/Afria's story demonstrates the complex process of renegotiating a "location of belonging" (Gilroy's term). All her life Constance/Afria tried to find such a location; tragically, her choice depended on acceptance by a community, and needed to be validated in this fashion. Not recognizing this limitation, Constance/Afria's search remained fruitless.

One of the strengths of Levy's novel is the dramatic irony resulting from reading Constance/Afria as Alter Ego to Faith. Both return journeys are on one level indebted to Garvey's teachings, but his plan for American and Caribbean people of African descent to "return" to Africa en masse aboard his Black Star Steamship Line in the 1920s and 1930s is known to have failed.[21] Constance/Afria's return to Africa has also failed and she deludes herself by claiming a heritage remote from her. Faith's return is not futile, but neither does it restore an unrealistically unbroken and undivided sense of belonging. This sense of partial failure is counterpoised with an idealized notion of "returning," together with its possible rewards, and any organicist overtones which such a sojourn might provoke.

■ ■ ■

The Jamaican part of Levy's novel assembles stories under headings such as "William's Story Told to Me by Coral" (Levy 1999, 239); and there follows a report of a conversation Faith had, for example, with her aunt Coral, containing her interlocutor's discourse as well as Faith's own voice. This formula is kept up when Vincent reveals how the family had been prepared by Faith's parents for her visit. Faith is embarrassed to learn that she was described as "a problem" (Levy 1999, 330–31), and that her mother had entreated her sister to accommodate Faith and to show her Jamaica (1999, 329).

When Faith herself becomes the subject of a story, she recognizes the contingency of the truths comprised in the stories she has gathered. The stories are inflected by her interlocutors' biases, their relationships to the subject, and by her own codes of understanding. This does not invalidate her wealth of stories, but it does put them into perspective. Just as her parents were able to utilize their narrative powers to procure Faith's invitation to Kingston, Faith can now take recourse to stories and employ them as needed.

Vincent tells Faith *her* story adjacent to a "wooden shack that leant dangerously." The structure is emblematic of Faith's newly gained and endangered confidence, which by implication also appears "as if one gentle prod could tip it onto the ground" (1999, 328). Having learned to fall back on memory and history upon her "discovery" of these structures to safeguard her, the end result of Faith's formation is expressed in terms of a building—an analogy which is nothing if not worn, and not only in black British literature.[22] But the newly derived powers are effective already: the house does not collapse, Faith withstands. Her growth over the preceding few weeks, her formation, is marked by her ability to simply smile at Vincent despite her acute disappointment and anger.

Stereotypes and Preconceptions

Jamaica is a mystery to Faith, as it is to the implied readers. Faith is perplexed at its language, food, and drink. In some places the novel employs a type of linguistic and cultural "glossing" toward Jamaican English. The Jamaican staple fried festival, for example, is dubbed "festival bread" (1999, 253), sorrel becomes "sorrel juice" (1999, 181), and Devon House in Kingston is explained to the reader in detail (1999, 322). Furthermore, some of the images of Jamaica are well known from travel advertisements, such as a description of "coconut palms" on a beach under a "blue sky," which is simply summarized as "Paradise" (1999, 321).

Fruit of the Lemon does not shy away from displaying some of the stereotypes Faith harbors toward the "land of crawly things"—a land which incorporates "things that bite, sting and kill you" (1999, 202).

With respect to her aunt's house, for instance, the young woman imagines a "mud hut" and is consequently surprised when "Formica worktops" and certain *mod cons* remind her of home (1999, 180). Her cousin's wife reminds Faith of "Black and White Minstrels" but she is "ashamed" (1999, 206) of this association, and is generally "careful not to offend" (1999, 197).

Fruit of the Lemon engages with the nature and effects of stereotypes in situations of unequal distribution of power. Constance is taught as a child to eat lemons with a spoon because her parents assume that this is what "the English do." The habit of eating fruit (maybe grapefruit) with cutlery is transferred to fruits which are not normally eaten on their own. Hence, when Constance moves to her paternal grandparents in the English countryside, they are understandably surprised at this peculiar habit. This act of cultural mistranslation is no longer recognizable as such in an English context. If seen as an act of mimicry, it is not of the agency-producing kind as theorized by Homi Bhabha;[23] it can rather be formalized as a case of imitating the colonizer in an attempt at upward social mobility on the part of Constance's mother.[24]

It is noteworthy that the novel is not only concerned with the growth of a family tree, but also takes its title from William Holt's song about a lemon tree.[25] As a young girl, Constance is made to eat the bitter fruit by parents who think it is for her and their own good. The child is geared to chase seemingly English ideals, only to reject them when older. But the technique of mimicry remains with her, even if the direction of her mimicry changes several times as she grows up. Constance/Afria's tragic story of failed identification would seem to indicate the pitfalls of misconceived intercultural transactions. Afria seems to have failed to establish her own ideals and is also not able to convincingly portray toward others those ideals which she follows as her own.

The fruit of the lemon thus stands for a failed intercultural transaction, an inedible food eaten for the sake of it. In so far as Faith has Constance as her alter ego, it is vital to note that her story differs from Constance's. The protagonist succeeds in making her own choices and breaks free from her own parents. However, she is not driven toward total opposition—something which, as in Constance's case, can paradoxically constitute an extreme case of dependence on what is protested. Rejection constitutes and presupposes an acknowledgment of that which is rejected.

Neither Faith nor Constance possesses the qualities of stability and resistance to change that their names suggest. While Constance undergoes quite dramatic mutations, Faith achieves change without any sense of total rejection, and without losing sight of her own basic premises. Her "return" journey to Jamaica helps to make her tree take root and flourish, and produce edible fruit. If she herself represents the product of such a lemon tree, Faith, to take the organicist metaphor slightly further, is geared toward successful horticulture upon her return to Britain.

The novel is careful to reveal Faith's preconceptions regarding Jamaica—preconceptions which signal that, despite the young woman's family ties, her perception of the country is not dissimilar from that of her white peers. The affiliations with Jamaica come about in the course of Faith's visit, and are constructed rather than "given." The genealogy which the novel develops is a *historically produced formation*—it does not result from a direct connection between Faith and Jamaica. However, as the following section will show, Faith is differently positioned to her white peers in Britain; the novel explores a variety of "contact zones" between nations, cultures, and regions.

Black British Pastoral

> [T]he country always looked so charming. Miles and miles of picture-book pretty that reminded me of trips to the seaside with Mum and Dad. "England is lovely—when you get out of the filthy city, England is a lovely place," Mom always said.
>
> Occasionally we used to stop, to get out of the van with the aim of running through a field or paddling in a river. But we were always greeted with fences and gates and barbed wire. And we never knew how to actually get onto "that green and pleasant land."
>
> —(LEVY 1999, 56)

The pastoral is a constant in black British writing, even in texts where the setting is predominantly metropolitan.[26] It was Raymond Williams who worked on the relationship of the country and the city, positing a similar structure of mutual symbolic and socioeconomic dependency between colony and metropolis (Williams 1973). While the English countryside appears charming and full of "picture-book pretty," Faith is always barred from entering it. She is not able to enter "that green and pleasant land." As if to underscore the analogy suggested by Williams, Faith faces similar impediments in Jamaica; the heavily secured, cage-like fortress that is the Kingstonian middle-class home is only open to her because she is her aunt's guest. Faith, who was once surprised by her father when she had left the key in the front door, is not as security-conscious as her elders, and would prefer it if fewer restrictions were placed on her movements.

When Faith considers herself a child of the empire (above), this indicates a sense of belonging; this, however, is thrown into relief by the qualification "bastard child," which suggests illegitimacy and unbelonging (Levy 1999, 327). This is borne out figuratively by Faith being barred access from the English countryside and by the other obstructions she suffers. In Levy's earlier texts, *Never Far from Nowhere* and *Every Light in the House Burnin'*, the countryside is portrayed as particularly resistant to the coexistence of white and black Britons. It is significant that Britain often imagines itself in pastoral terms when these are precisely the terms that exclude black Britons.

Historical connections to the British Empire are present in Faith's mind, whether she interprets her brother's drawing of a triangle as historically significant, or when she encounters Simon's safari-jacketed father who seems to have "stepped out of the plains of Africa after a hunting trip." Incongruously, it is in the heart of England that Faith meets this "white man" full of tales of Kenya (Levy 1999, 120). Faith notes how "old and frail" the man looks, how spent the ideas he embodies now seem. Ironically, *she* is considered exotic-looking (1999, 125), when it is Simon's father who seems to have emerged from a time machine.

In contrast to her parents' collection of boxes, and the transience indicated by the image, in the countryside Faith is impressed by an image of stability and continuity, of "Englishness" even: a sizeable mansion containing "[o]ld furniture passed down from generation to generation" (1999, 121). "Pa" may be the ex-colonial Faith supposes, but for all the stories he might have to tell, she perceives him as rooted in the countryside, and as belonging. His home apparently comes intact with a well-greased old-boy network (1999, 126), and an unwillingness to acknowledge history. Faith feels compelled to confront Mr. Bunyan, a valued family friend, who appears oblivious to the history of slavery, and merely recalls the so-called civilizing mission. With reference to a namesake he had met in Jamaica, Faith charges: "Your family probably owned his family once" (1999, 131).

This is a good example of colonial history having repercussions in Faith's everyday life. Her sensitivity is, crucially, not reciprocated by many of the white Britons she is confronted with. Although Faith questions Simon's notion of a "[q]uintessentially English" village (1999, 115), in Jamaica she actually becomes surer of what it might mean to feel English: "I had never in my life felt so English" (1999, 225). However, Faith is English in quite a different way to Simon or her father and her connection to the history of the British Empire is similarly distinct. She challenges Bunyan, when Simon, possibly with a view to his career prospects, refrains from criticism. Faith identifies "Pa" with the side of the colonizers; she identifies herself, however, with illicit progeny and even with unwanted immigrants.

Faith has been seen to have embarked on a voyage of discovery, a voyage that takes her not only to Jamaica but also into the "regions" of England and across distinct British cultures. Her voyage is not so much a discovery of roots as the charting of routes. Faith seeks to clarify for herself how she relates to her Jamaican and African family history, but her affiliations will impact on her identifications within London.

Lara: Sentimental Journey?

> The Negro, however sincere, is the slave of the past. None the less I am a man. . . . In no way should I dedicate myself to the revival of an unjustly unrecognised Negro civilization. I will not make myself the man of any past. I do not want to exalt the past at the expense of my present and of my future. . . . Have I no other purpose on earth, then, but to avenge the Negro of the seventeenth century. . . . My life should not be devoted to drawing up the balance sheet of Negro values. . . . *I am not a prisoner of history.* I should not seek there for the meaning of my destiny. *In the world through which I travel, I am endlessly creating myself.* . . . Am I going to ask the contemporary white man to answer for the slave-ships of the seventeenth century? . . . I am not the slave of the Slavery that dehumanized my ancestors. . . . The Negro is not. Any more than the white man.
> — (FANON 1952, 225–31; EMPHASES ADDED)

This quotation from the conclusion of Frantz Fanon's *Black Skin, White Masks* points to the dangers of idealizing returns. Fanon stresses the tension between the desire for restoration and the revenge of the past and, in Nichols's diction, the "charting [of one's] own future" (Nichols 1983, 86). At the same time, the non-essentialized human being, delineated merely by her or his shared humanity, is posited by Fanon; black man or white woman are seen not as essential characteristics but as (self-) created constructions.

Like Levy's novel, Bernardine Evaristo's *Lara* features a wandering protagonist. Lara's travels evoke the history of the European conquest of South America and the colonization of Africa, and they evoke the population movements these imperial enterprises induced. Lara travels backward through time, symbolically reversing the history of her ancestors while retelling it. That is, she "returns" to Africa *before* "turning" to Brazil. Her ancestors sought to travel across the Atlantic in the opposite direction; having been born in Brazil, they desired to return to West Africa.

As she works her way upriver to the interior of the Brazilian rainforest, Lara explores the limits of her own history, the limits of its retrievability, and the limits of her own consciousness. She succeeds in claiming personal and collective pasts and in giving new meaning to her present. In Levy's novel, Faith goes down the same route but is less self-determined; she therefore remains, to a higher degree, subject to external determination by the stories to which she is exposed. Lara develops from being enthralled by the past to being in a position where the lyrical I is strong enough to author herself in her own image. At the end of the novel, Lara, the artist, arrives at a crucial understanding of the creative process, vowing to paint the "Daddy People" (Evaristo 1997, 140) out of her thoughts, and thereby freeing herself of a recurring dream. In line with Fanonist thinking, Lara is now intent on working through the memory of slavery, and thereby both acknowledging and leaving behind ancestral historical experience. Her travels have led her to encounter her ancestors in order to disidentify herself from them, to underscore her separateness and her difference.

■ ■ ■

Lara is a formally innovative text. Although the book is often treated as though it were a novel, Evaristo has employed blank verse in her prose poem and the layout, comprising an index of first lines, is that of poetry. The lyrical form is well suited to honing Lara's voice, to conveying its evolving tune; but as in a drama, there are many voices that either add to Lara's story, or are incorporated by her. One reviewer has suggested that the verse form "channels and disciplines" Evaristo's narrative talent (Brown 1999, 84). The poem's flowing rhythm accords with the protagonist's peregrinations, evoking and orchestrating Lara's experiences and moods.

Stewart Brown has rightly celebrated Evaristo's début as "enriching the vocabulary of both form and utterance," ascribing to it a "multicultural British consciousness" which manifests itself in new and hybrid aesthetic forms (1999, 84). *Lara*'s formal and aesthetic properties reflect its narrative and ideological content. The narrative poem is told in a complex manner: Not only does it skip in time and space; the narrative perspectives constantly shift, sometimes between, sometimes within the fourteen chapters. Over one hundred and fifty years are spanned, and the protagonist's voyages link Brazil, Nigeria, and England. The connections that the reader has to make going back and forth from chapter to chapter, from focalizer to focalizer, from perspective to perspective, mirror the connections that are forged by and articulated in the text itself. While the poem *recites* the links of continents and generations, histories and characters, it at once *performs* these connections.

"Born into Whiteness"

Years before I'd made my teenage foray into Brixton, / awed by the vivacious tableaux of Atlantic faces. I was born / into whiteness, this was the moon, I was elated.
—(EVARISTO 1997, 88)

For Lara, as the excerpted passage suggests, life in the suburbs equals the absence of "Atlantic faces" and implies being surrounded by "whiteness." Her advances into Brixton, South London, with its large population of black people, constituted an eye-opener for Lara, and made clear that she did not have to live in the isolation of Eltham and Woolwich. Like Faith, at Kingston Airport, Lara is bewildered by Brixton which seems to her as strange as the moon. This early experience foreshadows her later travels, and pinpoints the significance of being taken outside one's surroundings and being confronted with difference—on one's way "home." While Brixton is alien to Lara at an early age, her later visits are elating experiences which make her feel self-confident.

Growing up in the London of the 1960s and 1970s to a Nigerian father and a mother of Anglo-Irish descent,[27] racism casts a shadow over Lara and her family's life, for it was during this period that the immigration laws for Commonwealth citizens were tightened and the police adopted repressive strategies such as " stop and search" against blacks and Asians. Taiwo and Ellen's marriage had been considered an "unspeakable union" (1997, 34) from its inception in the 1950s, and their eight children suffer from taunts in school as well as attacks by the National Front in the 1970s. Taiwo calls himself Bill—"after William the Great"—because he finds that "an African name closes doors" (1997, 5). Lara's father declaims: "How I tire of defending my right to exist on these/ great British isles," to which he adds sarcastically: "Hey! What a speech! I will write a play" (1997, 49). This self-ironic lament does not only try to make light of the state of affairs. It also indicates an awareness of topicality and points to *Lara's* narrative self-consciousness, a text aware of having to place itself among "rival accounts" of related histories and journeys.

Racism is shown to be occurring in Nigeria as well as in England, where it is much more marked. Taiwo's mother writes to her son that he had better find a Nigerian bride: "So! You choose an England-lady to woo? Eh! Eh!/ Son! There are plenty nice Nigerian girls here!/ Come home soon to look after your poor mama" (Evaristo 1997, 26). Lara's Irish grandmother Edith Burt was shocked when her daughter Ellen, Lara's mother, decided to forsake her vocation to become a nun in order to marry Taiwo: "A native from a colony! Good Lord!/ So he *is* dark! Have you no sense of morals!/ . . . Good grief, whatever next!" (1997, 29).

Racism is also an influence which has become internalized in Lara. Witnessing her father being taunted and assailed by racists proves a difficult experience for her. When the young girl objects that "it was bloody embarrassing having a black dad" (1997, 70), it is significant that her complaint echoes a racist remark made about herself by her friend's boyfriend (see 1997, 67). This indicates the problematic nature of Lara's situation, her imbrication in society and its patterns. Her character formation is subject to a whole host of influences, racist ones among them. While her assertion is but an explanation of how she feels—intended to clarify the difficulty of her position—the fact that she is seen to unwittingly mimic a racist comment points to the traces a racist society has already left on her. Given Lara's birth into "whiteness," her assertion can also be read as an indication that she has not yet come to terms with being black in England.

Lara's claim to Englishness is questioned in many contexts: her friends, for example, consider her skin tone to contradict her citizenship. In an all-white school in Woolwich, Southeast London, Lara at first does not notice "her" difference but becomes increasingly self-conscious.[28] Visibility, e.g., conspicuousness at school, is a burden not carried by all minorities. Lara's aunt Dora, for example, is married to Heini: after his escape from Nazi Germany, this couple "chose the invisible life" in London (Evaristo 1997, 45). But being black, this option is foreclosed to Lara. Moreover, she wants both "to be invisible" and "to be noticed" (1997, 70). This reveals the desire to be in control of one's representation, of how one is perceived, of what becomes noticeable and what remains unseen.

It is racism that seems to be central to Lara's desire to travel, to seek out her "origins," and to come to terms with her past. As in Levy's novel, the need for social and cultural transformation becomes apparent in the lives of the protagonists at home. It is partly racism that induces Lara, like Faith, to travel back in time and space as if to reach out to lost origins.

> Home. I searched but could not find myself,
> not on the screen, billboards, books, magazines,
> and first and last not in the mirror, my demon, my love
> which faded my brownness into a Bardot likeness.
>
> . . . .
>
> . . . up three flights to the roof
> where in the silence of the sky I longed for an image,
> a story, to speak me, describe me, birth me whole.
> Living in my skin, I was, but which one?
> (Evaristo 1997, 69; cf. 97)

These stanzas have to do with representation in all its complexity. Home is seen here as the locus of self-identity, of assured self-knowledge, and of being represented. The gendered and adolescent pressures of looking a certain way, and of fashioning the body in accordance with the icons of the day, make it even harder for Lara than her white peers to locate an image that could represent her intact. Since such an image cannot be retrieved, fragmentation is conveyed in these stanzas. Lara desires to feel unbroken, and seeks a *rebirth* which she likens to being represented by an image or a story "to speak" and "describe" her in her entirety.

In a relationship with Josh, during her sexual awakening, she is on her way to finding such a "home," to feeling at home within her skin: "I began to dip into my skin like a wet suit," Lara confesses (1997, 87). With growing confidence, Lara learns to inhabit the castle of her skin, until the scope granted her becomes too confined.

Lara aspires to "emerge,/ the sum of all [her] parts" (1997, 97), rather than having to choose which facet of her personality to emphasize, which of her "skins" to inhabit. "Skin" is here a dwelling place, a room, a dress; the implication of the plural form is that there are other skins, like facets of a personality. Lara then resists being reduced to one facet of her personality, to one "part," to one "skin." The text conveys a nuanced conception of identity as multiply inflected and subject to change.

In accordance with the novel of transformation, and like Levy's Faith, Lara tries out different roles, and "wears different skins," while she is growing. In addition to that, like Meera Syal's Meena, who wants to shed her "body like a snake slithering out of its skin and emerge reborn, pink and unrecognizable," and like Faith's desire for invisibility, for "whiteness," Lara wants her "brownness" to fade. This is coupled with the goal of being noticed—but as "Brigitte Bardot" and not as herself.[29] The recurrence of this topos[30] indicates that a color-conscious society is likely to make self-conscious those whom it regards and treats as "other." The exertion of such a homogenizing and normalizing power adds to the challenges depicted in the novel of transformation. Given her alienating experiences of racism, and her pursuit of a story which can express and convey her being, and ultimately deliver her in one piece, Lara embarks on a voyage of discovery.

Across the Dark Waters

> We have floated upwards from history, from memory, from Time.
> —(RUSHDIE 1983, 87)

The eponymous heroine of Bernardine Evaristo's novel in verse has a racially mixed background. The narrative traces both strands of history represented by Lara's parents (although the paternal side is clearly given emphasis). From early in her life Lara is interested in her parents' stories, like Levy's protagonist. However, in both cases the families do not seem to satisfy their children's curiosity. Lara first imagines traveling and creates her own dream world; however, later she travels for real and puts the pieces of "her" story together.

Lara grows up in a house called "Atlantico," near Woolwich Common (Evaristo 1997, 46). The Black Atlantic can be seen as the text's "terrain." Indeed, water is the central metaphor in *Lara*. The room of the womb is a sea left behind with grief when the waters break (1997, 43). The breaking waters at birth have conflicting connotations: affiliation and beginning on the one hand, severance and ending on the other. Birth and the cutting of the umbilical chord stand for belonging but also for dislocation throughout the text (cf. Bahia, 1997, 129).[31] On one level, this is a *donné*, a given, an experience shared by everyone, marking the *condition humaine*. Yet concurrent states of belonging and unbelonging, association and dissociation, are of particular pertinence for Lara. As a "mixed-race" person her "birthright" to live in England is under threat even before she is born. For her, dislocation and alienation are a norm. In the text, and by Lara's experience, belonging, location, and home are all rendered dubious.

It is not only Lara's claim to Englishness and her belonging to England which is questioned; of Nigeria Lara says: "I wonder if I could belong" (1997, 104). This distinguishes Lara from her father, Taiwo. He equates racism with England, writing to his mother that "in this country I am coloured. Back home I was just me" (1997, 4). However, it is precisely this experience of being "just me" which seems unobtainable anywhere for Lara. It is in this respect that her position is distinct from her father's position. In Nigeria, her experience of London mutates her into a "been-to" (1997, 105); this could equally apply to Taiwo, who has been to London as well. However, while perceived as black in London, in her father's birthplace, Lagos (and in contradistinction to him), she becomes "Oyinbo," that is "Whitey" (1997, 104). In this respect, Lara feels that she cannot be "just me" in either London or Lagos.

This also reminds us that the crossing of borders can entail a change in social status and role, and often a change of color (Pettinger 1998, xiv–xv). Lara's travels are marked by such shifts and transformations. When traveling with her friend Trish in the Asian part of Turkey, the young women hold their breaths "as borders fly into blurs, black geese flying amid white" (Evaristo 1997, 96). Lara finds that they "become/ more British" while they darken "with the Turkish sun, yet less aware of race for we are simply: İngiltere" (1997, 97). Traveling to Turkey allows Trish and Lara to inhabit the same category, *İngiltere*, English, whereas in Britain they had been perceived as distinct, as white and black Britons, respectively. Like water, Lara is evolving, in flux. She is not *one* thing, then: her cultural identity is relational; the tenets of constructivism are driven home by her experience.

Water, transformation, is Omilara's element, her name designating such an affiliation in Yoruba mythology. The waters which separate South America, Africa, and Europe at once conjoin these three continents, being the connective medium on which voyages take place. Traversing Europe, across the Bosporus into Turkey's Asian parts, and traveling on the Black Atlantic to West Africa and Brazil, Lara symbolically lays claim to different parts of her history and ancestry. The oceans are a realm in their own right, a space in between the continents which *Lara* reinscribes.

One of Lara's ancestors is Joana, a free black woman who gave birth to Gregorio in Bahia just after slavery had ended in Brazil. The father, "Baba," is an *emancipado* who was given freedom at the death of his "master." Baba remembers in the 1830s that his "son swam into this world cooked in Joana's juices,/ roped to his mother; a cord I knew I would cut" (Evaristo 1997, 129). This severance refers not only to birth but also to Baba taking his son along to Lagos, much to Joana's chagrin. A century before, his ancestors had been sold into slavery from there. Baba returns, closes a gap, but with Joana remaining in the New World a new gulf opens, this time between him and his wife. To her, Bahia is home, whereas Baba has to follow Tolulope to Lagos from where his grandson Taiwo in turn is to leave for London. Joana has claimed a home in Brazil, where she was born, and decides to stay in the New World, while Baba follows a different principle, that of trying to restore an earlier condition, by "returning" to where he has never been. Baba and Joana's choices resemble the options which Faith and Lara discover: They could stay in London, they could visit or "return" to their parental origins, or they could "re-return" to London. But Faith and Lara have the possibility to travel *and* to return; conversely, Baba can only "return" to Africa, Joana can only stay in Brazil.

■ ■ ■

While colonial history may indeed be frequently allocated to its victims, as Paul Gilroy has suggested,[32] *Lara* supplants a clear line between victim/perpetrator. Traveling to Nigeria with her mother and father, Lara finds that

> [the Agudas have] been back a long time.
> Shades style skins, stories colour sins: burnt almond,
> caramel, umber, ivory, rust—antiquities now, long dark
> weals form striped designs across some backs, others
> have the stamp of ownership burnt into baby flesh.
> All were marked for life. Ships sailing sugar canes,
> slave legacy surnames: Salvador, Cardoso, Damazio,
> Carrena, Roberta, da Souza, da Silva, and da Costa.
> (Evaristo 1997, 111)

Lara reads surnames and skin tone as signs of history; the effects of the triangular trade are palpable in *Lara* (the protagonist is traveling the triangular route herself). The text is interested in deciphering signs, and in maintaining their readability. But in view of what is here referred to as "colour sins," or intermarriage, clear distinctions between historical protagonists are not easily made. "*All*" bear marks, the persona insists; and while legibility prevails, clear distinctions have become impossible. Lara's travels indicate that there is no straightforward "belonging" for her; the multiple links and connections she forges through her travels do not merge into one larger strand. Instead they show up the fallacy of notions of original belonging and undoubted origin. But significantly, the historical imbrication and the complexity of Lara's ancestry do not isolate her, as the following section shows.

Using and Loosening the Thralls of History

> Where are your monuments, your battles, martyrs?
> Where is your tribal memory? Sirs,
> in that grey vault. The sea. The sea
> has locked them up. The sea is History.
> —(WALCOTT 1986, 364)

> London retreats, a dislocated memory, immaterial now.
> —(EVARISTO 1997, 97)

The first stanza of Walcott's poem "The Sea Is History" juxtaposes material and immaterial signs of history, suggesting that Caribbean history may be patterned differently to European history. Containing, for example, the remains of many Middle Passage deaths as well as Jamaica's sunken Port Royal, the sea is a repository of historical material traces, while it is on top of the "rocks" (27f), in the island states, that history was made. Lara's voyages are explorations of history, of her ancestry, and also of her own personal memory. Furthermore, the *workings* of memory are explored, its capacities and its functions. Abroad, Lara has the sensation of London retreating while in fact it is she who is withdrawing. But through such *subjectivism* it is possible to displace and dislocate the memory of London. It can be named and unnamed, evoked and revoked. Such productive play with memory facilitates its manipulation and is also indicative of Lara's agency. She is less enthralled by London when putting distance between herself and the city, or when she reconsiders her existence there, as this allows her to utilize her newly attained breathing space.

The above line from *Lara* further indicates that memory, though "immaterial now," *can* in fact be material. But Lara demonstrates her powers to reverse memory, to work with it, and to use it to her own ends, instead of remaining in its thrall. This is the central project of her text, the cultural work accomplished and documented by it.

"History is interviews with winners," Salman Rushdie quipped at a conference titled "London: Post-Colonial City." This phrase emphasizes the now much-criticized imbalance in the representation of "subaltern voices" in historiography.³³ Evaristo's prose poem can be read in this context, inasmuch as it circulates two distinct notions of history and memory. On the one hand, memory and history are seen as confinement. Feeling guilty about having left behind Joana (above), Taiwo's grandfather asserts that "memories are a fort in which I am the prisoner" (Evaristo 1997, 130). For Taiwo, memory of his life in Lagos becomes too painful after his mother, father, and grandfather have all died. At this point he feels compelled to "erase their memory,/ in order to live" (1997, 57). His need for amnesia turns him into a migrant to the mother country. In his London house it is to the mildewed basement that books and memorabilia are relegated (1997, 79). The symbolism of this action underscores the fact that for Taiwo, as for his grandfather, memory is a burden—if not a nightmare—from which he is trying to liberate himself. To him, London is the place of a new beginning; he tries to keep it free from his memories, a strategy which will impact upon his daughter, Lara.

Lara's view is diametrically opposed to that of her male forebears. She resembles more closely her "magical memory grandmother" who is, in allusion to Lara's Irish and African forebears, "churning stories into a babbling stream of poetry oratory" (1997, 124). Lara's journeys through Europe, to Nigeria, and to Brazil indicate a desire to reconnect with her ancestors' stories and with her history. And if identity construction signifies the process of creating a speaking position, then Lara's journey and her use of memory can be interpreted as such a process. But this process is not backward-looking for its own sake; rather it is characterized by movement, by flux, and by its *calculated* recourse to history. Lara hopes, for example, that in Salvador the "past will close in" on her (1997, 137), which indicates that she had felt distanced from her history; but from this experience she will learn to loosen the thralls of history.

It is ironic that former colonial routes are now traveled by postcolonial subjects in a mythopoeic quest for origins. Faith and Lara both peregrinate on colonial trade roots, where coffee, sugar, gold, spices, and slaves were once shipped. But *Lara* can be read as a revisionary project, as it tries to rediscover and remake connections that have been lost in history.³⁴

The final leg of Lara's voyage (before returning to London) is to Brazil's colonial capital, Salvador (the major port of entry for slaves transported from Africa), and on to the present capital, Manaus, in the country's interior. In Salvador she hopes to come into close contact with her past, but "Bahianas [sit] in white . . . as if no sea,/ no history separates them from the traders of Lagos" (1997, 138). Speaking of the Caribbean sea, Walcott envisages the sea as a receptacle of history where "entries" are kept as in an archive. *Lara*'s association of sea and history is reminiscent of Walcott's poem, and is apropos the protagonist's crossings across time and space. In this episode *Lara* takes a stance similar to Caryl Phillips in *Crossing the River*. The responsibility of West African slave traders is accented, and the different historical positions of the descendants of slaves to the descendants of traders are emphasized. Yet, the clear distinctions that Lara seems to be looking for she does not find. The "Bahianas" she encounters are inattentive to the history Lara seeks. The fault lines the protagonist is tracing cannot be seen from up close; they evade her as she approaches.

Still interested in her family, the da Costas, she discovers that "Hundreds of thousands" of da Costas are still around (1997, 138). Structurally, of course, their presence indicates precisely the history the novel traces (family history, slavery, return). In Brazil, the "slave legacy surname" is inscribed by its Portuguese origins but it does not have the unusual quality it has for Lara in London. As in Lagos, there are too many da Costas in Salvador for Lara to make out an individual ancestor on the basis of a name only. During the final stages of her journey, when Lara no longer knows what to seek, she embarks on a river journey. Travel into the South American interior as a literary topos goes back to Sir Walter Raleigh, who was in turn attracted by the myth of El Dorado.[35] The topos is taken up by South American and Caribbean postcolonial writers, such as the Cuban novelist Alejo Carpentier, and the Guyanese writer Wilson Harris. *Lara* partakes of this tradition. Lara's river journey in Brazil is akin to Carpentier's depiction of the search for aboriginal instruments for a museum of oganography in *The Lost Steps* and Donne's pursuit of Amerindians in Harris's *Palace of the Peacock*.

Traveling up the Amazon, Lara has an epiphany at a river stop which bears quoting fully:

> We move on into loneliness, my thoughts become free/ of the chaos of the city, uncensored, the river calms me:/ I become my parents, my ancestors, my gods. We dock,/ a remote settlement, I stretch my pins, earthed, follow/ my singing ears, Catholic hymns hybridized by drums,/ it is a hilltop church, Indian congregation, holding flowers/ and palm fronds. It is Palm Sunday! I hum from the door,/ witness to one culture being orchestrated by another,/ yet the past is gone, the future means transformation. (Evaristo 1997, 139)

Evaristo's poetry successfully uses contemporary language and is not shy about making use of technical and theoretical vocabulary. The organicist overtones found in Levy's novel could be said to be in evidence in this passage, when Lara describes herself as "earthed." However, *pins* is not only a colloquial term for her legs—she has her "pins . . . earthed" much like a microchip. Organicist connotations are thus counterbalanced by the electrotechnical provenience of the metaphor. Instead of being romanticized, Lara's "groundedness" is likened to that of an electrical gadget: the humorous incongruence is able to preclude pious seriousness.

It is Harris and Carpentier's literary project "to reveal the hidden traces of historical experience erased from the collective memory of an exploited and oppressed people" according to Barbara Webb; history can thereby "be reconceived as a future history to be made, *l'historie à faire*" (Webb 1992, 7). For Lara, the future not only means transformation; her travels also mean (re)connecting with ancestral history. Insofar as Lara manages to reinscribe herself into these histories, and into the history of England, history here too becomes "*à faire.*"

From Belem, on the mouth of the Amazon, Lara is swallowed up by the river as she travels upward for fourteen days and nights. Unlike the protagonists in Carpentier and Harris's texts—and unlike Marlow in Conrad's *Heart of Darkness*—Lara is not horrified at the source of the river she has traced. Calmed, her circuits earthed, the non-Catholic is ready for Palm Sunday in Brazil. Hers is not a triumphal entry into Jerusalem (or Belem or Manaus). Instead, Lara undergoes a cathartic transformation. The white noise of the city is released; Lara arrives, she "docks" at a settlement to become parents/ ancestors/ gods. But her transformation does not end with this return and her rebirth. Her auricles are tuned to a syncretic music that blends Catholic hymns with African drums beaten for an Indian church. Lara has a vision of permutation. She foresees an age characterized not by origin and the past, but by transformation and the future.

Lara's closing lines, sung in the Amazonian city of Manaus, are a manifesto to loosen the thralls of history. The desire to become her parents, ancestors, gods is only a means to an end, a passing phase en route to a future understood as transformation. Neither erasing memory (which her father attempted) nor any longer wishing to submit herself to memory (as she once did), Lara frees herself from subscribing to one origin, to one memory, to one history. Instead she claims a multitude. The text finally defies purity, the notion of an uncorrupted source to which a return might be possible. Histories, human beings, ways of life are inextricably bound up with each other: Bahia with Lagos with London, a concept of mutuality that is well rendered in the line "one culture being orchestrated by another."

In the spirit of the epigraph taken from Said at this chapter's opening, *Lara* renders traditions as *evolved*, as "live," as woman-made. Moreover, self-expression, whether observed in a remote Amazonian settlement or performed in metropolitan London, is also autopoiesis, self-creation. Ritual, rite, and work of art can constitute and effect transformation, as Lara herself experiences. Omilara, whose "family are like water" (1997, 43), understands that her history, like water, is everywhere. She is "baptised, resolv[ing] to paint slavery out of" her and to convey her "Daddy People onto canvas" (1997, 140). Personal and historical experience become not the source of anxiety but are transformed into a source for art. Lara is a painter whose influences are quite diverse: "Hackney, afro-beat and Blue Peter!" (1997, 95). Her mixed heritage constitutes a rich resource, and Lara vows to reconnect with Africa and South America again and again from her European location. Her lyrical voice and her compositions allow her to recreate herself. And they allow her to return to London, to "step out of Heathrow" (1997, 140).

Her voyage has taken her through the past and she has overcome belatedness. Her need to follow on and pursue has been exhausted, and Lara herself becomes a witness (1997, 139) and a participant of ritual, rather than a voyager through time in pursuit of previous witnesses and antecedent rites. The volume that opened with the scent of "sugar cane" (1997, 1), redolent of the plantation economy, closes with Lara stepping into the "future" (140).

The Diasporic Bildungsroman: Calling London

London calling The Empire! Calling The Empire!
—(EVARISTO 1997, 3)

It was this siren call that lured Lara's father, Taiwo, from Lagos to the erstwhile colonial capital. The famous *Caribbean Voices* program produced by the BBC, from which the refrain stems, was not only a haven for writers like Henry Swanzy and V. S. Naipaul when they came to England. Programs such as these were broadcast in the colonies and added to the attraction of London's calls, inducing migrants to seek their fortune in the metropolis. Ironically, the BBC program used to start with the phrase "Calling London"—a phrase which is, however, reversed in the popular imagination, as reflected in *Lara*. While the original radio chime appealed to the centrality of London in the world of broadcasting—relegating the colonies and former colonies to mere outposts—its reversal stresses the significance of the "margins" which are hence called "in."

Focusing on racism, both novels show the necessity for social, political, and cultural transformation in the lives of their protagonists in London. Both narratives, then, travel back in time *as if* to search for lost origins. In this movement, personal history is overlaid with family history and with collective history. The quest motif in fact suggests a mythical structure (separation, exile, and return) which also ties in with these three levels of history. But the protagonists do not actually pursue lost origins. Faith charts connections with her Jamaican family and begins to look to Africa before she returns to London. She has not found lost origins but has affiliated herself in new ways. *Lara*'s more complex travels and travails make it plain, too, that it is Lara's own efforts which allow her to construct connections and claim affiliations. She forsakes her initial attempt at salvaging and recuperating histories: en route she decides no longer to chase her destiny and discovers her own creative potential.

These processes involve a genesis of consciousness on the part of Lara and Faith. At the end of their journeys, both young women are ready to return to London with an understanding of the nature of their alienation, not only in a cultural sense but in broader existential terms. After their formation process the protagonists are enabled to return to London strengthened and equipped to position themselves in a satisfactory fashion.

A "return," as sought in *Lara* and *Fruit of the Lemon*, is prone to idealizations of the past, to notions of a mythical Golden Age. However, *Lara* is careful not to idealize the times and places that are revisited by the protagonist. The exploration of her past constitutes a process of demystification in which the protagonist sheds romantic notions of an earthly paradise. The quest for origins in both Levy and Evaristo's texts does not seek to reestablish a mythical Golden Age preceding European conquest and slavery. In the case of *Lara* it leads instead to an affirmation of the creative potential of the future in view of the past, a motif that was seen in Nichols's poem at this chapter's opening.

Levy's Faith seems to retain the romantic notion of being contained in her past, of originating from it, and of being authorized by it. Given a history of cultural and psychic dismemberment, this reconstruction of historical memory is not necessarily geared toward a positive or future-oriented goal. Although her travels have endowed Faith with a more positive outlook on her future, I have suggested that the precise nature of her transformation is not rendered clearly in the novel.

While Lara is more self-reliant and autonomous in dealing with "her" history, Faith simply collects stories, rather than actively searching for them. This is a fairly passive process, and allows her to potentially recollect "her" stories in London. But how, precisely, agency is produced (as the text implies), Levy's novel does not disclose. How is Faith changed; how is she strengthened? Why does her visit to Jamaica empower her as it seems to have done at the novel's close? These questions remain unanswered.

Although the bildungsroman resembles the picaresque novel, with both genres following a simple basic pattern of departure, growth, and return, there are important differences which *Lara* and *Fruit of the Lemon* render clear. The Picaro lacks self-consciousness and ultimately development; adventures are lived through for their own sake.[36] The bildungs-hero, however, follows a path that is far from inconsequential; instead, *formation* is achieved. Returning in this case denotes a return with a new consciousness, or even as a different person.

Faith and Lara both undergo such a development and return home with renewed strength and confidence. But theirs is a *diasporic* bildungsroman which leaves them aware of the condition of diaspora, aware of their own specific history. Certainly in Lara's case, it is this particular knowledge which invigorates her and facilitates her claims for an empowered subject position. Both journeys entail the genesis of consciousness, and a renewed assuredness in one's historical "origin" and in one's ability to position oneself. Faith and Lara come to construct cultural identities.[37] That is, they have learned to position themselves in narratives of the past without being overdetermined by these narratives of the past. They have exposed themselves to the play of "history, culture, and power," and learned to use these discourses productively, rather than being merely positioned (and used) by them.

As has been seen, Evaristo and Levy both use history, anecdote, and memory in their novels. This allows them to chart the developments of their protagonists, and to thereby explore problems of cultural identity and historical presence. In both narratives, Caribbean, Latin American, and African history, respectively, provide the contexts for a search for cultural and personal identity.

It is telling that both texts reach a conclusion with an arrival in London, with its emphatic embrace even. The double "returns" of Faith and Lara, first to their parents' birthplaces and then again to their own birthplace, signify their multiple attachments, and point to the condition of diaspora. At the end of her journey, and at the close of *Fruit of the Lemon*, Faith lands in England: "I was coming home" (Levy 1999, 339). The recurrent image of the banana boat—which to Faith is also a slave ship—is present at the novel's opening and close. *Lara* also ends on an imminent return to "my island—the 'Great' Tippexed out of it," with the lines: "It is time to leave./ Back to London, across international time zones, I step out of Heathrow and into my future." Faith and Lara arrive in London as their parents once did (deriving respectively from Nigeria, Ireland, and Jamaica). Although their journeys, in contradistinction to their parents' journeys, also originated from London, their travels have indeed changed them. Their travels have moreover changed their perception of London, and via acts of literary *estrangement*, possibly the readers' perception of London as well. Lara and Faith have sharpened, to borrow Stuart Hall's words, their "awareness of the black experience as a *diaspora* experience" (Hall 1988, 29).

The "quality" of Faith and Lara's diaspora experience, however, is not identical to that of their parents' generation. On their travels, the protagonists have also undergone a "process of cultural *diaspora-ization*" (Hall 1988, 30). Theirs is a *cultural* diaspora-ization, which is opposed to their parents' *historical* experience of diaspora. This condition calls attention to itself, and manifests itself in everyday life, as has been seen above. But the disruption and trauma at the root of a historical experience of diaspora is not remembered firsthand by Faith and Lara. It is assimilated and learned rather than self-experienced.

In the case of the protagonists' parents, their experience of diaspora is constituted by the rift between their location of residence and their location of belonging, to use Gilroy's terms. Faith's parents reside in London but they feel they still "belong" in the land of their birth. Lara and Faith, however, do not experience the same division. Their location of residence coincides with their location of belonging—to a point. But their "belonging" is of a more complex nature; their attachment to London, and to Britain, is not recognized and accepted by all. Moreover, by parents, peers, and others, the protagonists are pointed toward different "locations of belonging," as has been demonstrated above. These locations are explored in the course of both novels, and it emerges that there, too, their belonging is not recognized and accepted unanimously. In contradistinction to their parents, for Lara and Faith London remains a territory from which to grapple with aspects of multiple belonging, and to negotiate a form of acceptance. The metropolis constitutes a starting point of their navigations.

It is in this distinction between the parental generation's *experience* of diaspora and the *cultural* "diaspora-ization" of their progeny, that the radical generational conflict which is central to the novel of formation can be concurrently formalized as a *cultural* conflict between distinct generations for the black British novel of transformation.

IV. FOLLOWING ON

Returning does not need to take the form chosen by the characters Lara or Faith; for the diasporic writer, turning back, forging connections with preceding generations of writers and with these writers' origins, can also be a way of returning. Intertextual connections, turning to pretexts, are a common literary strategy. Indeed it has been argued that all texts can be deemed intertextual. It is not only the critic's desire to read a text in a certain context which propels us to categorize literature. Writerly practice, too, looks for traditions, for schools of writing, for alliances, not necessarily to fit in, or follow on from, or, conversely, to contravene; but other writers' texts constitute beacons and buoys when traversing an ocean of words.

Caryl Phillips has described his search for literary ancestry in a piece called "Following On: The Legacy of Lamming and Selvon" (Phillips 1999).[38] At the beginning of his writing career it never occurred to Phillips that he might become a "part of the other club of writers" (34), which included John Fowles, William Golding, Iris Murdoch, and Doris Lessing. Instead, he turned to Ralph Ellison, Richard Wright, James Baldwin, and other African American writers; at first he was able to identify with their sense of what it meant to be a black person in an urban setting. But in the end he was left "feeling that there was still something missing. Like their British contemporaries of the Golding-Lessing school, they were, at least to my eyes, from a different world" (35). At this point he turned to Caribbean writing which he had initially found alienating, mainly because of cultural references which meant little to him.

Phillips, editor of the new Faber Caribbean Series, had grown up in Leeds and

> would no more have known a breadfruit from a plantain, or a mango from a papaya. A hibiscus may as well have been a flamboyant tree for all I knew, and a palm tree was a palm tree was a palm tree. Who cared that there were a dozen varieties of palm trees, all with their

own specific names and histories. Caribbean literature in its broadest sense baffled me. And then I came upon Samuel Selvon and George Lamming. (Phillips 1999, 35)

What appealed to Phillips in Selvon's writing—and what induced Phillips's *return*—was his groundedness in London, coupled with Selvon's sense of rejection. As with the African American writers he had previously aspired to, Phillips recognized the urban landscape in Selvon's writing. But it is "the contradictory tension" (1999, 35) created by Selvon's attraction to and rejection by England which is an element crucial to Phillips, an element missing from his earlier models. The concept of "double consciousness," which W. E. B. Du Bois developed from Hegelian metaphysics, may within limits be applicable to the black British situation, but Selvon's generation arrived in Britain under much different political and historical circumstances than those experienced by African Americans (cf. Gilroy 1993b, chap. 3). While it was economic pressure that triggered West Indian migration in the 1950s and 1960s, the *choice* of the mother country as destination was made by the migrants.

Lamming, the other Caribbean ancestor claimed by Phillips in the same article, attracted him partly because of *Natives of My Person*'s aesthetic properties and formal experiments. Lamming's essays in *The Pleasures of Exile*, which speak of the relationship of language and colonization, of migration, reading and writing, and the influence of West Indian literature on English reading, were also crucial for Phillips's development as a British writer with West Indian origins.

In his chapter titled "Journey to an Expectation," Lamming addresses the question of where the West Indian migrants of the 1950s and 1960s thought they were going and where they actually arrived.[39] Conversely, Phillips makes it plausible that his quest for a literary lineage takes him from African American writers to certain West Indian writers. However, it is not entirely clear whether this lineage holds today, with young British-born writers.

Authors such as David Dabydeen and Caryl Phillips were dubbed in a recent edition of *Wasafiri* as "younger writers influenced by this earlier generation," and were said to have inherited a "legacy,"[40] and yet they actually constitute a middle generation. They are neither wholly party to the migrant writers who came to Britain in the 1950s and 1960s, and they are also distinct from the writers born in Britain between the mid-1960s and 1990s. As is well known, Phillips was taken to Britain when he was only a few months old, and Dabydeen spent his formative years in Guyana but was educated in Britain. Both writers, then, did not have a choice when coming to Britain, but they were not born there either.

We are thus confronted with a form of writing whose relationship to Britain is quite varied; an earlier group of authors who chose Britain (and in some cases chose to move on to other countries); a later group of writers taken to Britain with the option of staying or moving on; and a recent group of writers, such as Evaristo and Levy, who were born in Britain and whose connection to any other territory is more faint.

The situation is actually more complex than this tripartite scheme suggests. Firstly, the expediencies of the British Empire required a class of British-educated "natives" who, in various ways, acted as mediators, educators, and representatives.[41] There is a history, then, of coming to Britain for studies, a history that did not always entail a return to one's colonial origins, or the playing of the predestined roles upon one's return. Some of the leaders and thinkers of the various independence movements of India, Africa, and the West Indies passed through British academia and spent time in this country.[42] Some of the leading writers in post-colonial studies were also schooled in Britain.[43] But before the 1950s, these oscillations do not seem to have produced lasting local networks or "generations" of black British writers. The numbers may not have been sufficient, the circles too isolated and temporary, and the specter of returning loomed large. This changed with extensive migration.

The tripartite structure will also not hold since migration is, of course, ongoing. The novelist Atima Srivastava was born in India, and came to Britain at the age of ten with her parents. In terms of age she would be placed with Evaristo or Bidisha, but in terms of migration she belongs with David Dabydeen and Caryl Phillips. Ultimately, then, we have to go by the writing and not the writer's history, and maintain an awareness of the provisional nature of the categories we employ.

■ ■ ■

Lamming describes the so-called first generation of West Indian writers as living in exile; this entails the writer hungering "for nourishment from a soil" to which he or she could not return for he or she "could not at present endure" it. To this, Lamming adds that the "pleasure and paradox of my own exile is that I belong wherever I am" (1960, 50).[44] In Lamming's view, the West Indian writers exiled in Britain—a group which overlaps to a certain degree with black British writers—are marked by the attraction to and rejection by England, and also by a mutual rejection of the Caribbean homeland. "[A]nd yet," Lamming adds, "there is always an acre of ground in the New World which keeps growing echoes in my head." Lamming relies upon these echoes, and hopes that they "do not die before my work comes to an end" (1960, 50). These echoes and childhood memories have nourished expatriate writers; if the bildungsroman is chosen, it is often set in the "New World" which the writers have left behind. For writers who migrated to Britain early in their lives, the echoes of the Caribbean, the subcontinent, or Africa are mediated through family and friends, through society; therefore they are not as immediate as the echoes described by Lamming.

The middle generation would seem to rely on these memories to a lesser degree; but in a recent interview, the Guyanese-born writer David Dabydeen asserts: "I think of Guyana constantly. I've just come back from Guyana. The first ten, twelve years of your life are the formative years. I spent thirteen years there. Those are the experiences that form your character. . . . So in a sense: yes, I feel Guyanese." However, he adds that the "non-writing part of me, the restrained part of me is Britain. The imaginative part of me is Guyana. But then one can't have these easy dichotomies either" (Dabydeen 1999b, 28). To the middle generation, then, Britain is more in the foreground than it had been (and is) for the exilic writers, for whom Lamming speaks.

Dabydeen's comments also mark the difference between those West Indian exilic writers of the 1950s and 1960s and those who came to England later, and sometimes at an earlier age. Having been shaped by English culture, not only via colonial education but more directly by growing up in Britain, indicates a greater "investment." At the same time, a link to one's birthplace is retained.

While both Lamming and Dabydeen rely on their own distinct memories of their birthplace, British-born writers cannot fall back on the same unmediated resources. For Meera Syal's character Meena, the echo chamber which Lamming mentions has shrunk into a corner. Listening to her parents at a musical evening makes her realize "that there was a corner of [her] that would forever be not England" (Syal 1996, 112). Crucially, the echo chamber is here defined negatively, as "not England," rather than in terms of a more specific location. The reference, pointing not directly to the land of her parents, India, contravenes any sense of Indian cultural nationalism. Syal has Meena echo Rupert Brooke's famous World War I poem, which holds that the "richer dust" of an English soldier's body would transform "some corner of a foreign field," and make it "for ever England" (1915, 44). The reference to Brooke inverts his meaning, underscoring what is "not Engl[ish]" in Britain itself, and thus counters Brooke's chauvinism. In Syal's text it is not the "foreign field" that contains an English corner; Meena herself becomes the battleground containing an "un-English" corner.

Lamming has said that for the novelists of his generation "the new Caribbean" may not emerge. "It will be, like the future, an item on the list of possessions which the next generation of writers and builders will claim" (1960, 50). Phillips and Dabydeen have made this claim; they *follow on* while they stand on different ground than their literary fathers and mothers. A similar point can be made for Fred D'Aguiar and, up to a point, Grace Nichols, and it may also be true of certain writers with African or Asian connections, such as Ben Okri or Romesh Gunesekera.

However, a "return," while already problematical to Lamming or Selvon,[45] is far less possible for the middle generation, as the novelistic travelogues by Caryl Phillips suggest.[46] But British-born writers such as Hanif Kureishi, Andrea Levy, Bernardine Evaristo, Diran Adebayo, or Ravinder Randhawa—writers who are also under investigation in this study of the novel of transformation—do not possess this dual allegiance in the same way. The returns staged by Andrea Levy and Bernardine Evaristo's protagonists lack the vibrant echoes which Lamming describes, and are not evidence of a desire to return; the protagonists (and authors) are not exiled in Britain. But at the same time, a tension between attraction and rejection remains crucial, if not in the terms laid down by Lamming. Faith and Lara undertake "return journeys" *and* are attracted back to London. But they are positioned differently, abroad and in London, to those who have themselves migrated. Likewise, writers such as Kureishi, Adebayo, or Randhawa are still not by default considered as belonging to British literature—but there is no default "alternative belonging" available to them either (cf. chapter 5).

In Diran Adebayo's first novel, Dele describes himself as a Londoner "yet to set foot in his home country," and feels "nostalgia without memory" for the Nigeria he misses without ever having visited it (1996a, 29, 169). Likewise, among British-born writers, the echoes of ancestral home cultures may be present but the echo chambers are filled with other sounds too; the heritage is a complicated and multilayered one. Meena finds within herself a corner of "Otherness" or "Indianness," but Lara, Meena, and Dele also embody a great deal of Englishness. Arguably this is taken further with "mixed race" protagonists as deployed by Andrea Levy and Zadie Smith (see chapter 3 and the conclusion, respectively).

Generating Generations: Literature of Belonging

> However far the stream flows,
> it never forgets its source.
> —Yoruba proverb
> —(EVARISTO 1997, i)

In 1762 Olaudah Equiano, one of the ancestors of black British literature, was sold on the river Thames, near Deptford, Southeast London (Equiano 1789, 58). He could not reach the shore where the law would have protected him. The river can thus be considered an extension of the oceans and of the British Empire that reached into London, or that emanated from it—a question that *Heart of Darkness* leaves pending.

This chapter has reflected upon lineage, genealogy, and generations. It has been argued in chapter 1, however, that the notion of generations, in the sense of one category neatly bringing forth the next, is inappropriate particularly with respect to black British literature. The debts and sources are multiple and multidirected, and the future course seems similarly multidirectional.

Members of three "generations" are all writing concurrently; the appearance of a successor does not entail the silence of those succeeded. But despite this apparent synchronicity, their writings do not share the same historical and cultural moment and are marked by synchronous asynchronicity. Their writings partake of and contribute to different cultural moments—at the same time.

■ ■ ■

In 1998, the year of the fiftieth anniversary of the arrival of the SS *Empire Windrush*, a major celebration took place at the Royal Festival Hall. Turning to literature, a number of black British writers were celebrated on this occasion.[47] E. R. Braithwaite, Beryl Gilroy, and George Lamming were celebrated as pioneers; the black British writers Caryl Phillips, David Dabydeen, and Mike Phillips read from their work in later sessions. What was striking in this parade of two generations was the absence of a third one. And it may be precisely this sort of exclusion that Adebayo has in mind when he distinguishes between his peers and "the kind of people who wrote books" already before his time:

> The whole vibe of London has changed in the past 20 or so years—and
> a lot of that has to do with the black presence here. Huge things have

been happening in language, style, culture, but just below the level of the kind of people who wrote books. (Adebayo 1996b, 27)

The author's claim that London has been changed decisively by the presence of black people is not to be doubted. But interestingly, Adebayo emphasizes the changes which have happened during his own lifetime—changes for which his particular age group, born in the mid-1960s, might stand. This is coupled with his insistence that this group's writing differs from earlier literature in that "language, style, [and] culture," which lie "just below the level of the kind of people who wrote books," are now represented. In other words, writers like Selvon or Naipaul or Gilroy, and maybe even Dabydeen, Phillips, and Nichols are accused of not noticing important cultural changes, and of being "out of touch," or at least not representing these changes.

Adebayo's phrase "just below the level" contains a charge of aloofness, and smacks of the divide between popular and high culture, and of the class difference between "the man in the street" and the "ivory tower." Hanif Kureishi's work—to be discussed in the next chapter—could be cited as a counterexample because it breaches this very divide. In fact, Adebayo's own novel can be read very well in conjunction with Kureishi's *The Buddha of Suburbia*.

Adebayo's comment points to the unfolding of a vigorous scene of popular black British literature, which is indeed a recent development. Brought to the fore by the publication of *Yardie*, this writing aims primarily at a black readership. It is mostly entertaining rather than cerebral or somber. Often it is characterized by a marked nationalism which stresses "difference" without pursuing a particular course (or cause). Kwame Dawes has addressed recent developments in black British literature, and has focused particularly upon what could be termed the atomization of black British literature. Joseph Johnson (fig. 1), a black beggar walking the streets of Covent Garden in the early nineteenth century, is represented by cartoonist John Thomas Smith in *Vagabondiana*.

Johnson is depicted wearing an elaborate ship on his head, a wooden replica of the *Nelson* with sails and riggings. In his hand the beggar carries another hat, which he hopes to fill with money in the course of the day. In his provocative long essay, included in a *Wasafiri* special issue on black British literature, Dawes discerns in this image Johnson's self-conscious effort to explain his presence in the British Isles. To Dawes, the ship on Johnson's head is an indictment of British society, and confronts it with "the very ship of abuse, enslavement and adventure" (Dawes 1999, 19).

FIGURE 1
Joseph Johnson, by John Thomas Smith, Vagabondiana (1815)

Clearly, Johnson could be considered one of the black loyalists turned "sadblacks" who people S. I. Martin's historical novel *Incomparable World* (1996). These black characters represented in Martin's novel were provocative insofar as their despondency accused white England of neglect after having enlisted their support during the American Revolution. As Dawes himself admits, however, he may well be over-reading Johnson's hat when he posits the ship as the offensive sign, worn to produce white guilt. For in a sense, this hat is *doubling* Johnson's blackness (which Smith so stereotypically emphasizes). In and by itself blackness was offensive to the white Briton; schemes to remove the growing black population of London were instigated by Elizabeth I, and after the American Revolution, for example (Innes 2002, 8f).

In a sense Johnson's headgear is not a hat; he is wearing his hat in hand, not as a sign of greeting and submission but as a sign of begging. The ship on his head confronts white guilt by making it more explicit; but it turns Johnson into a spectacle of otherness and helps him to generate cash. How often Johnson wore this particular hat (or another symbolically charged headpiece) we do not know, but the sign of blackness is "worn" by him at all times, and continues to be "worn" by black Britons today. I say "worn" since black skin is often noted, seen, and read in opposition to white skin, which is routinely not noted, not seen, not read, and whose normative power renders it invisible in many British contexts.[48]

Dawes's article faults several young black British writers, such as Diran Adebayo and Courttia Newland, for not writing in the tradition of black British literature, and for being too concerned with the American market, and therefore appropriating what are inappropriate traditions in Dawes's view. Young black British writers are seen as not properly "wearing [their] hat" on their head, and not properly negotiating blackness in the light of the traditions they have inherited. Bernardine Evaristo is accused of missing her chance of writing something relevant by refusing to forge new black British myths and by allegedly shunning inherited African or New World mythology (1999, 21). The pop icon Q, like Newland and Adebayo, is criticized for taking up an American iconography and mythology, and for writing market-geared novels (Dawes 1999, 21–23).

But why do these writers need to display a particular consciousness, and wear the ship on their head, in the way Dawes sees fit? And why are they expected to continue a tradition, or inscribe themselves into a particular tradition? Why are they burdened with "the crucial task facing the black British writer, which is to contextualise the black British experience within the larger British socio-political world" (1999, 22)?

American-style gang fighting *is* ongoing in big British cities, much in the way described in Newland's thriller *The Scholar: A West Side Story*. Police and prison *are* the reality for a disproportionately large number of young black men. And poverty and "estate" life *are* an experience many black families go through.[49] Newland's protagonists' wish to escape by any means indeed points to dreams which may be American dreams, but that does not make them inimical to black Britain. The strong influence of African American culture on black British youth culture (and through them on white British youth culture) is not only a reality; it is also dealt with in the diegesis of *The Scholar* where the influence of hip-hop culture on language, for example, is debated, and certain limits to imitation are drawn by the youths themselves. In this respect, then, *The Scholar* reflects the shift from African and African Caribbean terms of reference of the 1970s and 1980s to African American culture.

In the light of Evaristo and Levy's inquiries it also seems particularly surprising for Dawes to demand a particular brand of cultural nationalism from younger writers, a specific "following on" in the vein of earlier writers and the politics of contemporary Britain. Clearly, both writers do follow on in certain ways; but their writing emerges from contexts which are different to those of earlier writers, whom Dawes prescribes as models. Pondering the possibility and impossibility of "returning," the travels of Faith and Lara, and the thematics chosen by Levy and Evaristo, indicate the concern with being black in Britain, which Dawes demands. But even if they did not have this concern: would that constitute a flaw? Such specific expectations unnecessarily increase the "burden of representation."

The quest for a position among a variety of literary precursors, as exemplified by Caryl Phillips, can be considered related to the quest of the protagonists Faith and Lara. The notion of an unencumbered sense of belonging is crossed out. But at the same time, the condition of unbelonging is not accepted but contested. In both cases, a search for ways of belonging is undertaken.

The black British novel of transformation, as a diasporic bildungsroman, is a means of describing the condition of diaspora. It is also, as has been seen, a means of combating alienation and unbelonging; Faith and Lara return to London strengthened and ready to position themselves as they see fit. In depicting racism, both novels demand social, political, and cultural transformation.

"The 'mongrel' nation that is Britain," Caryl Phillips asserted recently, "is still struggling to find a way to stare into the mirror and accept the ebb and flow of history that has produced this fortuitously diverse condition and its concomitant pain" (Phillips 2000, 11). Faith and Lara are a part of this diverse condition Phillips so vividly describes; they need to find a way of bearing the view in the mirror. The novels themselves in which the two young women figure, and the problematics the texts pursue, can also be seen as part and parcel of the process Phillips describes and requests. Faith and Lara's genesis of consciousness, while embarking on prolonged literal and symbolical journeys of discovery, have equipped them well upon their return to London. They can now demand—and also bring about more effectively—a form of belonging. Their formation allows them to combat alienation. They are also prepared for generational and cultural conflict, and can therefore meet the challenges which are pronounced by Dawes.

Ships of Kin

> As citizen
> of the English tongue
> I say remember
> the ship
> in citizenship
> for language
> is the baggage
> we bring—. . .
> I'm here to navigate—
> not flagellate
> with a whip of the past . . .
> for is not each member
> of the human race—
> a ship on two legs . . .
> and diversity
> shall sound its trumpet
> outside the bigot's wall.
> —(JOHN AGARD, "REMEMBER THE SHIP" (1998)

Poets in residence are the order of the day. Bernardine Evaristo held this office at the Museum of London from 1998 to 1999; in Ian McMillan, the company Northern Rail had its very own rolling poet in residence (Walsh 1999, 1); and in 1998, John Agard took up his Internet-residence with the BBC. It seems very appropriate that the corporation should choose a West Indian migrant and black British writer for this position in the year of the fiftieth anniversary of the arrival of the *Windrush*. As poet in residence, Agard published the poem "Remember the Ship" (1998). Agard is aware of a history of displacement and demands living up to this memory. But the interpretation of what this may mean is not prescriptive but rather evocative in the work of the poet.

While to Dawes, the ship on Johnson's head represents "abuse, enslavement and adventure" (1999, 19), to Agard it is a much richer symbol: "I say remember/ the ship/ in citizenship," he admonishes in his poem (1998). Citizenship is understood to pertain not to nation but to language, so that English citizenship covers many parts of the world.

At the same time, it implies "a call/ to kinship/ that knows/ no boundary/ of skin" (1998). Connectedness is promoted as opposed to division, with Agard positing a universal humanity. The poem likens the individual to a "ship on two legs," and beseeches Europe to "offer its wide harbours" so that a "new voyage" can begin (1998).

The punning on the word *ship,* and the poem's humorous tone, do not belie the seriousness of its intentions. The image of the ship conveys sufficient gravitas, and indeed evokes the slave ship, the refugee's boat, the exile's vessel. The concept of the navigating individual who does not use the past as whip—and is not whipped by the past—resembles Lara's final development toward self-creation. Just as the journeys Lara and Faith undertake question barriers which are drawn for them, Agard's ships navigate a continuous ocean that does not tolerate the strictures of poetics or politics. The image of the ship is not only apropos at this chapter's end; it also prefigures the following and concluding chapters which are concerned with making and perusing "amorphous connections."

4

Of Aunties and Elephants —Kureishi's Aesthetics of Postethnicity

> Everyone looks at you, I'm sure, and thinks: an Indian boy, how exotic, how interesting, what stories of aunties and elephants we'll hear now from him. And you're from Orpington.
> —(KUREISHI 1990, 141)

I. ASCRIPTIONS AND INSCRIPTIONS: THE "WALK-IN" UNION JACK

In a one-room gallery of Brick Lane, an area wedged precariously between the East End and the City, where a formerly Jewish district of London is now inhabited by a large number of Bengali migrants, I came upon an exhibition titled It Ain't Ethnic. The sculptor Said Adrus, who has Indian parents and grew up in Uganda, now lives in Switzerland.[1] His works raise the question of what is and what isn't "ethnic"—both within the arts and outside them. Entering the gallery I first came across a range of small empty rice sacks adorned with patterns I had seen in India. Like little artifacts these pieces of coarse cloth were framed and on display behind glass. On closer inspection it became clear, though, that the material (Hessian, a mixture of hemp and jute) pointed not to India but to Europe, the rice sacks bearing an address in Switzerland. So "it ain't ethnic" after all? The display raises many questions: What is "ethnic" art? Does the artist's ethnicity endow it with this quality? If so, then all art would be "ethnic" on one level. Is the represented subject matter decisive? Are the artifact's formal and aesthetic properties crucial? Or the provenance of the materials? Could the context possibly be significant, Hessian being as "ethnic" in one place as Indian is in another? And what is it that marks out these readymades as art? These rice sacks shipped not only grains of rice—they also contained the germ for my readings.

Adrus's main exhibit on display was a "walk-in" Union Jack. Assembled out of wooden beams, the national flag covered most of the exhibition floor. But the emblem was at once *disassembled*, since it had been made open and penetrable: It permitted entry and solicited passage. Visitors walked between the beams making up the emblem, as if walking down a path. These pathways, including the openings they represent, became part of the national ensign. Therefore the visitors, too, became part of the "walk-in" Union Jack, and of its assembly and its disassembly.

It is in the light of such entries and passages, and the questions raised above, that I read Hanif Kureishi's bildungs-literature. This chapter initially pursues the concept of postethnicity, by looking at the reception of artist Chris Ofili, and by critiquing David Hollinger's term *postethnicity*. Next Kureishi's novels are examined within the context of the black British novel of transformation, and read as postethnic texts. *London Kills Me,* Kureishi's postethnic film about the formation of Clint within a symbolic family, is subsequently analyzed. The chapter closes with observations on the relationship of postethnicity, visuality, and the politics of black representation.

Chris Ofili's Canvas: Multicultural or Multivalent?

The Turner Prize, established in 1984, is awarded to a British artist under the age of fifty for an outstanding exhibition. In 1998 Ofili won the prize and is noted as "the first black recipient," following the "Asian artist" Anish Kapoor, who was the winner in 1997. Ofili employs a wide variety of techniques and materials in his paintings and collages. From a distance his brightly colored canvasses reveal their overall composition; from nearby it becomes clear that he often uses tiny dots to create shapes and figures in a manner much like Australian aboriginal paintings, but actually inspired by Zimbabwean cave drawings. Likewise, the small cuttings from magazines (which range from images of black leaders to pornography) are noticeable only from close-up.

In a review of Ofili's recent exhibition, Richard Dyer claims that Ofili both courts and undermines the art establishment and "the politically correct agenda of the multicultural lobby" (Dyer 1999, 79) by using elephant dung, "African" hair collected in London's barbershops, and various references to black popular culture. Ultimately, however, Ofili is merely interested in marketing his works, according to this critic; he is "far from being subversive," and practices "exploitation of exploitation" when "play[ing] the minstrel" to his own ends and grafting onto formalist paintings the topic of "racial identity" (Dyer 1999, 80). According to Dyer, this is required in the face of an art establishment which accepts black and Asian artists only if two conditions are met: first, "the cultural neo-colonialism of a post-socialist, New Labour Britain" and, second, the "'ethnically authentic' and identity-centred agenda of multicultural arts . . . patronage" (1999, 80). Dyer's unforgiving critique cuts two ways then: the so-called art establishment is charged with being deeply prejudiced, and Ofili is indicted for playing along. Had he not, the Turner Prize would not have been his, thinks Dyer (1999, 80).

But such a reading of Ofili's paintings as unambiguous locks them into a market-conscious corner of ethnic kitsch. Their striking playfulness is read out of the works, while the ready and uncritical accommodation of clichés is read into Ofili's œuvre. The fact that Kapoor (a detail of whose untitled sculpture decorates Homi Bhabha's *The Location of Culture* [1994]) won the Turner Prize before Ofili—with works that are unashamedly modernist and formalist, and free from explicit references to Asian popular culture—would seem to contradict Dyer's attack on the Turner judges. And it appears that Ofili's works speak a language more nuanced than that of his critic.

Ofili has indeed explained that he meets the expectations confronting a black artist, which include "the witch doctor, the drug-dealer, the exotic, the decorative." But he "package[s]" these clichés differently and sees himself as dealing with stereotypes by subverting them (Searle 1998, 10). Confronting an audience with their own expectations can indeed be more than mimicry; Ofili's work is not so much a bow to the multicultural lobby as a celebration of multivalency.

While the references to black popular culture merely constitute one level of his work, the various levels of Ofili's palimpsests need to be seen as related. Some of his work is reminiscent of batik, while other aspects seem to be adorned with Indian paisley patterns; "Captain Shit and the Legend of the Black Stars" is more reminiscent of the Mandarin pantheon. It is not easily established what his use of dung as a "ready-made" object (generated by Asian elephants in the London Zoo) indicates, or what and where it refers to.

The problematics of reading Ofili's œuvre are posed by the attempt to contextualize it within the various influences of contemporary Britain: his traditional training (Chelsea School of Art and the Royal College of Art) has to be considered, rather than emphasizing unduly his "African heritage," which, materially, consists of Nigerian parents and one visit to Zimbabwe. Similarly, in post-colonial writing, this problem arises with texts that are marked by numerous and (culturally and historically) divergent influences. While Flora Veit-Wild has charged Chenjerai Hove's novel *Bones* with cultivating "an exotic and romanticized image of Africa and the African soul" (1993, 5), for example, the South African critic Dan Wylie extols: "there is something almost despairingly hopeful about invoking the smell of dung, as if it were a cultural artefact, as a symbol of survival" (1991, 59). Wylie here celebrates a dung heap, albeit a fictional one, for flaunting "Shona-ness"; and he suggests implausibly that "it is 'Shona-ness' itself . . . that appears to speak" in *Bones* (1991, 49). These two readings of the same Zimbabwean novel could not be further apart. Texts such as Hove's are not uncommon in post-colonial writing. And in both visual art and literature, some cultural products, such as Opal Palmer Adisa's *It Begins with Tears*, are geared toward a readership feeding on the "exotic" (cf. Huggan 2001).

Wylie contrasts Hove's work with that of Marechera, who has expressed anxiety about being confined to such expectations: "Would I go out like the last speck of a spectacular fireworks display of unending conferences on Black Culture?" one of his characters muses (Marechera 1980, 77). Here fears of commodification and the reduction to a specimen of academic inquiry, or to a spectacle of "ethnicity," are expressed. Undue aggrandizement, or the valorization of "ethnicity" and "Africanness," are rejected by a narrator who wants his writing to be received in terms of "art" rather than as social or ethnographic text.

Post-colonial literatures are often conceived of as "ethnic literatures," deriving from other, distant cultures. They derive from, say, the Orient but surely not from Orpington. Reading from an exoticist paradigm is a way of "shedding light on any area of darkness"—as well as a way of bringing these texts to light.[2] There is a sense in which critics retrieve, for metropolitan consumption, writing from former colonies in Asia, Africa, the Caribbean, and the settler colonies. On one level, these are the brokers of alterity without whom post-colonial literature would be less popular in Europe and North America. Beyond relegating literatures to the realm of the ethnic, such reading strategies resemble colonial power structures as Tobias Döring has observed: The metropolitan critic discovering the ethnic text (1996a).

The Concept of Postethnicity

Hanif Kureishi's postethnic work can be seen as an intervention connected to the debates outlined so far. But why another *post*-word; why *postethnic?* Moreover, why *postethnic literature?* I'm using the term here *not* to build upon and thereby defend the category "ethnic literature"; hence *post* is not being used in the temporal sense of superseding, but rather in a contestatory fashion. In my usage, the term *postethnic literature* characterizes writing that shows an awareness of the expectations that so-called ethnic writing faces; I apply it to texts working through these expectations and going beyond them. "Postethnic," then, does *not* try to *transcend* the "ethnic." Instead, it disputes the confinements of the very category.

Our point in history is marked by numerous complexities: There are large-scale migrations across the globe for a whole host of reasons; there is a genealogy of admixture, of syncretism, and hybridity; and we are going beyond a politics of left and right. Both postindustrial and developing societies are characterized by a high degree of internal sociocultural differentiation. Official multiculturalism is upheld while ethnic divisions are breaking down at street-level; crossovers take place as the ethnic and gender divides are being permeated and perforated. At the same time, class divisions have become less clear-cut, although economic distinctions have not disappeared; crippling poverty stifles development or induces movement, removal, and migration. Although "ethnicity" may be *en vogue,* the "other" celebrated, and rootlessness fetishized, there are areas in London today which, depending on the color of your skin, you will only cross with apprehension. It is in this context that I look to David Hollinger's work.

In his study *Postethnic America: Beyond Multiculturalism,* the Berkeley historian develops a postethnic perspective which synthesizes some features of multiculturalism while criticizing others:

> A postethnic perspective favors voluntary over involuntary affiliations, balances an appreciation for communities of descent with a determination to make room for new communities, and promotes solidarities of wide scope that incorporate people with different ethnic and racial backgrounds. (Hollinger 1995, 3; cf. 116)

Hollinger's definition acknowledges the contingency of social collectivities and insists on the usefulness of solidarity *across* narrower, filial collectivities to form new (comm)unities; these are reliant upon choice rather than tradition and descent, new formations which are thereby marked by variety and variability.

One of the problems I see with Hollinger's manifesto is that it does not sufficiently consider the limitations that impinge upon the charting of the voluntary affiliations it favors. His concept seems modeled on those white European ethnic groups which, over a long period in history, have amalgamated to form "American culture." Hollinger himself declares that "many middle-class Americans of European descent can now be said to be postethnic" (1995, 129). The group on which he models his concept is not only white and therefore in the United States "socially invisible," but also middle class. Social mobility, the freedom to affiliate which Hollinger advocates, is highly dependent on the means to afford such movement. There is an ethnic and also a class bias, then, at the bottom of Hollinger's concept.

In a sense Hollinger is suggesting something akin to upward social mobility, a mobility which is charted not in terms of class but in terms of ethnicity. But what is "up" or "down" on this scale? The question is not only who can "afford" this mobility, but also what, precisely, is the "cost" of such mobility for different ethnic groups. What are the "losses," and what the potential "gains"?

Despite these reservations, the concept of postethnicity is adapted here in order to stress that the boundaries of cultures, or what is often termed subcultures, do not necessarily coincide with formations that have an ethnic, "racial," or historical lineage. In other words, ethnicity, "race," or history are only *some* of the possible determinants delineating the symbolic boundaries of cultures. Not only in multiculturalist discourse is the notion of cultures often blurred with *ethno-racial classifications*. I do not accept the more radical forms of constructivism—nor do I deny history or biology, or the need for affiliations which can be crucial in group formation. But in my view neither history nor biology constitutes a primary basis for the fashioning of affiliations, and this is signaled by my use of the term *postethnic*.

This is not to suggest that there is no referent to the notion of "ethnicity"—at present, wars are being waged in the name of "ethnicity." Nevertheless, "ethnicity" is not by default a key feature of black British literature. When labeling Kureishi's novels *postethnic* (to varying degrees), I thereby mean to indicate Kureishi's play between external ascriptions and active affiliations, and the assumption that ethnicity is partly chosen.

II. READING KUREISHI'S NOVELS

Hanif Kureishi is now mostly recognized as a novelist and the author of film scripts, but he started out as a dramatist, writing plays from 1979 onward. Since 1984 he has also been publishing short stories, and these are collected in several volumes (1997a, 1999b, 2002b). During the mid-1980s he started to concentrate on film scripts, and in the 1990s began publishing novels.

Postethnic Authorship and "Posed Ethnicity": Stalling the "Otherness Machine"

> It is difficult for a person of colour to evade the definitions settled upon him.
> —(KUREISHI IN DODD 1991, 11)

At the beginning of his career, over twenty years ago, Kureishi was aware of certain expectations relating to his times, his cultural background, his ethnicity, and the color of his skin. These expectations enter his fiction; he thematizes them head on.

When Kureishi started writing he was expected to tell "stories about the new British communities"; the Royal Court Theatre, the Riverside Studios, and other new writing venues required "cultural translators" who could "interpret one side to the other" (Kureishi 1992, xvi). At this early point in his writing career, then, it was already implied that Hanif Kureishi could translate across divisions. In his own words, he started writing at "the end of something—the psychological loosening of the idea of Empire—and the start of something else, which involved violence, the contamination of racism and years of crisis" (1992, xvi). This historical phase and its requirements can be considered the background to many of his texts to date.[3] Kureishi concludes that the "questions that a multi-cultural society had to ask had hardly been put," a remark which implies that he may wish to bear out some of this responsibility (1992, xvi).

In Kureishi's most famous novel, *The Buddha of Suburbia*, a retired academic and critic, Dr. Bob, is ridiculed as "an enthusiast for the 'ethnic arts.'" His office is reminiscent of the loot amassed in the Pitt Rivers Museum in Oxford: It is full of "Peruvian baskets, carved paddles, African drums and paintings" (1990, 243). The only thing that these artifacts share is that they hail from faraway places, and that the artisans and artists have brown faces. The inclusion of the image of this not entirely unfamiliar colleague is indicative of Kureishi's awareness of the expectations his texts may meet. And the derision Kureishi has his narrator heap upon the academic suggests that Kureishi clearly does not favor reception of his writing in terms of "ethnic art."

Kureishi's writing thrives on unpredictable encounters and affiliations. *My Beautiful Laundrette* (1985) spins around the multilayered partnership of two schoolfriends, Omar, of Pakistani parentage, and the white Johnny, a former member of the National Front. *The Buddha of Suburbia* also contains unlikely alliances, such as that between Jamila and Shinko, the one being Changez' wife, the other his friend and prostitute. This novel disrespects conventional boundaries and refrains from placing its characters exclusively within *one* type of formation, be it an ethnic group, a cultural group, or a class. Instead, characters are "afloat" within the orbit of divergent groups. Affiliation is actively sought and not inherited. And affiliation can be revoked, not at will, but within limits. These limits are thereby subjected to negotiation, a negotiation which is part of the novel's brief.

The Buddha of Suburbia (1990) and *The Black Album* (1995), Kureishi's first two novels, bear a relationship to colonialism and post-colonialism and mediate what it means for a text to be so positioned. They can be considered *self-consciously* post-colonial. By this I mean that the expectations of the field are neither rejected wholesale nor noiselessly imbibed. Instead, these expectations are embraced, parodied, and tampered with. Kureishi's first two novels self-consciously—and excessively—fit the mold of "post-colonial writing"; in the process the mold not only overflows but also cracks in places.

Kureishi's first two novels invite a pun on the term *postethnic:* they provide a *posed*-ethnic perspective.[4] It is with some irony that Kureishi self-consciously deploys ethnic markers in these texts. The irony lies partly with the registers of these markers: They belong primarily to the realms of food, religion, and clothing; the smell of curries wafts through *The Black Album.* The irony is furthered by the ostentatiousness with which ethnic markers are deployed and by the frequent references to performances and stagecraft (discussed below). The highly syncretic Buddha of Suburbia himself is described as "a renegade Muslim masquerading as a Buddhist" who is heard wailing "Christian curses" when making love to the suburban Amazon called Eva (Kureishi 1990, 18). At the same time, the very notion of "ethnic writing" is denounced and ridiculed. The "ethnic markers" deployed by Kureishi are not what they seem. Nevertheless, *The Buddha of Suburbia* and *The Black Album* feature protagonists who have to come to terms with their ethnicity and its implications for their position in society. Both texts emphasize the significance of the protagonists' own positionings and affiliations in spite of the external pressures which seek to determine them.

In the following I trace Kureishi's attempts at stalling the "otherness machine"—a phrase I borrow from Sara Suleri's well-known *memoir* (Suleri 1989, 105)—and suggest that this project exemplifies a trend in post-colonial British cultural production. The posed-ethnic texts *The Buddha of Suburbia* and *The Black Album* both show an awareness of the expectations so-called ethnic writing faces, and they go a certain way toward working through these expectations. Both novels *dispute the confinements* of the very category, but "ethnicity" remains of importance to their characters Karim Amir and Shahid Hasan. Kureishi's third novel, *Intimacy* (1998), is most clearly written from a postethnic perspective. Historicizing his extended flirtation with the post-colonial, *Intimacy* attempts to leave behind colonial cultural and oedipal anxiety. The novel, therefore, also seeks to divorce itself from the bildungsroman genre—but it succeeds only up to a point.

Staging "Asianness": *The Buddha of Suburbia*

> My name is Karim Amir, and I am an Englishman born and bred, almost. I am often considered to be a funny kind of Englishman, a new breed as it were, having emerged from two old histories. But I don't care—Englishman I am (though not proud of it), from the South London suburbs and going somewhere. Perhaps it is the odd mixture of continents and blood, of here and there, of belonging and not, that makes me restless and easily bored.
> —(KUREISHI 1990, 3)

The opening paragraph of Kureishi's first novel establishes Karim's self-consciousness which results from being socially visible and from eliciting comment ("I am often considered . . ."). The passage indicates that Karim regards himself as the product of an "odd mixture" and of "belonging and not." The adjectives he uses (funny, new, not proud, odd, restless, easily bored) by themselves leave his image blurred. His self-characterization remains either vague ("going somewhere") or relies on antithetical terms such as *here and there*. He finds it hard to describe himself precisely and depends on approximations ("almost," "but not"): there seem to be no terms that fit him comfortably. Three variations of the phrase "I am an Englishman" occur; this is what Karim seeks to establish. But what he does in fact establish is that he is "an Englishman" with qualifications.

Karim's story indicates the significance of his particular ethnic background to his personal development. Initially Karim wants to become Britain's first black football player, but he then decides to become an actor and, after a début in *The Jungle Book,* comes to act an "Asian" part in a soap opera at the novel's close. His career choices indicate that Karim being recognizably Asian impacts heavily upon his formation.

The Buddha of Suburbia opens with Karim accompanying his father, Haroon Amir, the "future Guru of Chislehurst" (Kureishi 1990, 25); they make their way from Bromley to Beckenham (both in London's South East), where Haroon is to preach a motley of Eastern wisdom to Eva Kay's guests while Karim is enthralled by his schoolfriend Charlie Kay. Haroon develops a relationship with Eva and eventually leaves his wife, Margaret; Karim follows his father to live with Eva and Charlie. The novel subsequently focuses less on the father and more on Karim's peregrinations. He not only commutes between various households across London, but follows Charlie as far as New York while pursuing everything but his schoolwork. The novel develops the theme of self-transformation by emphasizing stagecraft and acting (Haroon, Karim, the theater workshop), remodeling homes as a way of remodeling life (Eva and "Heater"), dressing up and wearing make-up (Allie, the actors). Despite all these transformations, *The Buddha of Suburbia* closes with Eva and Haroon announcing their marriage (a state which both had previously escaped), and with Karim finding a position as an Asian character in a soap opera, a role which he had previously sought to evade. In view of this lack of progression, *The Buddha of Suburbia* can be considered an anti-bildungsroman in the tradition of Günter Grass's *The Tin Drum*.[5]

Unusually, Karim Amir and his father grow up alongside each other. It is the father, Haroon Amir, who gives the novel its title when he embarks upon a radical trajectory of growth, and starts to minister as the Buddha of Suburbia, dispensing Eastern wisdom to London suburbanites. Karim is taken along on his father's adventure: "I like having you with me, boy." He assures his son further that they are "growing up together" (Kureishi 1990, 22). Karim's career resembles his father's in that both are theatrical characters who "invent" an "Asian" personality for the consumption of their audience. Growing up with one's father clearly goes against the conventions of the novel of formation and in this respect, too, *The Buddha of Suburbia* can be considered an anti-bildungsroman. However, Karim does break free from his father once he has the opportunity to seesaw between Eva's, Margaret's, and other friends' and relatives' houses.

In the first epigraph to this chapter (from *The Buddha of Suburbia*), the theater director, Shadwell, brings into play an appetite for aunties and elephants. According to the director, these cravings are spawned by the protagonist himself. Significantly, the director emphasizes that it is not he who expects "stories of aunties and elephants." Rather, it is "everyone" else, excluding the rarefied Shadwell. In this way he attempts to thematize Karim's Asian background (on which he intends to draw for his production of *The Jungle Book*) while distancing himself from any stereotypical expectations this may trigger. But due to Karim's *deflating provenance*—"And you're [not from India but] from Orpington," Shadwell notes disappointedly—Karim cannot easily satisfy the desires he stimulates. The director solicits Karim to play the part of Mowgli, because he needs "an actor just like you" (Kureishi 1990, 140). Karim is quick to pick up on the implications of this proposal: "An actor like me in what way?" and at first remains unwilling to act as an "Indian boy" for Shadwell (1990, 140, 141).

Being confronted with sedate suburbanites who worship a "porky little Buddha" (1990, 84), the readership of *The Buddha of Suburbia* is made wary of going down the same alley. Haroon Amir, who was "hissing his s's and exaggerating his Indian accent" after spending "years trying to be more of an Englishman," is now "putting it [an Indian accent, *Indianness*] back in spadeloads" (1990, 21). Likewise, the novel itself pulls one ethnic register after the other, and thereby self-consciously inscribes itself into the genre. It is not only Karim Amir (with respect to his father) who wonders: "Why?" The same question is insinuated to the reader. What is the meaning of the excessive and stereotypical references to ethnicity? Does Shadwell's production of *The Jungle Book*, with the loin-clothed, browned-up, lilting Karim, constitute the blueprint for the novel as a whole? Or is not this *excess* indicative of the novel not conforming to but parodying the sometimes constricting expectations directed toward post-colonial literature?

Kureishi is at pains to overcome the constraints he meets with when taken as a representative of an ethnic group. He does not wish to be conscripted as a participant in "ethnic minority discourse" (as Abdul Jan-Mohamed and David Lloyd [1987] might have it). This can be illustrated by a brief example from the film *My Beautiful Laundrette* (1985). When Omar's Pakistani uncle turns against notions of solidarity among distinct black British groups and explains that he can evict a black tenant from his apartment block because he considers himself not "a professional Pakistani" but a "professional businessman," this also acts as a caution to the reader. For Kureishi feels himself to be neither a "professional Pakistani," nor a "professional Black Briton," but merely a professional writer. Ironically, the uncle's Thatcherite profession could be considered as equally provocative to various audiences as Kureishi's stance as a writer. His novels and his other writings display an awareness not only of the expectations with which the author's work is met. There is also an awareness of the possibility, and the need, to negotiate and intervene in these expectations. This negotiation is accomplished by using and emphasizing artifice and theatricality.

In *The Buddha of Suburbia* nothing is what it seems; acting is not only a theme of the novel: theatricality is its central trope. Haroon's friend Anwar, who migrated with him from Bombay to London, wants his daughter Jamila, Karim's intimate friend, to marry Changez. The novel thus features an arranged marriage (almost a cliché in Indian writing in English), which is enforced by Anwar's hunger strike. But when the feminist Jamila actually marries Changez to prevent her father's suicide, this apparently happens "out of perversity" on *her* part. Karim assumes further that the wedding was in the bride's mind "a rebellion against rebellion, creative novelty itself" (Kureishi 1990, 82). Is this, to paraphrase Rushdie (and, in his wake, Bhabha), how newness enters the world? It is difficult to produce a stable reading of this episode involving a reluctant and later willing bride of an arranged marriage who turns into a political activist. Does Karim's reading of her marriage as a "perverse" rebellion simply prove his naïveté? Or are stereotypical notions of arranged marriages being lampooned?

The novel wants to have its cake and eat it, too. An arranged marriage is featured and criticized as authoritarian insofar as it disregards the bride. Concomitantly, that stereotypical notion of an arranged marriage is itself undermined through Jamila's creativity. She moves into a commune, permitting her Indian husband to join her. As the French imperative of his name would suggest, Changez adapts well, indeed, he becomes the child minder to the communal baby. He develops from would-be patriarch into a "maternal" caring figure (which is even underlined by his rounded physique that earns him the nickname "Bubble"). Hence any stereotypical notion of an arranged marriage is made redundant. The effect is a defamiliarization of the signifier "arranged marriage"—it is hardly recognizable and thus marked as unstable. This is achieved by Jamila's "theatrical" arranged marriage; she acts the willing bride—but to her own ends.

This is reminiscent of Ravinder Randhawa's novel *A Wicked Old Woman* (1987) whose central British Asian character, Kulwant, self-consciously transforms herself into a range of "signifier[s] of Indianness."

In the words of Lyn Innes, these roles include "that special feature emphasised by Europeans as the mark of difference and unacceptability, the arranged marriage" (1995, 31). This novel, "the first *explicitly* Asian British novel" according to Susheila Nasta (2002, 182), crucially empties out preconceptions of an arranged marriage in the way the concept is used in her novel. The instability of the signifier "arranged marriage" exemplifies how Randhawa and Kureishi's texts can simultaneously feed readerly expectations and challenge them.

The Buddha of Suburbia's negotiations with readerly expectations are complex because it is aware of a plurality of audiences. In other words, Kureishi's first novel calculates its relationship with a *range* of potential readerships. It displays impatience with the liberalism of some readers as, for example, the following exchange bears out: "'We old Indians come to like this England less and less and we return to an imagined India.' Helen took Dad's hand and patted it comfortingly. [And now comes the stock liberal response, a dripping cliché:] 'But this is your home,' she said. 'We like you being here. You benefit our country with your traditions'" (Kureishi 1990, 74). This response is lampooned with the characteristic hyperbole that Helen was "driving [Jamila] to suicide" with her patronizing attitude. Such impatience with Helen's white-liberal response to multiculturalism is aimed at a specific type of reader.

The text also treats with humor the stereotypical expectations supposedly held by those from a migrant generation: "I thought it would be roast beef and Yorkshire pudding all the way" (1990, 24). In this self-deprecating statement, Anwar acknowledges his misguided expectations about coming to Britain. He neither finds the ease of life he himself had hoped for, nor does he succeed in becoming a lawyer, as his parents had wished; his only call to the bar coincides with the opening hours of the Public House. This exemplifies how the expectations of migrants are ironized in the novel which constitutes another example of Kureishi's targeting a plurality of readerships.

While Karim, the budding actor, is drafting his first role for a coauthored play, and is forced by the director into researching a black character, he faces equally rigid expectations from another side as well. Jamila requests: "Don't leave your own people behind, Karim" (1990, 136). Later, his first character (based on the hunger-striking Anwar) is rejected by the black woman Tracey (and in her wake by the entire theater workshop) on the grounds of not showing "black culture" in a sufficiently good light. The pressures exposed to be working on Karim point to those faced by black British writers, and in certain ways postcolonial writers more generally. Pressures on the author to portray positively the Anglo-Pakistani community are taken up in the novel. Karim asks Jamila whether he can tell his white friend Helen about her father's hunger strike: "'Yes, if you want to expose our culture as being ridiculous and our people as old-fashioned, extreme and narrow-minded'" (1990, 71). These are precisely the allegations which Kureishi has faced and which other writers face when being claimed as group representatives.[6]

Earlier in this chapter it has been seen that Richard Dyer has charged Chris Ofili with overcompliance, by yielding to expectations too easily. I would argue that Kureishi (like Ofili) has taken this tug-of-war on board and is trying to negotiate the conflicting expectations levied on his works. If Kureishi's novels work through the expectations which "ethnic writing" faces from various sides, as is argued here, then this does not imply that *The Buddha of Suburbia*, for example, is in denial about the troubled state of "race relations" in Britain. But it does imply that Kureishi reserves the right to poke fun at the same time. So the novel acknowledges that the "lives of Anwar and Jeeta and Jamila were pervaded by fear of [racist] violence" (Kureishi 1990, 56), without resorting to reverence when portraying the despotic Anwar.

Ethnicity does play a part in Karim's quest to fit in; he notes that Jamila, Changez, and himself are "bound together by ties stronger than personality" (1990, 214). Despite this pertinence of ethnic affiliations, however, Karim does not understand the language of his father, a trope that is present across Kureishi's œuvre:[7] "They weren't speaking English, so I didn't know exactly what was said" (1990, 81). Karim Amir, the outsider within, concludes in an apparent paradox that "[w]e became part of England and yet proudly stood outside it" (1990, 227).

> But I did feel, looking at these strange creatures now—the Indians—that in some way these were my people, and that I'd spent my life denying or avoiding that fact. I felt ashamed and incomplete at the same time, as if half of me were missing, and as if I'd been colluding with my enemies, those whites who wanted Indians to be like them. (Kureishi 1990, 212; cf. 214, 216)

This remorseful conclusion acknowledges two things: Karim Amir not only belongs to "these strange creatures . . . Indians," but to British society and culture as well—a society which has also been characterized as "strange." Karim sees himself as consisting of torn halves, a conception he introduces in the novel's opening paragraph (quoted above). This raises the question of how these halves interact, how they feed upon each other, and in how far they remain irreconciled to each other.

Karim Amir often takes an outsider's perspective when speaking about white English society. One page into the novel we are informed that "Englishmen looked like clumsy giraffes" (1990, 4) while the way they "sleep and eat is enough to make you want to emigrate to Italy" (1990, 220). On stage it is not so much the size of the audience that is daunting ("with four hundred white English people looking at me"), it is apparently the color of their skins that induces stage fright in Karim Amir (1990, 228).

Representing the idea of free choice and self-determination, his play-acting role model Charlie is a social chameleon whom Karim won't quite follow. Difference is acknowledged in the novel, different lifestyles are portrayed, but the emphasis is always on transformation and on acting out cultural change as well as individual change—something which makes it hard to insist upon a notion of a core identity that is beyond redress.

In the spirit of postethnicity (with *The Buddha of Suburbia* being a novel about individualism), Karim Amir insists on forging his own affiliations and reserves the right to reject those parties who have all too fixed expectations of him. He is not beyond recognizing and forging "ethnic" affiliations. But, in a postethnic vein, such affiliations are indeed *forged*, are made and appreciated as provisional, as Karim's peregrinations indicate. While his peregrinations come to an end at the novel's conclusion, Karim continues to "act" Asian—but in a soap opera. *The Buddha of Suburbia* emphasizes performative elements in the characters it deploys—they themselves try their hand at creation. The novel disrespects conventional boundaries and shows its characters to be imbricated in a number of formations, be they ethnicity, culture, or class. Karim, Charlie, Eva, and Haroon are all "afloat" and within the orbit of divergent groups. They actively seek affiliations instead of inheriting them or obeying ascriptions. Within limits, affiliations can be revoked. The limitations placed on such "movements" are thereby subjected to negotiation, a negotiation which is integral to the novel's brief. The trope of theatricality allows *The Buddha of Suburbia* to treat ethnicity as *partly* chosen and accords with its posed-ethnic stance. The novel seesaws between external ascriptions and active affiliations, between using ethnic ascriptions (as on the stage) and subverting them.

Traveling Affiliations: *The Black Album*

At the center of *The Black Album* stands Shahid Hasan, a would-be writer, who ironically pens his first story on "Papa's headed notepaper" (Kureishi 1995, 72). Writing is therefore portrayed as an act of inscription into preexistent texts and contexts. Should Shahid have acted on an Oedipal need to distinguish himself from his prior other, the choice of paper would indicate this attempt doomed. The short story reveals some of Shahid's childhood experiences and is angrily titled "Paki Wog Fuck Off Home" (1995, 72–73). He is to learn later from his friend Strapper that "outsiders" are fashionable—but only within narrowly defined borders (1995, 175). The novel self-consciously plays with the limits of fiction and with the limits of what is considered acceptable.

The Black Album resembles a campus novel with Shahid taking a course on Cultural Studies and the novel being partly set on campus. But London, not the campus, frames the novel; it is a text not about university life but about life in the metropolis. Shahid is new to the very run-down London college and at first feels quite lost and lonely. "[S]eeking interesting Asian companions" (1995, 15), he is happy when befriended by Riaz and Chad who live on the same corridor of his hall of residence. Shahid is able to tell his new friends that in the past he had felt self-conscious as a young Asian British man because he was often the only dark-skinned person (Kureishi 1995, 10). At first it appears that their shared background means that "he didn't have to explain anything," and their relationship is one of mutual trust (1995, 57). Their relationship develops quickly since Shahid feels that they "were the first people he'd met who were like him" (1995, 57).

His connection with his Cultural Studies lecturer, Deedee Osgood—which soon transcends the boundaries of classroom and orthodox pedagogy—fills him with pleasures of a different order. Her hedonist Marxism enlightens him not only about himself and his position in society: introductions to sex, raves, and drugs follow suit. Lacan is supplemented by Prince and Ecstasy.

As the story develops, Riaz and his "brothers," as the group of religious activists is derisively labeled, turn out to be increasingly dogmatic. They make heavy demands on Shahid's time, disrespect his privacy, and are suspicious of his life and family background. Ironically his friends were sympathetic in their very first discussion, when Shahid talked of the effect of reading Rushdie, while it is precisely over the question of tolerance and freedom of speech provoked by Rushdie that Shahid breaks with the "posse." It is not only an aubergine which allegedly contains a Koranic inscription that Riaz and his allies want to display in the town hall, possibly beside a picture of Nelson Mandela (1995, 241). They also organize a book burning of *The Satanic Verses*.[8]

Shahid comes to realize the narrowness of their beliefs and the absence of any doubts toward their tenets.

The publication of *The Satanic Verses* in 1988 was an extremely significant event, not only for black British literature but also in the context of British politics. The publication of Rushdie's novel antagonized British Muslims, and indeed many Muslims worldwide, who considered the text blasphemous. When the *fatwa* was declared in 1989 by the Ayatollah Khomeini, Rushdie had to go into hiding for nearly a decade. At the same time the heterogeneity among Asians in Britain, and Asian Muslims in Britain, became all too obvious, with some defending the right to freedom of expression while others felt personally and spiritually antagonized.[9]

Shahid is placed neatly between two opposing forces, Deedee's secular individualism and Riaz's fanaticism. This strict dichotomous structure is reminiscent of a morality play which underscores the didactic nature of Kureishi's novel. Over a large part of the novel, the protagonist remains skeptical of both positions. His quest to resolve his conflicting attractions can be seen as a novelistic device to develop an understanding for youths who turn to Muslim "fundamentalism."[10] Yet the extremity of the two poles casts doubt on the sincerity of Kureishi's attempts to understand the nature of "fundamentalism." There is a glibness, a flippancy to *The Black Album* which makes it a funny text but one that cannot be taken entirely seriously. Humor is an important feature of Kureishi's writing, and in itself is not at all averse to serious themes. *The Black Album* seems to hover on the line that divides the weighty from the ephemeral.

In both *My Son the Fanatic* and *The Black Album* there is a gap between the migrating and the British-born generations where those who migrated aspire to English ways of life, are "Westernized," and at best follow a secularized version of Islam. Shahid's late father ran a travel agency selling exotic package holidays to the English—as *authenticity* has itself become commodified. Expected to take over the agency, Shahid was criticized for writing his first short story because his father took "bookishness" to be indicative of effeminacy (Kureishi 1995, 41). Surely Mr. Hasan would have had no patience for Shahid's flirtation with "fundamentalism." In *My Son the Fanatic,* Parvez's son Farid becomes an ardent Muslim. Parvez is a taxi driver who carries his customers to the local brothel and who himself starts a relationship with one of the sex workers. Farid leaves his English fiancée and later turns into a "fundamentalist." By attacking a Bradford brothel he turns not only symbolically against what he considers a corrupt and corrupting society, but also against the livelihood of his father and he even endangers his father's girlfriend.

In contradistinction to their "Westernized" parents, the British-born sons and daughters realize the degree to which their parents remain rejected by the host society—despite their attempts at assimilation—and feel themselves rejected. In turn, some of them renounce the path of assimilation and practice a "spiritual return." Shahid does not choose this path, but Farid seems to travel it a long way. This feature of Hanif Kureishi's work relates to the previous chapter, which followed Lara and Faith's attempted returns in the light of generational tensions.

Racism severely limits its victims' potential to disaffiliate themselves from their ethnic background (and it also limits the potential to affiliate with their background). It marks the point at which a black or Asian Briton cannot merely decide to foreground *other* postethnic affiliations, due to the power of racism and racist discourse. Racism is also a key feature of *The Black Album:* it considers both its pernicious influence on individuals as well as on society as a whole. Shahid notes that in Britain black people are "third-class citizens, even lower than the white working class," and that racist violence was on the increase. He fears that his father, who expected future generations to be accepted as English, may have been deluded: "We haven't been! We're not equal!" Shahid adds desperately: "However far we go, we'll always be underneath" (Kureishi 1995, 209). Racism is not only seen as an external force; perniciously, it can become internalized, and thence even harder to tackle. The influence of internalized racism not only drives Shahid to self-hatred—he confesses to "becoming a monster" and to wanting "to be a racist" at the novel's opening: "'My mind was invaded by killing-nigger fantasies'" (1995, 11). The novel suggests that the alienation Shahid, Chad, and "the brothers" experience at the hands of a racist society potentially drives them into groups that counter unbelonging with blind certainty, and racism with mutual support. Clearly, a racist climate curtails the potential for postethnic affiliation; it can reinforce bonds within victimized ethnic and religious groups and exacerbate tension between discrete ethnicities who are victimized in distinct ways.

The story of Chad best illustrates this: Trevor Buss alias Chad had been transracially[11] adopted and his "soul got lost in translation," as Deedee Osgood puts it (Kureishi 1995, 107). Confronted with the effortless belonging of the white children with whom he grew up, Chad found it difficult to belong similarly. White Englishness is experienced as an ethnicity which forestalls Trevor's affiliation. "[C]hurch bells" and "English country cottages and ordinary English people . . . the whole

Orwellian idea of England" signaled exclusion to the boy (1995, 106). In white England people habitually mistook him for a street robber. However, when asking for salt in Southall, he was mocked for his accent despite Urdu language classes (1995, 107). "But in Pakistan they looked at him even more strangely. Why should he be able to fit into a Third World theocracy?" (1995, 107). Trevor can't forge affiliations in the white countryside, nor in Asian Southall, nor in Pakistan. He leaves his family at an early age, changing his name to Chad. Becoming involved in crime, he is later "rescued" by Riaz: Chad's life is saved when he is converted into one of Riaz's "spiritual brothers." Tragically, Chad's various attempts at voluntary, postethnic, transethnic, and ethnic affiliation fail until he meets the tightly organized "brothers."

Shahid derives from a more stable background than Chad but he, too, is afraid of inhabiting a "no man's land" (1995, 92), and of falling through the grid of received identities. Despite the ironic tone, he is convinced that:

> These days everyone was insisting on their identity, coming out as a man, woman, gay, black, Jew—brandishing whichever features they could claim, as if without a tag they wouldn't be human. Shahid, too, wanted to belong to his people. (Kureishi 1995, 92)

However (in the logic of the "posse"), Shahid has to know how to pray in order to belong and his friend, Hat, offers him a swift induction into the practice. He tries to explain Islam to him and even dresses Shahid up in a white Shalwar Kamiz (1995, 124). This scene corresponds to a later one in which Deedee undresses her young lover, applies make-up, and feminizes Shahid. Though Shahid had resolved to leave Deedee, this second cross-dressing redresses the first one. Shahid derives pleasure from it and feels liberated, and his association with Riaz and Chad is consequently relativized.

Although his friends cast a spell on him when they are together ("their story compelled him"), he cannot visit a mosque for worship without humming a Beethoven tune. Shahid embraces a double consciousness—to him leaving his friends is like "leaving a cinema": once through the door he finds his world to be more perplexing and subtle than his friends admit (1995, 133). His jarring emphasis on "coming out" with a suitable identity, likening the company of his friends to the "illusions" provided by a cinema visit, and employing and then revoking cross-dressing, all emphasize subjectivity as ongoing, unstable, and performative, rather than tightly locked to ethnicity. Shahid is seeking to reposition himself throughout the novel and in so doing develops a postethnic perspective, yet conflicting affiliations threaten him with rupture.

The text can be said to take sides in that Shahid is eventually seen to distance himself from his friends. Structurally opposed to Riaz's rigid position and his unquestioned certainties is the trope of *motion*, which is central to *The Black Album*. Shahid is thus marked out as Riaz's opponent, with images of movement abounding while Shahid's peregrinations are described. Within its dichotomous structure, *The Black Album* ultimately comes down on the side of tolerance and freedom of speech. The text is laced with Kureishi's characteristic irony, as "the brothers struggled over the vegetable" with its divine inscription (Kureishi 1995, 253) and Deedee confronts her young lover with an ultimatum: "[I]t's me or the enchanted vegetable." While the young "fundamentalists" are initially portrayed with sympathy, their positions are at length marked as untenable, and their actions rendered ridiculous.

In view of the ups and downs of his relationship with Deedee, and of their limited knowledge about each other, Shahid concludes they "had been tourists in one another's lives" (1995, 240). The text closes with the couple's departure for the countryside where Shahid is determined to "embrace uncertainty" (1995, 227). Ending with a weekend jaunt behooves a novel whose main characters are in near-constant motion. It allows Shahid to escape his increasingly violent friends and facilitates his reconciliation with Deedee. In *The Black Album* it is the trope of motion which undermines states of rigidity and points toward the mutability of ethnic and postethnic affiliations.

"How could anyone confine themselves to one system or creed? Why should they feel they had to?" Shahid asks, echoing the textbooks Deedee must have prescribed. He asserts that there "was no fixed self" and speaks of "several selves" that melt and mutate daily (1995, 274). In another act of inscription (he has moved on from his father's notepaper to his lover's desk), Shahid is seen writing among Deedee's letters, clippings, and unmarked essays, echoed intertextually in his above ruminations on identity. Ironically the protagonist of this post-colonial novel takes a "course on colonialism and literature" (1995, 30), and is keen to explore "innumerable ways of being in the world" (1995, 274). The fixity of religious or political dogma is rejected when Shahid sings a praise song for the several selves. His praxis not only of *mutation* but crucially of *traveling affiliation* is counter to the stagnation which is represented by Riaz and his group.

While London is seen as a potentially perilous place, an amorphous megalopolis in which you "could drive for two or three hours . . . and not come out the other side" (1995, 57), there is comfort in movement—"at least he was in a London taxi," he muses at one point (1995, 55). According to James Clifford, the "everyday practices of dwelling *and* traveling" can be fused as "traveling-in-dwelling, [and] dwelling-in-traveling" (Clifford 1997, 36). Shahid indeed dwells in travel. With all his wanderlust, soul-searching, and questioning, Shahid, ironically, seems most at home when he is *not* in one particular place, but on the Tube, in transit, en route from Deedee to the "posse," or on the way back. Whenever he is frightened, rummaging or walking through London's wastelands, he is often relieved at finding a Tube station. This to him not only signifies shelter, or a means of escape, or the possibility of retreat: significantly it also represents a move toward the next affiliation. London Transport becomes a machine for postethnic affiliation; the Tube, with its hundreds of points of entry and exit, emblematizes the sheer joy Shahid senses in exercising choices which his friend Chad has never had.

The novel endorses this type of voluntary affiliation and disaffiliation of which Shahid becomes conscious toward the end of the text. Equipped with a fountain pen, he begins to write, poised to make sense of his recent experiences: "he wanted to know and understand" (Kureishi 1995, 274). While not quite the same as the Romantic notion of autopoiesis, Shahid's affiliation at will by public transport (and his self-authorship by fountain pen) promises him freedom to enjoy the moment, instead of "swallow[ing] one old book," the Koran (1995, 272). Deedee and Shahid take off for the seaside, looking forward to a bed-and-breakfast, beach walking, and "lying wrapped up like pensioners in deckchairs on the pier." They have the intention to celebrate their relationship until "it stops being fun" (1995, 276).

■ ■ ■

In the previous section, *The Buddha of Suburbia* was seen as placing notable emphasis on what is often termed *subculture*. This is indicative of an engagement with the question of why some cultures are termed *ethnicities*, while other cultures are merely considered lifestyles, and yet other lifestyles are deemed "cultured." The conglomerate of ethnicity, race, class, sexuality, age, gender, region, and religion cannot be disentangled into neat composita, as the complex make-up even of Kureishi's minor characters makes clear. Omar's Thatcherite uncle in *My Beautiful*

Laundrette is one example of this conundrum, while another example is Uncle Ted (the electrician) in *The Buddha of Suburbia*. He is not only susceptible to Haroon's gospel, which regularly moves him to tears, he is also prone to mood swings and "short-circuits." While on the train with Karim, for example, he suddenly snaps, mutating into a hoodlum and a racist (Kureishi 1990, 43–45). The feminist Jamila belongs in this league of intricate characters, as does *The Black Album*'s Labour councillor Rudder. These characters are portrayed in too complex (and volatile) a relationship to ethnicity, class, religion, gender, or electorate to be schematically reduced to one particular determinant.

The theme of theatricality is used in *The Buddha of Suburbia* to undermine notions of a stable ethnicity, while the trope of flux and movement serves this purpose in *The Black Album*. Unlike *The Buddha of Suburbia*, which ends theatrically with the protagonists being arrested at a dinner table and the announcement of a marriage, *The Black Album* ends without stifling its momentum. Instead, Shahid and Deedee prepare for a new departure which promises that Deedee and Shahid will celebrate their affiliation despite their numerous differences. Their relationship is a positive sign since partnership and marriage metaphorically stand for the interaction between and affiliation of different social collectivities in *The Black Album*:

> It takes several generations to become accustomed to a place. We think we're settled down, but we're like brides who've just crossed the threshold. We have to watch ourselves, otherwise we will wake up one day to find we have made a calamitous marriage. (Kureishi 1995, 54)

These are Uncle Asif's words of wisdom which advise patience and restraint in the matters of postethnic affiliation as well as in personal relationships; but Shahid is determined to follow a different path, breathlessly. Likening cross-cultural affiliations, which are a result of large-scale migrations, to personal relationships and their attendant pitfalls and instabilities, *The Black Album* demonstrates that neither can be resolved in a comprehensive or dogmatic manner. Anticipating an aspect of Kureishi's next novel, Deedee volunteers the following with respect to relationships: "One would hope . . . that intimacy would leave more of a mark, that more of it would remain." But she finds this not to be the case. Instead you "just end up thinking, who is this person?" (Kureishi 1995, 49–50). The radical individualism which Deedee and Shahid represent at the end of the novel is closely connected with Kureishi's next novel, *Intimacy*, where it is taken further;

this underscores a development in Kureishi's writing from a politics of engagement to individualism.[12]

Intimacy and the Crisis of the Pronoun "We"

> My children hunt through their toy boxes, chucking aside the once-cherished to drag out what they need to keep themselves interested. . . . Can we do this with people? . . . We must treat other people as if they were real. But are they?
> —(KUREISHI 1998, 52)

Kureishi's third novel contemplates the possibility of intimacy, in its various forms, and identifies it with happiness, contentment, and romantic love (cf. 1998, 47, 101): intimacy between partners in a relationship, between sexual partners, between confessor and listener (or reader, in the absence of a priest), between father and son, between Jay and Victor. But, significantly, hurting someone is also "an act of reluctant intimacy" (1998, 4), and Jay's pursuit of happiness and movement is bound to hurt his family. The awareness of this problem constitutes Jay's and the novel's dilemma.

Walking through Islington, Shahid had noted how rare it was to see anyone "over forty, as if there were a curfew for older people." With publication of *The Black Album*, Kureishi himself passed that threshold; in *Intimacy* the curfew is lifted. It portrays a middle-aged, unmarried couple with two sons. Susan works in publishing, while Jay is an independent screenwriter. In a confessional mode, Jay narrates how he is dissatisfied with the life he and Susan share. He has an affair with a younger woman, Nina, but has recently lost touch with her. *Intimacy* relates the twenty-four hours preceding Jay's decision as to whether or not he should leave his partner and their children.

Intimacy is characterized by differences and continuities with the author's previous writing. It can be read as a sequel to the earlier novels: His first novel is about the 1970s,[13] *The Black Album* is about the 1980s, and *Intimacy* can be considered a 1990s novel. Although Kureishi has asserted that he will not "write any more fathers for a long time to come," absent or leaving fathers are a central motif in his œuvre (Kaleta 134). *The Buddha of Suburbia* revolves to a certain extent around Karim's father, who, like Jay, leaves his family; moreover, in *The Black Album* Shahid's relationship to his late father is important. While the first two novels showed young men growing up and can be formalized as black British novels of transformation, *Intimacy* is not overtly part of the same genre. However, it does share the concerns of the novel of formation, and even seems to grow out of this genre (Jay egresses, travels, matures, and returns). Jay is explicitly concerned with what his role might be in the context of a novel of formation—he is afraid that he may have "become the adults in *The Catcher in the Rye*" (1998, 111). Thus, when he enters a nightclub he is not party to the youthful crowd but feels removed, like a scientist: "Igniting my lighter, I push through the crowd, as if I am exploring a cave" (Kureishi 1998, 110). When he does see younger people in another nightclub he wonders whether "they have all, simultaneously, been afflicted with head pain, as they clutch their skulls as if posing for Munch's *The Scream*" (Kureishi 1998, 105). This description of youths speaking into their mobile phones reveals an observer who is at many removes (with respect to age, class, and use of communication technology), and who uses terms of reference (Edvard Munch) that are possibly beyond the lexicon of the subjects of his anthropological inquiry.

There remains a romanticization of popular youth culture in *Intimacy*, but the cynicism toward it has grown stronger.[14] When Jay feels excluded, this is because of class and age, and not ethnicity. Having hidden his dress shirt behind a bush in order to enter the nightclub with only a T-shirt under his jacket, Jay comes to understand that simply bowing to youth culture does not get him far. Unlike its predecessors, *Intimacy* constitutes a novel of *prolonged* formation, a liminal narrative in which Jay experiences the irrevocable loss of his youth: "For most of my life, until tonight, I have been young" (Kureishi 1998, 110). Therefore, the novel not only covers the period leading up to Jay's decision about leaving his family, but concurrently the last twenty-four hours before becoming aware of his loss of youth.

Much of Kureishi's work to date had been concerned with migration, with "race," and with ethnicity. *Intimacy*, like *The Body* and *Gabriel's Gift*, does not overtly share this preoccupation. These texts are not heavily embossed with "ethnic markers," as the preceding texts had been. The reader is not invited to acknowledge explicit ethnic backgrounds of characters, in contradistinction to *The Buddha of Suburbia* and *The Black Album*. In *Intimacy* there is instead a certain vagueness about the ethnic background of the central character, Jay, a vagueness which constitutes a counterpoint to Kureishi's first two novels. *Intimacy* is most clearly written from a postethnic perspective; apparently transgressing the concerns of post-colonial literature, *Intimacy* attempts to leave behind colonial, cultural, and oedipal anxiety.

In sketching the notion of postethnic literature my concern here is not whether Jay is white or Asian, or to which ethnicity he lays claim.[15]

Ethnicity is not a key concern in *Intimacy*, unlike the earlier novels. Yet there is a concern with whiteness in this short novel. Jay is blinded by his partner's whiteness; Susan looked "so white I could write on her" (1998, 95). And when naked, his girlfriend Nina can be compared to "a white grain of rice" (Kureishi 1998, 109).[16] The concern with the symbolism of whiteness is again not new to Kureishi's writing; Karim Amir, for example, had noted his mother's "almost translucent white legs" in *The Buddha of Suburbia* (1990, 72).

In these two examples from *Intimacy*, woman is turned into an object. A grain of rice evokes an embryonic state of a seed that needs growing, unless, of course, it is used for cooking and eating. In either case, Nina is represented as diminutive and in need of transformation. Susan's body, since passion is now absent from their relationship, seems a blank to Jay. In *Intimacy* (as in the previous novels) the protagonist is a writer, and the act of writing, of inscription, is likened to the male gaze. There is a concern with writing and the body, with writing *on* the body, with the sensation of pen on paper, of "fountain pen" on "good paper," of a finger gliding "over young skin" (1998, 48). Writing implies authorship and posits Jay as exerting the power of definition. While we are led to believe that Nina is more yielding to Jay's fantasy—she likes to sit *under* his desk when he is writing—his perception of Susan as a neat slate clashes with the novel's reality. Susan runs the house, Susan is in charge, and this seems one of his motives for considering leaving her.

Intimacy is an instance of self-writing. To Jay, his own experience is a resource for the book he is composing (of which Kureishi has been accused upon the publication of *Intimacy*).[17] Jay's gaze seeks to objectify women, turning them into parts of his narrative. He claims that his writer's sensibility won't allow him to "forfeit any important emotion," even as he leaves his family, and he therefore requires writing paper for his journey (Kureishi 1998, 47). His creative process involves not only autobiographical writing, "as I read myself within" (1998, 47), but also his writing of others; the "intimacy" between himself and Nina, and himself and Susan, therefore appears a precondition for his self-writing. It is salient that Jay is both intimate with and far removed from the women around him, and that he is in a position to inflict pain. Insofar as Jay feels unable to understand Susan, or Nina, the gender divide is thematized and becomes axiomatic in any definition of Jay's subjectivity. But the concern with age, gender, and whiteness does not, in and by itself, define and delimit the protagonist; whiteness is not foregrounded to the point of the text becoming an *overt* inquiry into ethnicity, or whiteness.

In her study of black British writing, *Cultures in the Contact Zone,* Susanne Reichl has astutely observed that Jay "talks about his home as if he were an outsider" (Reichl 2002, 118). With respect to whiteness and womanhood, Jay is so positioned as well. Furthermore, his close friend Victor is described as speaking slowly, "as some Englishmen do" (Kureishi 1998, 6). Maybe this too is an outsider's observation (but alternatively it might be an insider's view).

Importantly, these instances of exteriority with respect to whiteness, youth, femaleness, and Englishness do not allow Jay to be positioned according to the implied opposites. But the Romantic notion of the artist as an outsider, committed only to his art, is evoked; one way of accounting for Jay's positioning himself as an outsider is his commitment to his writing, a commitment which requires of him the external perspective of an observer as against the entrenched perception of the insider. Ironically, however, Jay is at once the center of this story. Like Karim Amir, Jay is best described as an outsider within. His constant play between rebuff and intimacy (which for him also implies license) allows him to hover on the edge, to be both outside and inside at once. With the help of this strategy, Jay constructs his own identity; however, for Jay the construction of any sense of "we" is difficult since the other is merely instrumentalized.

The following series of quotations suggests that in *Intimacy* there is a notion of a common "we" which comprises a shared secular position and Christian background, similar careers and lifestyles, a shared middle-class background and political leanings, and a shared sense of aging and mortality:

> Not many beliefs come spontaneously to mind. *We* have reached such a state that after two thousand years of Christian civilization, if I meet anyone religious—and, thankfully, I do only rarely these days—I consider them to be mentally defective and probably in need of therapy.
>
> [*W*]*e* went on the dole for five years in order to pursue our self-righteous politics, before starting work in the media and making a lot of money.
>
> If *we* dropped out to become carpenters and gardeners it was because *we* wanted to share the experience of the working class.
>
> Most of my friends seem to spend most of their time on their backs, sleeping, fucking, or having therapy and talking about their "relationships" on the phone.
>
> I am invited to more funerals than dinner parties.... *We* are going down already.... (Kureishi 1998, 100, 53, 53, 54, 80; emphasis added)

Intimacy thus presupposes a shared middle-class background in its deployment of this "we." But the pronoun remains ambiguous. The reader learns that *"we* like: *English* seaside towns. ... Long discussions about *English* mod groups of the sixties" (1998, 76, my italics). But who is "we"? Who are "we"? How wide is the scope of this "we"? Who resides inside; who remains outside? In this particular case, reference is made most probably to Susan and Jay. But ultimately the novel plays with this pronoun's vagueness. Its ambivalence accords with the inside-outside dyad and is of particular significance for the novel's ending. Throughout the duration of the text, suspense is built up as to whether Jay will actually take the step he has contemplated for over eight months (1998, 63) or whether he will give in to his affinity for happy endings (1998, 103). Although happiness (read: leaving) or staying constitutes mutually exclusive options in the text, the novel in a way ends happily. The final sentence reads: "It could only have been love." But Jay's final decision remains a secret, and the novel's premise that Jay must leave in order to rid himself of unhappiness is thus unsettled.

"We walked together, lost in our own thoughts. I forget where we were, or even when it was" (1998, 118). Or *who* it was, one might be tempted to add. Crucially, the reader does not learn with whom Jay is walking. The final paragraph leaves many questions unanswered and provokes various speculations. Is Jay walking with Susan and has not left her? Or has he left Susan and found Nina again? Or is it Victor and Jay who are walking? Or has Jay postponed his decision, as he has done throughout the text? The ending could then be read as a flashback to Jay's childhood, to a walk with his affectionate father. Does Jay's happiness lie in sustaining memory, or, conversely, does it require oblivion and forgetting? Or does his happiness indeed lie with the sustained pursuit of new partners? The intimacy between narrator and reader is suspended when the outcome of the novel—and hence the source of Jay's happiness—is withheld. It is now the reader who is positioned as an outsider, looking in, looking on.

Jay's questioning of marriage, partnership, gender, age, and ethnicity unsettles determinants that could otherwise more readily identify him. On the one hand, Jay is confronted with his aging body; on the other hand, his agility leads him to question these determinants, and thus demonstrates their instability, and their contingency. Although "ethnicity" is not foregrounded in this novel, the text fits the postethnic mode suggested here; however, if only indirectly, ethnicity *is* a concern of the text, as has been seen. It is contextualized and contrasted with other relevant determinants, a feature which *Intimacy* shares with the preceding novels.

Thus I am not claiming that Jay is without "ethnicity"; this is clearly an impossibility. But it is not foregrounded in the narrative. The near absence of ethnic markers for Jay (unless we take the above-mentioned class markers as such) can be seen in relation to Kureishi's other writings, where ethnicity and ethnic markers did matter. In a sense Kureishi is teasing the reader, and provoking questions such as: Why does the ethnicity of the character matter? Or, Why does it *not* matter? What is the reason for Jay's metaphorical "passing"? And what are the consequences? This exemplifies some of the ways in which postethnicity puts pressure on the regime of ethnicity.

There is a subtle difference between making an effort *not* to meet expectations, and not meeting expectations. In the former case, these expectations are paradoxically heeded by being circumnavigated. In the latter case they have not disappeared but are losing their grip. The tension with respect to the significance of ethnic markers and the thematics of ethnicity, which can be delineated from *The Buddha of Suburbia* to *Intimacy*, can be found in the later works by Kureishi as well. Like *Intimacy*, some of the stories in *Love in a Blue Time* (1997a) can also be labeled "postethnic," and some of them are older than the collection's publication date would suggest.[18] Included in his second collection of stories, *Midnight All Day* (1999), "The Umbrella" reads like a sequel to *Intimacy*, even though its protagonists bear different names. Likewise, Bidisha's first novel, *Seahorses* (1997), resists the categorization "ethnic," as does V. S. Naipaul's much older *Mr Stone and the Knight's Companion* (1963). The development traced here reflects the emergence of a body of writing which self-consciously sidesteps and disputes the confines of ethnicity. With this body of literature emerging in Britain it becomes possible to widen the scope of post-colonial writing to encompass "other" British writing (see chapter 5).

III. VISUALITY AND POSTETHNICITY

> [W]e must, at last, don the empowering mask of blackness and talk *that* talk, the language of black difference. . . . [W]e see no true reflections of our black faces and hear no echoes of our black voices. . . .
> —(HENRY LOUIS GATES JR. IN MOORE-GILBERT 1997, 196; ORIGINAL EMPHASIS)

In the final section of this chapter I review Hanif Kureishi's film *London*

Kills Me with respect to the interconnections of "visibility" and postethnicity. It is argued that Kureishi's postethnic aesthetics are transferable to the visual medium of film. The chapter closes with a brief observation on the relationship between postethnicity and the politics of black representation.

Kureishi's Politics of Representation: *London Kills Me*

In an unforgiving review in *The New Statesman and Society* (written before the television adaptation), Gilbert Adair suggested that *The Buddha of Suburbia* resembles an "extended movie treatment" (Adair 1990, 34), and that it should have been a film rather than a novel. Nevertheless, he conceded one redeeming quality to Kureishi's choice of genre: It allows Kureishi to play "The Skin Game."

> But [the novel] does possess one virtue that operates with greater force on the printed page than it could ever have done on any screen. *The Buddha of Suburbia* is an utterly, unselfconsciously multiracial artefact. . . . [W]hat lends his story its consistent energy and ebullience is the fact that none of the races in Kureishi's beige-y spectrum is accorded narrative supremacy over any other. Here at least, from surface to psyche, the equality is absolute. If such a strategy works more effectively in a literary context, it's simply because, the characters' racial origins not being infallibly determinable by either their names or their behaviour, one gradually finds oneself forgetting just which are white and which are not. This is an exploit impossible, for an obvious reason, in the cinema. For that, much may be excused. (Adair 1990, 34)

To this critic, literature constitutes a brave new world where "absolute" equality is possible; it allows for ambivalence, whereas film and TV only offer crippling forms of overdetermination. His position reminds me of the 1970s when "color-blindness" seemed desirable in what was then known as "race relations." On one level it is a truism to suggest that print leaves more to the imagination than the screen. But it would seem that "absolute" equality does not come about by sheer ambivalence. On a path toward equality, is not one requirement the *destabilization* of the definite nexus between race and identity? And does this destabilization not also require that the unambivalent visibility of what is sought be overcome?

What is the relationship between visuality and a postethnic perspective as suggested here? Visibility of difference, visuality, is a key concern to black British literature. While it is more obviously pertinent to dramatic and cinematic writing, it is of import for narrative texts as well. But is postethnicity—a contestatory perspective which is characterized by the play between external ascriptions and active affiliations, if not by the absence of ethnic markers, and which treats ethnicity as partly chosen—a phenomenon that is limited to narrative texts? In the context of Kureishi's œuvre, the question of whether postethnicity is of relevance, and whether it bears translation to screenplay and drama, needs to be pursued.

The vagueness about the ethnic background of the central character of *Intimacy* could be considered to arise merely because the reader does not see him. In this first-person narrative, Jay is invoked by his own voice, and any form of direct visual access (such as on stage or film) is precluded. It could be argued that if we were to *see* Jay, then we'd know. This view is in danger of romanticizing visuality, and claiming that it permits a more direct or *purer* form of perception. Since visual difference is often considered synecdochical of ontological difference, much like the use of a particular linguistic variety, texts that are visualized on stage or screen might undercut what might be left indeterminate in narrative.

However, this rests on the assumption that the relationship between the visual or observable and a particular ethnic positionality be a stable one. A postethnic perspective, however, starts from the *instability* of this very relationship. Postethnic writing in fact destabilizes this relationship by subverting it; here I can merely touch upon the question of how far this feature is inflected by generic conventions in dramatic, cinematic, and narrative texts. Kureishi goes beyond sheer oppositionality and thereby contributes to this instability. Hence counterethnic positions are not produced, but rather new, hybrid positionalities are imagined.

Given the centrality of visuality, a distinction between narrative texts (where visualizations take place in the reader's mind) and cinematic and dramatic texts (in which visualizations occur on film or stage) is plausible. However, whether a particular actor is conspicuous depends highly upon circumstance. For not only are the ethnic and "racial" backgrounds of the actor of relevance, so also are the backgrounds of the audience.

In this context, Kureishi's film *London Kills Me* (1991) is of particular interest. Whereas his previous films had been directed by Stephen Frears, this one is screenwritten and also directed by Kureishi. The narrative centers around Clint and the couple Muffdiver and Sylvie who, though not related, form a *family* with Burns, Bike, and Tom Tom. Their complex net of relationships ironizes the emphasis on family under the Conservative government of Margaret Thatcher. The symbolic family is an enterprising (and entrepreneurial) clique of drug dealers who live in a squat and try to squeeze out a living. The film opens with the bildungs-hero Clint resolving to change his life and escape the squalor. As the story unfolds he secures the promise of a job, but on one condition: he needs to find a pair of shoes. The film humorously charts his progress—and his numerous setbacks—on his way to well-heeled employment.

The film title *London Kills Me* is a double entendre: It refers not only to the living conditions depicted in the film, it also cites a group of tourists to whom "London is a cool place" which they then restate in the phrase "London Kills Me." The film thereby stresses its ironic politics of citation. In accordance with that, the central character's name is another citation: he calls himself Clint Eastwood, a young white man adopting the stage name of a reggae singer who has in turn appropriated the name of a Hollywood actor.

The tourist couple is present in key episodes but excluded by their complete incomprehension of the situations which they witness. Importantly, the viewer is likely to mistake the title's significance (possibly as an indication of social realism) before seeing the film; *London Kills Me* thus ironically likens the viewer to the naïve couple. The audience is as distant to the story as the tourists are, and the film imagines its viewer at many removes. Though both may be English-speaking, cultural and class distinctions separate audience and characters. At its opening, then, the film hints at the complex nature of the story it tells, by turning the audience into spectators and voyeurs.

London Kills Me is neither about racism nor ethnicity. The protagonists' class-positions are foregrounded, not their respective ethnicities. The Asian actor Naveen Andrew plays a character, whose name, Bike, does not register a particular ethnic background. Bike is down and out, like the other "family members." His ethnic background is not central to *London Kills Me*. It could be argued that the character Bike is without an Asian ethnicity, although he is played by an Asian actor. The film can therefore be considered alongside *Intimacy* in its deployment of a postethnic perspective. A type of ambiguity which Adair claims to be reserved to the novel, then, can also be found on film.

Naveen Andrew returns in the television adaptation of *The Buddha of Suburbia* (1993) where he plays Karim Amir. But for Karim, of course, ethnicity *is* of relevance. Likewise, Dr. Bubba of *London Kills Me* (played by the well-known Roshan Seth) returns as Karim's father,

Haroon Amir, who mobilizes his ethnic background in order to act as Buddha.

What we are witnessing is more than a return of the same actors. While there was, according to Kureishi, a shortage of Asian actors when making his first film, *My Beautiful Laundrette* (1985), this was certainly no longer the case when *The Buddha of Suburbia* (1993) was being produced for television. Seth and Andrew's return is therefore a conscious gesture. They return as "relations" of the previous characters, wearing almost identical costumes, and showing similar mannerisms. In Haroon Amir (the "Buddha" of Suburbia) we recognize Dr. Bubba (a near homophone); in the cyclist Karim we recognize Bike. It is as if the same personalities have been included in a different production. However, while they were minor characters in *London Kills Me*, Andrew/Karim and Seth/Haroon return as central characters in *The Buddha of Suburbia*.

Two distinct aspects of the same personalities appear: once with and once without an emphasis on ethnicity. Depending on the story that is being told, and on its perspective, ethnicity either is or is not of importance. In this sense, *London Kills Me* is a postethnic film which does not foreground the character's ethnicity. Conversely, *The Buddha of Suburbia* is a television film which can be considered postethnic by virtue of its excessive and defamiliarized performance of "ethnicity" which clears space in ways similar to the novel.

Speaking about *London Kills Me*, Kureishi commented in an interview:

> It seems to me progress to *assume* that we live in a mixed society. Before [as writers of ethnic texts] it was your job to say: "Oh, by the way, there are amazing people here who do live here and are part of Britain." Now we can integrate that into our work while not forgetting it. (Kureishi in Dodd 1991, 12)

In accordance with Kureishi's aesthetics of postethnicity, Bike needs no glossing. *London Kills Me* does not have to explain why Bike "looks" Asian. The consciousness of a multicultural London is embedded into the film; but the film does not need to establish it—it is taken for granted. The casting of the Asian actor Naveen Andrew in a role that does not specifically call for this background indicates that the ties between (visible) ethnic background and permissible social roles are loosened in the film. Like Karim's father in *Buddha*, Bubba provides New Age spiritual services to the chanting classes. But in terms of the film *London Kills Me*, he is a neighbor whose profession and background are no more extraordinary than any of the other characters' professions or backgrounds. In fact, the benevolent Bubba is a transethnic father figure not to Bike but to the white Clint Eastwood. Given his wish to end his career as drug dealer, the narrative is driven forward by Clint's quest for a pair of shoes required on the first day of his first job. Significantly, Dr. Bubba offers Clint his own pair of sandals, thereby indicating his guardianship over Clint.

The film opens with Clint denuded and reborn, vowing to start over again; he needs clothing for his protection, and shoes to leave his marks. *London Kills Me* is a formation narrative charting Clint's process of maturation, and includes recapitulations of his childhood and adolescence. But his potential role models and father figures are themselves *poseurs* and the protagonist cannot construct a clear line of descent; however, he does not seem to require one. Clint Eastwood's stepfather likes to dress up as another show-biz personality, Elvis Presley; and Clint's symbolic father, Bubba, may well be another "renegade Muslim masquerading as a Buddhist." At the close of the film, Clint follows in the footsteps of an American entrepreneur: wearing stolen boots, he has become a waiter in a chic "World Food" restaurant. This choice of footwear—their Native American design constituting another faux lineage—serves him better than any other pair he wears during the film. For Clint's lineage is messy, his ancestry is unclear. *Whose* shoes he wears is of no import to him, as long as he has a pair with which to start his new job—and new life—by the time the film draws to a close.

Clint, however, is aware of the symbolism of wearing someone else's shoes. He rejects Dr. Bubba's offer of sandals, and thereby the spiritualism the character represents. When presented with a brand-new pair of "Dr. Maartens" boots, he also rejects Sylvie and Muffdiver's birthday present, for its acceptance would reaffirm his ties to drug dealing and street life. A pair of stolen boots—the most unclear lineage—suits him best. But the fact that Clint has unwittingly stolen the boots from his future boss corroborates the fact that he cannot avoid stepping into someone else's footsteps, even if by accident.

Every square inch of London has been trodden and trodden again—as Clint observed firsthand when "sleeping rough" and living in the streets. In this (modern) condition, finding his own way does not, and cannot, involve discovering new ground. Be the source text Hollywood, New Age spiritualism, or World Food, *citation* takes the place of originality, as the examples of Clint's stepfather, Bubba, and the restaurateur show.

The postethnic "family" at the center of *London Kills Me* does not share any common roots; it is a hybrid family, including English, Asian, and Irish members without being rooted in these backgrounds, a family that stabilizes itself. This family of social outcasts is resourceful, ironically, in the spirit of Margaret Thatcher. It "visibly" stands out, but not in terms of its members' ethnicity. Through the exclusion of the viewer (noted above), the film raises the question of who has the right to exclude whom and on what grounds. In creating its own family space (through squatting), two points are made: Both the possibility of forging affiliations and the invention of new traditions are emphasized. Like Clint Eastwood's messy lineage, the ancestry of the family remains unclear.

Pipes and tubes and cables are ubiquitous on the outside of many English buildings; they seem affixed like an afterthought. But they also constitute an ideal entryway for those who are barred from using the front door. In *London Kills Me,* the squatter Clint Eastwood enters his future flat by way of a very English drainpipe. And yet, he does not feel out of place, intrusive, or in the wrong. The group of squatters seem to "own the territory ... *they occupy a new kind of space at the centre,*" to echo Stuart Hall (1987, 44). Is an author like Hanif Kureishi similarly placed? Are the Monica Alis and the Zadie Smiths, the Evaristos and Equianos "intruders" in English literature? "Squatters" even? Come in through the wrong door? Or does the makeshift entry which *London Kills Me* so poignantly represents indicate an unease of staying, of belonging, or of owning?

Both V. S. Naipaul and Hanif Kureishi have been criticized for "selling out," and for *not* adequately representing "their own" background; at the same time, both have been inhabiting (or enjoying?) mainstream attention via publishing houses which do *not* specialize in black British literature. The main difference appears to be that Naipaul, bearer of a knighthood of the Empire, is less ambivalent about his position—"one has been compared to Orwell," Paul Theroux reports in *Sir Vidia's Shadow.* But Naipaul enters the house and hopes to stay, as the autobiographical fiction of *The Enigma of Arrival* illustrates. In contrast, Hanif Kureishi enters the "heart of whiteness" to mock it and then to move on; he criss-crosses, in and out, in and out. His practice is one of passing and of space clearing, a transgressive act that is not contained.[19] This motif will also be pursued in chapter 5, with respect to David Dabydeen's *The Intended.*

I have suggested above that Kureishi's *My Beautiful Laundrette*, in depicting a homosexual relationship between a Pakistani man and a former member of the National Front, is a film grappling with the politics of representation. It takes the liberty to neglect the orthodoxies of ethnicity and black representation in order to stress heterogeneity, and to chart new, postethnic affiliations. The variation between Kureishi's texts with respect to postethnicity should not be seen in terms of a chronological development. Rather, there is a parallelism of different strategies of postethnic writing. The film *London Kills Me* and the novel *The Buddha of Suburbia* appeared at roughly the same time, but with the film sidelining ethnicity and the novel foregrounding it, they pursue distinct postethnic and posed-ethnic strategies. In other words, I'm not suggesting a linear development, whereby Kureishi has achieved some sort of transcendence called *postethnicity*. Rather, his works signal a consciousness of the aesthetics of postethnicity and the politics of black representation. While they are not trying to simply avoid ascriptions of ethnicity, they nevertheless do not meet any obligations of dealing with ethnicity as a topic, or of furthering the project of black representation. Instead, ethnicity is displaced but not evaded, without entirely ceasing to be of concern.

Ethnicity enters Kureishi's texts by way of the expectations and projections of his audience inasmuch as they consider him an "ethnic" author; it is also there on a thematic level; and it affects his texts in formal and aesthetic terms. As we have seen, however, Kureishi works through ethnicity on all three levels. His aesthetics of postethnicity compels the reader to consider his or her own positionality. Without discarding ethnicity, its essentialist character is undermined by Kureishi's post- and posed-ethnic texts: As in Said Adrus's Union Jack, Englishness is interrogated and opened up. Donning ethnic roles like masks, Kureishi's characters squat in a porous, penetrable Englishness, as in a disused house, only to move on when that is desired.

5

Amorphous Connections —Post-colonial Intertextuality

THE EMPIRE CHRISTMAS PUDDING
according to the recipe supplied by the King's Chef, Mr. CEDARD, with Their Majesties' Gracious Consent

1 lb Currants	Australia
1 lb Sultanas	Australia or South Africa
1 lb Stoned Raisins	Australia or South Africa
5 ozs Minced Apple	United Kingdom or Canada
1 lb Bread Crumbs	United Kingdom
1 lb Beef Suet	United Kingdom
6½ ozs Cut Candied Peel	South Africa
8 ozs Flour	United Kingdom
8 ozs Demerara Sugar	British West Indies or British Guiana
5 Eggs	United Kingdom or Irish Free State
1½ oz Ground Cinnamon	India or Ceylon
¼ oz Ground Cloves	Zanzibar
¼ oz Ground Nutmegs	British West Indies
¼ teaspoon Pudding Spice	India or British West Indies
¼ gill Brandy	Australia, South Africa, Cyprus or Palestine
½ gill Rum	Jamaica, or British Guiana
1 pint beer	England, Wales, Scotland, or Ireland

—(EMPIRE MARKETING BOARD 1932)

The controversial representation of British imperial and naval history in the National Maritime Museum (NMM) in Greenwich, London, raises a number of questions which are pertinent to this chapter. By considering two exhibits of the NMM, this chapter touches upon the particular complexity of historiography in a heterogeneous society. It then investigates the use of the book as an emblem of colonial power, before pursuing those themes in David Dabydeen's novel *The Intended*.

I. UNDOING THE EMPIRE?

The British Empire cannot be *undone* in the sense of reversing it, or restoring preceding historical conditions. Likewise its effects cannot be annulled or canceled. However, *unfixing* the discourse of empire, opening it up, and interpreting its history and its current efficacy, such types of *undoing* are both possible and necessary.[1] This *unfixing* of the discourse of empire is one vital aspect of black British literature and, more generally, post-colonial writing.

One example of such undoing is the grand display of a recipe for an "Empire Christmas Pudding" in the Wolfson Gallery of Trade and Empire at the NMM. This dish comprises ingredients from around the globe, allowing the metropolitan center to ingest Britain's Empire. Effortlessly drawing upon its rich resources, the recipe represents the empire's reach and its power. Australian currants are commanded along with a measure of cinnamon from India; West Indian sugar and Jamaican rum are also mixed into His Majesty's Pud. All of this not only underscores the expansiveness of the empire, but also points to its power to legislate across very large distances.

The recipe allows for a number of different readings which can only be touched upon here. On one level, it can be read as a mark of the empire's expansiveness. On another level, since the effortless representation of His Majesty's pudding is central (with the various colonies and dominions falling into place at the periphery), it is indicative of the power commanded by the empire. This power is not only represented but at the same time produced by such a representation. Moreover, the recipe can be read as a strategy of the Empire Marketing Board to deal with various *colonial* governments' requests for a larger share of the trade within the empire.[2] Furthermore, and following on from this, the recipe can be read as indicative of the increased agency, and the heightened power of the colonial governments in relation to the Crown in the 1930s. Finally, the image reminds us that Britain's imperial history has for many generations yoked together nations, cultures, and peoples around the globe in an unequal exchange of culture and commodity, an exchange which has left its imprint both on the colonizer and the colonized.

In view of such a multiplicity of possible readings it becomes clear that a simple artifact which was originally meant to celebrate Empire also yields itself to other, conflicting readings. The artifact bears out multiple significations. It evokes different subjects in different subject positions, ranging from the sugar-producing person in the West Indies to pudding eaters throughout the empire; it also relates to agency-endowed colonies which necessitate action on the part of the metropolitan power.

The recipe card is displayed at the NMM in Greenwich, where the introduction of eight new galleries has entailed a fierce public debate about the modern nation's relationship to the British Empire, and about how that relationship should be represented in a museum space.[3]

The Drawing Room, one of the most controversial exhibits of the Wolfson Gallery of Trade and Empire, also speaks to the collusion between domesticity and empire. We encounter a woman dressed in finery, who is enjoying a cup of tea in the privacy of her drawing room. The table is laid out with a white cloth on which bread, butter, marmalade, and sugar are served on china plates. The style of her dress points to the 1750s, before there was a movement for the abolition of the slave trade. The table is set for two, with ample food and a second, unused cup.

Seen from another perspective, however, from the far end of the room, the first impression has to be corrected: The white woman is not alone. Though not acknowledging it, she shares the oval space of the exhibit with a black man in bondage, who is represented only by his shackled hand, which emerges eerily from the hold of a slave ship. This resonates with the emblem of the British Society for the Abolition of Slavery's emblem which is well known from Josiah Wedgwood's china plaque.

The exhibit's shape is reminiscent of a ship, and also of an eye; it also represents an island, Britain. Its mere outline, then, indicates its thematic concerns. It is concerned with transportation (ship), with perception (eye), and with the borders of Britain (island), as well as with their transgression. This space, this ship, this eye, this island are shared by a slave who is on his way to produce sugar under the whip, and by a woman who is drinking this sugar in her tea without noticing her connection to the triangular trade. Not only elliptical in shape, The Drawing Room is also about ellipsis, about the strategy of omission.

> People like me who came to England in the 1950s have been there for centuries; symbolically, we have been there for centuries. I was coming home. I am the sugar at the bottom of the English cup of tea. I am the sweet tooth, the sugar plantations that rotted generations of English children's teeth. There are thousands of others beside me that are ... the cup of tea itself. (Hall 1991, 48)

The symbolic and literal historical presence of black Britons, of which Stuart Hall reminds us here, is often ignored. In fact, historical elision and structural invisibility are so deeply ingrained that their undoing remains a formidable task. The Drawing Room is an exhibit that constitutes an intervention in this context. It is performing "cultural work" toward creating visibility and countering the elision of the historical presence of black Britons.[4]

The sphere of The Drawing Room, which a black man and a white woman coinhabit, actually implies numerous intricate connections, as we know with historical hindsight. At the same time, the *confrontation* which the exhibit suggests only takes place in the viewer's mind. Visitors themselves have to *see* the connections, and to forge the connections of which the represented woman is not mindful. The exhibit, therefore, interrogates the ability to perceive the moral and economic ties between the two waxwork figures; it dramatizes the tensions between ignoring and acknowledging those ties. Similarly, the connections I will suggest below, with respect to *The Intended*, are connections whose potential is contained within the novel and the discourses it addresses. These connections, however, are made explicit in the pages of this chapter.

Intriguingly, the new gallery has sparked a fierce public debate which has been conducted in the press, on radio, and on TV.[5] The issues which have been covered concern the writing of history in a multicultural society, where distinct constituencies have potentially irreconcilable claims to the history of Empire, or rather to its representation. Empire, it was argued by many, was depicted too negatively in the new gallery, with the benefits to the colonized being neglected and the legacy of the empire tarnished.

The historian Lawrence James, author of *The Rise and Fall of the British Empire*, seems to have initiated this debate with his article "Heroes No More" in the tabloid *Daily Mail*. His essay sparked off many further articles and letters to the editor. James accuses the NMM of an "appalling misrepresentation of our past," and concludes that "we are being grossly misled" by the new gallery. His second complaint is that "[w]e are urged to toe-a-line [*sic*] of national self-deprecation and depart feeling ashamed of our past" (L. James 1999). What stands out from James's contribution—and many of the responses—is an understanding that the past should by definition be praiseworthy and a source of pride, irrespective of particular historical detail. This is as surprising as the ease with which James uses the homogenizing pronouns "we" and "our." Most striking of all, however, is the notion of a single history. James's position is marred by a lack of differentiation between the divergent histories of the museum's heterogeneous visitors, and indeed, of Britain's heterogeneous populace. James is in denial of the fact that there is not one single referent to the signifier history. Rather, there is a plurality of narratives which seek to adequately represent the mutually entangled histories of those who make up modern Britain.

Traditionally, museums are expected to strengthen national identity, rather than endangering any such identity by raising uncomfortable questions. The controversy over the gallery also touches upon the question of who gains representation in the new museum gallery, and who ought to be targeted by the new halls. This is then also a conflict about the function of a museum: Should it be a seemingly apolitical space of leisure and edification or, conversely, a place of critical labor, cultural work, and public historiography?

The galleries also show many exhibits which originally served to celebrate the empire. However, as one of the notices in the Wolfson Gallery of Trade and Empire puts it, "these objects can also tell other stories."[6] From the outset, then, the gallery indicates the contingency of representation. The viewer learns that displays are far from innocent or neutral and instead possess a potential for multiple significations. The celebratory intentions with which many of the artifacts were first acquired and displayed is palpable. But this purpose is confronted and supplemented by the way in which the exhibition is arranged, how it is commented upon, and how artifacts and displays interact with each other. What is contentious is not only *what* is displayed, but more importantly, *how* it is displayed. Trophies of empire are not shown in an antiquarian manner but rather in an interrogative mode, and emphasize the polysemic nature of signification. By implication, then, the history of empire is depicted as being open to interpretation, and as being multifaceted.

The National Maritime Museum has striven for self-transformation, to move away from celebrating maritime achievement in order to engage in a critical representation of the involvement and complicity of British naval history. The ensuing debate highlights how sensitive the area of public historiography is, particularly in a heterogeneous society, where a museum is required to take into consideration not only the complexity of the represented subject matter, but also the distinct and varied relationships its audiences have to this subject matter. The complex mode of representation in the Gallery of Trade and Empire heeds the intricacies of signifying processes, and corresponds to the complex cultural and social mix of viewers a national museum located in Southeast London can expect. It reflects negatively on the museum, though, that it has recently given in to pressure by removing the offending exhibit (The Drawing Room) and relocating and paring down others. In the debate about the celebratory and critical agenda of museology at the NMM, those in favor of celebrating maritime achievement seem to have gained the upper hand.

What is borne out by the (former) exhibits of the NMM is the multiplicity of connections across time and place, and the intricate ways in which they have repercussions in contemporary debates. The map of the Christmas pudding (still in place) points to both historical legacies and contemporary connections which are presently negotiated within Britain. The Drawing Room spoke of the imbrication of the discourses of trade and domesticity, and culpability and responsibility, provoking the question of how to write history *from* the perspectives of a multiplicity of historical subjects and *for* a multiplicity of readers. The novels discussed in this study are marked by similar connections across time and space, and feature characters who can be "menacing" insofar as they are *from* England and insist upon their rightful place vociferously and self-confidently.

II. THE ENGLISH BOOK

> 'The horror! The horror!' must not be repeated in the drawing-rooms of Europe.
> —(BHABHA 1994, 107)

> [T]he Slaves lie in two rows, one above the other, on each side of the ship, close to each other, like books upon a shelf. I have known them so close, that the shelf would not, easily, contain one more.
> —(NEWTON 1788, 33–34)

John Newton (1725–1807) worked his way from mate to master of a slave ship before being converted and ordained into the priesthood. At this later stage in his life he developed into an abolitionist. In his pamphlet *Thoughts Upon the African Slave-Trade*, he employs the image of a library to describe the inhumanely packed hold of a slave ship. Equating an individual with a volume, he fuses the symbol of one of civilization's high points, the library, with one of its low points, the transatlantic slave trade. The energies invested in ordering a library are related to the energies that went into organizing and rationalizing the slave trade. The book can thus be seen not only as an emblem of European "civilizing" and colonial power; by being aggregated to a library it also represents an epistemological order which incorporates and disciplines colonial subjects.

In his essay "Signs Taken for Wonders," Homi Bhabha is interested in the authority of the "English book," that is, the Bible. He pursues the question of how authority is asserted under circumstances of colonization and witnesses the book "doing its own work"—but not quite. His contention is that the position of the colonizer was inherently unstable, as it undermined itself in the iterative process of establishing itself; it is "through an act of repetition, that the colonial text emerges uncertainly" (1994, 107). This formulation conveys Bhabha's fondness for discursive instabilities in forms of colonial discourse, as opposed to forms of material resistance and forms of anticolonialist discourses.[7]

Bhabha's central argument is that the English book is not only the fetishized sign glorifying Europe's epistemological centrality; the book is at once an emblem of colonial "ambivalence" which makes it susceptible to discursive subversion. "[T]he very ground for or source of authority is unstable, ambivalent and thus [lends] itself to intervention, to resistance. Resistance, then, becomes something of an inbuilt possibility; crucially, it is relegated to the realm of the discursive" (Stein 1996, 45).

In Bhabha's essay, a passage from *Heart of Darkness* is juxtaposed with one from V. S. Naipaul's *The Return of Eva Peron*. In these two passages Marlow and a young Trinidadian, respectively, read a section from Towson's *Inquiry into Some Points of Seamanship*.

> Marlow turns away from the African jungle to recognize, in retrospect, the peculiarly "English" quality of the discovery of the book. Naipaul turns his back on the hybrid half-made colonial world to fix his eye on the universal domain of English literature. (Bhabha 1994, 107)

In Conrad's novella, Towson's *Inquiry* is characterized by a "singularity of intention" to which Marlow aspires. Traveling up the Congo, remote from the epistemic support that would sustain him at home—and yet attracted by its very absence—the *Inquiry* is not just a manual on seamanship but representative of the order from which it derives. As such, Marlow derives strength from it in Conrad's novella. Dabydeen's *The Intended* also seeks entry to the "universal domain of English literature." In contrast to Bhabha's estimate of V. S. Naipaul's narrative, however, Dabydeen pursues this with an eye to the colonial world of Guyana, and, crucially, its interrelationships with Britain. This will be explored in the following sections.

III. LOGOVOROUS READING: *THE INTENDED*

> For that is the law of the human position: the spectator or interpreter has to live with, and within, the knowledge that "somebody began it"—the story, the web of human relationships, the *inter-est,* (the) painting, the installation, the verse, the critique—while acknowledging the fact that nobody is its author.
> —(BHABHA 1996, 15)

The Intended relates the unnamed narrator's formation up to the point where he succeeds in forging a literary voice. This he accomplishes by breaking with his life in London and by entering university—he has to egress and to ingress before he can belong. He also leaves the land of his birth, Guyana, to join his father in London when barely aged fourteen, only to be abandoned soon, growing up in an institutional "home." Seemingly unable to belong anywhere, his formation is marked by multiple divisions: he is removed from Guyana, socially excluded in London, and cannot empathize wholly with his friends, who have different ambitions and backgrounds.

The narrator's story is told alongside that of Nasim, Shaz, Patel, and Joseph. If the bildungsroman can be considered "a sort of laboratory in which the hero conducts an experiment in living," as Colin Wilson has suggested (1956, 51), this experiment is conducted by a group of friends in the case of *The Intended*. As a *multiple* bildungsroman, the depiction of a variety of character developments allows the narrator-protagonist's formation to be seen in context, with Joseph in particular functioning as his foil.

"The Immigrant Must Invent the Earth Beneath His Feet"

> Go and don't look back . . . or else Albion ghosts go follow you all the way to Englan. [*sic*]
> —(DABYDEEN 1991a, 70)

This is the advice given the young narrator by his grandmother as he leaves behind Albion Village and rural Guyana to join his father in London. The narrative structure of *The Intended*, however, effects just that, looking back from adolescence in London to childhood in Guyana. The novel does not progress in a chronological manner, but is told in a series of prolepses and analepses. It is haunted by the ghosts which the grandmother had warned against. Marlow's inquiry into the play between order and disorder is represented, on one level, by the narrative structure of *The Intended* that is inflicted on Albion.

Being a fictional narrative, however, ghosts are deployed as much as those whom they haunt in the novel's diegesis. It is fitting then that the ghosts who are poised to follow the narrator to England are "Albion ghosts," that is, on one level, English ghosts.[8] The young protagonist carries with him an "imperialized" identity (Gikandi 1996, 191) and a history that cannot be disentangled from British colonial history. In that sense, the narrator had already been at his destination in Albion Village; he had already arrived in England (having historically been a part of it) before his departure. This mutual entanglement is symbolized by the novel's anachronic narrative structure.

The notion of arrival before departure, or of connectedness, is not only exemplified by *The Intended*'s narrative structure but also characterizes Dabydeen's poetics. In an interview with Wolfgang Binder he explains:

> [T]he academic work that I have been doing on eighteenth-century England[9] has never been divorced from a personal quest to belong to twentieth-century England. . . . I tend to think that Britain depended upon us heavily for its material and cultural advance. So when I say that I want to belong, I mean I want to recognize that. To recognize that I (and by "I" I don't mean just myself, but the tribe) have had a very important say and impact in their development. *The sense of belonging only comes about when the British recognize that.* . . . Ultimately, you come to a kind of vision: Our cultures have become so intimately enmeshed over the centuries, that you cannot be Guyanese without being British, and you cannot be British without being Guyanese or Caribbean. (Dabydeen 1989a, 164–65; emphasis added)

Before he had published any of his four novels, Dabydeen suggested that his academic writing and his literary works are connected by the theme of interrelated histories. They share the aesthetic and political program of seeking out historical connections and making them visible. Creating *visibility* for this nexus is understood as achieving recognition, which is in turn considered a precondition for "belonging." According to Dabydeen, a "sense of belonging" can only be achieved "when the British recognize" the long-standing historical, economic, political, and cultural connections with black Britons, who are often relegated to the status of migrants despite citizenship.

The connections Dabydeen articulates are precisely the ones The Drawing Room at the Wolfson Gallery seeks to elicit. This exhibit points to an imbricated history of Britain and its former colonies which has entailed the entanglement and interdependence of which Dabydeen speaks. He sees "belonging" as being sanctioned by such long-standing historical connectedness, but it can only be achieved by the recognition of an overlapping and conjoint history.

It is interesting to note that the Wolfson Gallery has triggered considerable attention—which presumably entails a recognition of connections and responsibility, and thereby contributes to the kind of belonging of which Dabydeen speaks—while academic and creative writing seem rarely to produce this kind of widespread public interest, even when pursuing similar goals.

Elsewhere, Dabydeen has commented on another facet of his artistic practice. With reference to Wilson Harris, he described his aesthetic project as an attempt at rewriting "the pornography of Empire":[10]

> [T]he "Empire" was a pornographic project; it wasn't just an economic or a sociological or a political project, it was also a project of pornography . . . ultimately, the plantation experience had severe and traumatic psychic impacts that had to do with the loss of, or the traumatic changes in epistemologies and philosophies, but overwhelmingly had to do with what is the very ground of our being, which is our body.
> (Dabydeen 1994a, 220)

Here he suggests provocatively that it was the human body which primarily bore and still bears the experience of Empire. The body is almost conceived of as a repository of cultural memory, an idea which Dabydeen, however, seems to discard elsewhere.[11] Considering physical experience to be fundamental partially explains the emphasis which is placed on the body in Dabydeen's three books of poetry and in his first two novels.[12]

In The Drawing Room at the Wolfson Gallery the body is also of significance: It is the mere presence of a black waxwork hand which gives the display its uncanny power. While the slave ship is evoked only by the iron manacle and the wooden door of its hold, the museum visitor casts his or her gaze upon the scene from the outside and witnesses the stark contrast between the leisured lady and the imploring hand. Any other scenes are generated only in the mind's eye, but the viewer, on account of his or her spectatorship, is implicated in a visual display that one might refer to as "pornographic" for it risks titillation at the suffering of others.

Incorporating the voice of Dabydeen's comments on his own

poetics and creative writing is problematical inasmuch as it has the potential to short-circuit the critical process. Yet considering such commentary alongside other critical voices—without attributing it any primacy—reveals that Dabydeen's presence in the archives of literature and criticism has been characterized (from *Slave Song* onward) by a conscious and pronounced transgression of the borders between writer and critic. His novels are written with post-colonial critics in mind; and their expectations—of which Dabydeen seems painstakingly aware—are at once heeded and frustrated in his work. With reference to *The Intended* and *Disappearance*, the critic Mark McWatt has warned that Dabydeen's "self-consciously postcolonial" poetics are in danger of merely scoring theoretical points rather than constituting narrative works in their own right. He charges that both his fiction and the reader are "diminished" by his "literary gamesmanship" (McWatt 1997, 122). In the light of this critique it seems warranted to critically consider the author's own commentary when reading his fiction. This reading of Dabydeen's first novel sets it in dialogue with two programmatic notions expressed by the author: his understanding of the discourse of Empire as a pornographic project; and his claim that belonging to modern Britain is validated by colonial history while being conditional on the recognition of this interdependent history.

One of the connections mentioned in the context of The Drawing Room becomes visible in the narrator's relationship with his girlfriend, Janet. The young woman is seen as an inheritor to Britain's history of Empire. At the novel's close she is poised to leave the country with her parents—something about which the narrator is delighted. He explains that it is "a new beginning" for his girlfriend, in "a new, clean country" (1991a, 242). Janet is thus likened to settlers going out to find the New World five hundred years before her.

Chapter 2 suggested that Britain's iconography is redressed by the black British novel of transformation. *The Intended*'s portrayal of England is a further instance of this because it contrasts Janet's clean New World with "messy and violent and drugged up" England, where "everything is going to pot" (Dabydeen 1991a, 242). This indictment sums up the novel's portrait of the condition of England, as it is witnessed by the narrator and his friends: it is a place of violence, crime, prostitution, pornography, and drugs. However, as the next paragraph reveals, the narrator is not merely a witness. His own conduct is proof to him of the corrupted condition of England: "I was right," he argues, "for I had already betrayed her with Monica." Significantly, the narrator sees himself as implicated in the condition of England, rather than beyond the scope of his own judgment. With reference to his drug- and pornography-peddling friend, he adds: "I was as shop-soiled as all the things Patel dealt in" (1991a, 242). It behooves the theme of historical interconnectedness to note that the text indicts Janet's "inheritance" of Empire and concurrently recognizes the narrator's imbrication in England's "corruption."

In order to equip him for his studies at Oxford, Janet buys a new shirt for her boyfriend:

> She made me try it on in a booth and inspected me. . . . I felt like one of Shaz's whores, or a slave on an auction block. . . .
>
> As I stripped off in the booth I noticed my body in the mirror. It looked meagre and unworthy of attention. I was glad there was no one to see me in my nakedness through some slot. (Dabydeen 1991a, 243–44)

The narrator's glance at the reflection of his body triggers not only feelings of shame. Significantly, he also feels "unworthy of attention." In view of his physique and phenotypic features, the narrator experiences the problematics of post-colonial representation which he also ponders theoretically, as will be discussed below. Under Janet's gaze the narrator is reminded of his forays to a peep show and feels his own body becoming the object of unwanted stares which seek to take possession and imprint ownership. Janet's voyeuristic gaze is likened to both contemporary and historical commodification of the body, enacted through pornography and enslavement. The violence of such a gaze, where one is financially empowered to bare, debase, and purchase the other, is associated with the violence of the slave trade. Dabydeen's critique of the pornography of empire is born out by Janet "inspecting" and appraising the narrator's physique: "'It fits your body well,' she said, 'it goes nicely against your brown skin'" (Dabydeen 1991a, 244). As if to correct a slip of the tongue Janet swiftly adds that she "'love[s] the colour of [his] skin,'" only to shift her attention back to the shirt, admonishing him to "'wash it properly and keep it white'" (Dabydeen 1991a, 244).

In Britain, the narrator is motherless and describes his father as "utterly careless" (1991a, 237) whereas in Guyana he had been cared for by both his mother and grandmother. So it may well be her maternal counseling to "wash [his shirt] properly" which attracts the narrator to

Janet, who also demands that he honor her present by keeping it white. The narrator is in fact searching for a mother figure, and for a surrogate family, throughout the text (see Dabydeen 1991a, 26, 27, 168, 169, 192, 214), and his friend Patel accuses the narrator of wanting England to mother him: "Just because you ain't got a mother don't mean that England will mother you" (1991a, 246).[13]

But it seems slightly odd for Janet to comment on his skin tone and to immediately insist on the need to keep the shirt as its spectral opposite. Janet is not only an allegorical maternal figure who represents both England and its imperial heritage. She also pays attention to the narrator's body and skin, precisely the kind of attention which he wants to avoid. It is significant that while she is appreciative of his pigmentation, Janet presents him with a white shirt and admonishes him to keep it so. This is not only an expression of her wish for his faithfulness. Inasmuch as the white shirt covers the narrator's body, of which he feels ashamed, Janet is seen to be complicit with his desire for social invisibility, encouraging the narrator to enshroud himself in white. The shirt is moreover a visible and yet covert mark of his connection to Janet whose "dark secret" he represents in the terms of the novel (1991a, 245). It is visible because it can be seen by everyone, covert in that the shirt's significance can remain unknown. In the manner of an "illicit pregnancy" and an "undeveloped child" (1991a, 245), he has been kept hidden from Janet's parents who would not approve of their daughter's Indo-Guyanese boyfriend. However, the couple hopes his studies at Oxford will render him acceptable, "education compensating for my colour in the eyes of her parents" (1991a, 245).

The narrator's formation is represented as a process of cultural whitewashing which the white shirt symbolizes. Prior to his departure to Oxford, the narrator experiences the changing room on Oxford Street as an auction block. The shirt he is presented with then constitutes a token not only of attachment but also of Janet's ownership—obtained on the "auction block" on the road to Oxford.

Before Janet and the narrator's relationship is explored further, I want to briefly consider Dabydeen's second novel with respect to a particular mode of reading and writing. *Disappearance* (1993) is narrated by a Guyanese engineer who has been called upon to construct a sea dam to support Kent's crumbling coast. Confronted with his landlady, Mrs. Rutherford, and in the presence of her book collection which gives off the "damp smell and the fine dust of another age" (Dabydeen 1993, 9), the engineer feels that he is of another world. He feels emphatically "West-Indian, someone born in a new age" (1993, 10). Although they share the same house, the protagonists partake of discrete worlds and times. In fact, they belong to opposed epistemological orders, as their sense of history indicates. The decaying volumes' print, which is fading, recalls the coastline succumbing to the sea. This sense of decay, and of a fading history, distinguishes the engineer from Mrs. Rutherford and from England, as his future is not "bound to the past like pages in a book" for he "had cultivated no sense of the past" (1993, 10).

To the engineer the volume which he is holding in his hand, and which is made porous by insects, contains knowledge in a code "resembling Braille" so that "even the blind could have access" to it (1993, 9). Confronted with "the pathós of the leather-bound volume," he imagines an alternative mode of reading (1993, 10). His "culturally blind eyes" allow him to transcend sequential modes of reading, and permits him to "look through the tunnels made by the termites, . . . through the whole text, and beyond" (1993, 10).

His tunnel vision assumes an angular relationship to the archives of the "Western tradition," and his alternative (post-colonial?) mode of reading affiliates him with insatiable parasites which destroy what they eat/read. Furthermore, his probing is at once an exploration and a piercing, a reading which constitutes a "space clearing" in the archives of an exclusive tradition (Dabydeen 1993, 10). Significantly, the destruction of the archive's substance (entailed by this act of rereading) occurs in the act of its appreciation, and is concurrently a reconstitution of the archive. The texts are transposed (eaten, digested, and turned into dust) *and* in effect rewritten (as in Braille), as they become legible to those who were formerly excluded from the archive. This reading process can be called logovorous reading.

Disappearance's fantasy of effacement and depletive reading, and of raping archives, may not be concordant with the fiction of a narrating engineer. Nevertheless, it signifies a *logovorous* mode of reading whose practice can be observed in the preceding novel, *The Intended*.[14] This novel of transformation ingests pretexts and therefore recycles them, while at the same time punching holes in them. Destruction and recirculation go hand in hand. *Heart of Darkness*, for example, is alluded to in many ways but it is neither simply paid homage (one form of recirculation) nor is it merely parodied (another type of intertextuality which can be contrasted with the above).

On the last page of *The Intended*, the narrator's friend Patel envisages that "England will be one tribe of Patels." Alluding to Caliban's desire—"I had peopled else/ This isle with Calibans" (*The Tempest* I, 2, ll. 352–53)—he predicts that "names like Lucinda Patel and Egbert

Smythe-Patel" are becoming more and more commonplace (Dabydeen 1991a, 246). In a novel where erudition is measured in terms of knowledge about sex, it is not surprising that the less erudite narrator at first holds a position quite distinct from that occupied by Patel. He is not speculating upon peopling Britain, far from it. In fact, the narrator is intimidated by his girlfriend Janet's body. In a sequence of similes he transposes her body into a sphere with which he is conversant. Steeped in English letters, the novel's "professor" (1991a, 94), who wins an award to read English, imagines his girlfriend in terms of punctuation marks. Janet is curled "like a comma . . . her naked back . . . straightened like an exclamation mark and her nipples . . . like a colon daring me to conclude what I had timidly begun or to explain it away" (Dabydeen 1991a, 145). The narrator's anxiety and inexperience are shown up in this passage by way of irony. Initially he elects the second option, explaining "away" Janet's daunting body by perceiving it as text, as a cipher. His *logovorous* reading, which transposes Janet's body not into Braille but into punctuation marks, is reminiscent of the transformative fantasies of the engineer in *Disappearance*. The present narrator appears not to denounce the "cultural grammar of Englishness," to borrow Simon Gikandi's term (1996, 192); instead, he follows it to the dot, reconfiguring Janet accordingly.

However, the *logovorous* mode of reading can be more consumptive than the term *reconfiguration* suggests. Exposed to pornographic materials by his friend Shaz, the narrator also harbors sexual fantasies which seek transposition of a different order. Envisaging "smearing blackness over all that genteel Englishness," he speculates "how her parents would react if she returned home bruised and bitten and impregnated" (1991a, 169). The preceding fantasy confers upon the narrator the role of a reader, whereas the second vision exposes him as fiercely inscribing and violating Janet's body.

The narrator's vision (and possibly impetus) of violating Janet in various ways could be seen as a transference of the epistemological violence experienced by him as a black Briton into the domain of gender violence. It constitutes a translation of his experience of racism into misogyny toward his white girlfriend. But, significantly, he wonders about her parents' response, which suggests that the imagined violations are partly directed at them.[15] In his relationship with Janet, then, racial tensions which mark the narrator's world are lived out in fantasy; in these constructions Janet is subjected to violence on account of her gender and phenotype. Now it is not she who clothes him in white but he who dreams of rendering her black. His impulse to impregnate her moves him closer to his friend Patel's dream of peopling England in his own name and image. But the narrator remains unnamed in the novel and dissatisfied with his image: To him, Patel's Calibanesque dream is an option which remains foreclosed.

Although it is overwritten and verges on the grotesque (with Englishness no longer being synonymous with gentility), the above citation conveys a sense of anguish which is not dampened by this jarring rhetorical mismatch. The potent antithesis between "genteel Englishness" and bedaubing "blackness" signifies the violent alienation that the narrator has experienced. Tragically, he has imbibed societal biases against black and Asian men to a point of being unable to divorce himself from racist preconceptions. The fact that their relationship is kept secret from Janet's parents has corroborated his feelings of insufficiency and inadequacy. His experiences and his self-doubt trigger fantasies of violent misogyny. However, when he rejects his violent thoughts, he relapses into his protective attitude toward Janet, protecting her even from himself and from what "blackness" represents in his own eyes.

In view of the novel's ending it could be argued, in a Freudian context, that the young man succeeds in sublimating his desire and instinctual energy when turning into a writer at Oxford. This reading rests upon the assumption that the writer's profession is more socially acceptable, an assumption which, however, *The Intended* ironically undercuts. The narrator's *logovorous* fantasies point to a tension between *reading* marks and *leaving* marks, or between reading and writing. Insofar as the protagonist is poised to become a writer, he opts for the latter, although not in the destructive sense of his fantasy. This would suggest that he chooses not simply to be beguiled by English Heritage, but rather that he is bent on making a mark and remaining "true" to his conflicting desires.

Patel's vision of peopling the island on the novel's last page is followed by one further paragraph, which concerns the narrator's self-effacement. It contains a highly theatrical scene which constitutes an alternative to Patel's vision:

> I am wearing her clean white shirt as I wait for my taxi. . . . Soon the black cab will come scuttling along the road like a beetle. Its bright eyes will pick me up like prey, and soon I'll be gone, me and all my things. One last breath, then I'll climb in and be gone. (Dabydeen 1991a, 244, 246)

Here the first-person narrator announces his stage exit which naturally entails the conclusion of his narrative, once the last breath is taken. Instead of leaving behind offspring, however, self-eradication is thematized in this passage. Equated with a prey animal, the narrator is about to be absorbed so that he will leave behind no trace. This disappearing act is reminiscent of a ritual sacrifice for which the oblation is dressed up in white. Yet having himself called the black cab suggests that his eradication is not entirely imposed on him. Moreover, in this excerpt the narrator emphasizes that "I'll climb in," implying that he could also choose *not* to climb in and so escape absorption by the beetle. His eradication is therefore presented as courted, and as willed.

The taxi is to take the narrator to university so that the willed eradication of selfhood is attributed to his studies at Oxford. This accords with his experience of Oxford Street as an "auction block." He himself has chosen Oxford—which has of course also chosen him. In that sense, his desired and dreaded "rebirth" (which will be discussed below) is self-inflicted and is in character with his earlier experience of "reincarnations." The theme of migrant reincarnations—where rebirth is the lot of the immigrant—is pervasive in *The Intended:* "I wanted to stop moving. I didn't want to be born time and again. I didn't want to be an eternal, indefinite immigrant. I wanted to get off" (Dabydeen 1991a, 243). In her essay "'A Different Kind of Book': Literary Decolonization in David Dabydeen's *The Intended*," Karen McIntyre has read *The Intended* as a liminal text, situated between post-colonial and postmodern discourses (1996, 155). It is not surprising, then, that the narrator's wish to "get off" is reminiscent of Fredric Jameson's famous will to egress from the Los Angeles Bonaventure Hotel (1984). To Jameson the building is a symbol of postmodern epistemology which entraps the theoretician in search of the "curiously unmarked" exit. While Jameson is determined to get beyond the doors of the hotel, and out of the reach of consumer capitalism, the desire to egress is more ambivalent in *The Intended*.

On one level, the narrator's desire to egress simply refers to his wish to leave the bus on which he is traveling down Oxford Street as he is suffering from motion sickness. But the repeated "I wanted to get off" also refers to his weariness at the immigrant condition, which the novel visualizes as a succession of rebirths and a series of transplantations. The novel charts the journey from rural Guyana to Oxford via metropolitan London. In Guyana the narrator was seen to live between the rural Albion Village and the town of New Amsterdam. When called to London by his father, he has to leave behind both lives. Moreover, at the end of the novel, the narrator is about to leave London, which suggests that he is about to start all over again.

The narrator knows that leaving for university is a step from which he cannot retreat: "I would never return" (1991a, 211). Studying at Oxford, he understands, will entail not only his induction into another world, but also his alienation from his previous life: "a new accent in my voice, bigger words for bigger ideas, all of which would be beyond" Shaz and the others (1991a, 211–12). His new accent signifies a new class affiliation and a new identity which obliterates his previous position. Thus the narrator feels that he is part of a sequence of events which he cannot stop—he does not feel in control, yet he desires control: "I wanted to stop moving. . . . I wanted to get off" (1991a, 243).

Education seems to present a way out of this predicament. While the narrator wants to halt, and stay in one place, he is at the same time dissatisfied with the squalor of life in Balham, South London, and with being hidden from Janet's parents. Given his experiences of racism and exclusion, he feels that he cannot "belong to the crowd" and therefore aspires to do "something serious," such as "write books, and one day become a celebrity" (1991a, 113). The narrator is thus possessed by conflicting goals, wanting to be both a celebrity and part of the crowd; he seeks the future which Oxford seems to offer and at once wishes to stay away from it. He wants to find a literary voice (making the novel a *künstlerroman*) which would make him heard and give him visibility, and yet, at once, he desires invisibility (1991a, 15, 246).[16]

Into the Heart of Whiteness

> I screwed up the poem, bored by the project of universalising the petty death of Mr Ali's sister. Everything was petty, Mr Ali, his family, Peter, myself, and words were only ways of falsifying the pettiness, words were a fancy lie.
> —(DABYDEEN 1991A, 155)

The Intended is essentially about reading and writing. Throughout the text its protagonists are involved in discussing literature and other types of reading matter; they also debate their own essays on *Heart of Darkness* and other set texts for their A-level examinations. Moreover, the narrator self-consciously queries which literary exemplars are suitable for a post-colonial text, and which choice of language is appropriate.[17]

On one side, the novel raises the question of *how* to represent life in Guyana, life in the Caribbean, or life in the former colonies more generally—a question which is certainly a mainstay of post-colonial criticism. Parallel to this project, the narrator's grandmother, as a formative character, is remembered[18] and commemorated throughout the novel. Her wisdom, her rootedness, and her shrewdness are celebrated. *The Intended* amounts to a eulogy of her, and of her way of life.[19] Nevertheless the novel raises the question not only of how, but also of whether this form of representation can be achieved.

The concern with how to write in a post-colonial fashion is raised via a task set for the bookish narrator: He is asked to write an epitaph for a Pakistani peasant woman's gravestone. At first he is excited by his landlord's request, hoping that his first venture into poetry will mark the beginning of a literary career (Dabydeen 1991a, 143). But in searching for something to say about Mr. Ali's sister he finds "no landmark" in her life—a life that was "as plain as the ground in which the village stood," and as regular (and regulated) as the tilled earth that has for centuries been tended in the same fashion (1991a, 143).

This equalization of black people to mud is taken up again later in the novel:

> I suddenly longed to be white, to be calm, to write with grace and clarity, to make *words which have status*, to shape them into the craftsmanship of English china, coaches, period furniture, harpsichords, wigs, English anything, for whatever they put their hands and minds to worked wonderfully. . . . *We are mud, they the chiselled stone* of Oxford that has survived centuries and will always be here. (Dabydeen 1991a, 197–98; my italics)

The narrator's Anglophilia, his desire to be white, and his aspiration to write in a metropolitan fashion all permeate *The Intended*. He seems to fall for Oxford's historicist façades and is overawed by the British predilection for histrionics. But there is a tension between the narrator's intra-diegetic feelings (which are rendered plausible within the novel's diegesis) and the *implied author's* distance from the same feelings. This tension is highlighted by the irony toward post-colonial (and tomb-) writing which characterizes the excerpted passage. The narrator's Anglophilia is clearly exaggerated and is contradicted by the history of Empire which did not simply "wor[k] wonderfully." The oxymoron "English china" also points to the fact that "Englishness"—in its pure form and without the Empire—is but a fiction.

At the same time, the motif of mud, of earth, needs to be connected with the narrator's inquiry of how to write in a post-colonial fashion. In composing the epitaph for a woman whose life has been as "plain" as the ground of her village, he seeks inspiration from Milton. However, his friends are quick to point out that he "can't write about Mrs Ali like that" and that "Black people have to have their own words" (1991a, 147). This post-colonial brief, however, is puzzling for the budding writer to whom "'black words' meant the language of Albion Village" and "the vivid curses" of the drunkard Richilo (1991a, 148). Instead, he covets words with "status." The implication is that the narrator feels that he cannot possibly employ "black" English and that he cannot represent "mud." This draws upon the Aristotelian distinction between form and matter, where representation can only occur when matter is modeled into form; yet under such conditions the unformed (mud) cannot be represented.

■ ■ ■

The post-colonial critic Diana Brydon defines "post-colonial critique" as a "theory of engagement" (1994, 282). But this expectation is parried by the writer depicted in *The Intended*. His anticipated commitment is ironized when the versifying narrator muses that *his own* "immortality" could be achieved "by the verse on her tombstone" (1991a, 141). He can thus be described as engagé merely on his own behalf, rather than on behalf of Mrs. Ali. The narrator swerves from seriousness to sarcasm in view of his task. On the one hand, he is writing "[s]omething that will last," a life story for his landlord's sister; on the other hand, he is reminded of his friend Joseph's nihilism which renders his task absurd. While the writerly task is ironically portrayed as being worthy (in accordance with Brydon), the subject in this particular case renders it less so: the woman is described as an illiterate peasant, "draped in rags all her life" (1991a, 141). This should not, of course, deter the writer's commitment, if we follow Brydon's advice.

Following again the ironized brief of the post-colonial writer, the protagonist returns to drafting the epitaph and takes up his "pen and tried to fabricate verse with an exotic flavour." Soon he "paused in self-doubt, wondering whether I could ever rival Conrad and the other white writers when it came to jungle scenes" (Dabydeen 1991a, 144). The narrator not only jibes at Conrad, with whom he sees himself in competition; he also lampoons the post-colonial critic's alleged taste for non-European "exotic" writing, as he labors over "jungle scenes" (scenes which are *not really* favored by most post-colonial critics). This double-edged denunciation is characteristic of the novel, and also accords with the narrative's attentiveness to intertextual relations and critical expectations. The previous chapter on Kureishi has made similar observations on *The Buddha of Suburbia*. Kureishi and Dabydeen's novels negotiate with their critics' expectations, and try to circumnavigate and subvert them.

While I have described *The Buddha of Suburbia* as lacking development on the part of Karim and Haroon, *The Intended* charts its narrator's formation. Despite his doubts regarding post-colonial eulogies, the narrator proceeds to eulogize his grandmother and thereby constructs a powerful post-colonial voice:

> [H]ow cracked the soles of her feet were. There were lines everywhere, running in all directions, like a spider's web or a complicated map of the world tracing roads and rivers and other routes. She was born in Albion village, had never travelled out of the village, and would eventually die there, yet her feet mapped all the pathways of the world. (Dabydeen 1991a, 37)

The desire to take his task as the composer of an epitaph seriously, and thereby derive from it the status of authorship, alternates with the narrator's ridiculing his assignment with regards to the subject of his verse. The sardonic portrayal of the writer focusing upon his or her own self-aggrandizement contravenes the fondness for the engagé author, which characterizes much post-colonial literary criticism. At the same time, however, the world map on his grandmother's feet is successfully (and unironically) lauded. *The Intended*, therefore, performs the task of the "post-colonial" writer and at once questions it.

This description of the grandmother's cracked feet which embody a comprehensive map of the world (although she does not know the outside of Albion Village) reminds me of the opening passage of Roland Barthes's *S/Z*: "There are said to be certain Buddhists whose ascetic practices enable them to see a whole landscape in a bean. Precisely what the first analysts of narrative were attempting: to see all the world's stories (and there have been ever so many) within a single structure" (Barthes 1973, 3). The structuralist dream of finding a limited set of metanarratives may have been at the back of the Dabydeen's mind when writing the passage on the cracked feet. More so since, in some forms of post-colonial criticism, there is a tendency to see all post-colonial stories as rewritings of colonial narratives—and a *small* canon of colonial narratives at that.[20] The bean containing a landscape, a foot bottom describing the whole world, a single structure relating all stories—this pattern of correspondences points to Dabydeen's understanding of enmeshed and connected cultures, and indicates *The Intended*'s involvement in forms of intertextuality.

Intertextuality, the recirculation of source texts, paradoxically implies the acknowledgment of the valency of texts which are abrogated in their reuse.[21] However, the irony with which sources are employed in *The Intended*, and the context into which source texts are set, can be considered an attempt to circumnavigate the valorization implied by imitation, parody, recirculation, and rewriting.[22]

On one level, *The Intended* does the expected: it "writes back" (in Ashcroft, Griffiths, and Tiffin's famous phrase)[23] to Conrad's *Heart of Darkness*. One of the many echoes of *Heart of Darkness* resounding in *The Intended*, for example, is Marlow's journey up the river Congo, narrated on the Thames, a journey which is subjected to a bathetic revisit. In Dabydeen's text it reappears as a "World Cruise" on the Battersea Fun Fair. Young lovers take advantage of the darkness in which they travel for fifteen minutes, rather than viewing the exoticizing exhibits.

> I stood on the prow of my boat, torch in one hand, spiked aluminum rod like a fearsome weapon in the other, the artificial ventilation blowing back my hair, gliding down the canal in quest of debris. . . . Past Austria, the boat was enveloped in darkness, the air not so much brooding and mysterious as dank and still, the smell of unclean water filling my nostrils. (Dabydeen 1991a, 77)

This comic image, steeped in artificiality, pokes fun at the seriousness of Marlow's metaphysical journey into the heart of darkness by citing Conrad's vocabulary (brooding, mysterious, quest, darkness) and by juxtaposing a sober Marlow with the garbage-collecting narrator of *The Intended*.

It cannot be overlooked that *The Intended* addresses a favorite of the colonial canon, *Heart of Darkness*. That *The Intended* constitutes such a "rewriting" is a well-established point,[24] and is evident even from Dabydeen's title which evokes Kurtz's "Intended." The novel also refers repeatedly to Blake's poem "The Tiger," and Shakespeare's *The Tempest*, another post-colonial favorite. These overt references (and reverences) are particularly interesting, for the novel contemplates the act of writing and inquires specifically what it means to write a post-colonial text. But the treatment of both, this inquiry as well as the rewriting of colonial pretexts, is laced with irony. One single clear intention alone cannot be distilled from *The Intended*.

However, the novel also addresses some of the textual critiques, revisions and rewritings, to which *Heart of Darkness* has given rise. Indeed, the relevance of the rewriting trope within post-colonial studies is addressed and implicitly disparaged by the novel. The textual history of *Heart of Darkness* is floated in *The Intended,* and the intellectual climate, in which well-known critiques appeared, is portrayed. This representation, as I hope to show, is not neutral but ironic in character.

In his famous article "An Image of Africa: Racism in Conrad's *Heart of Darkness,*" Chinua Achebe attacks Conrad's text as racist, pointing out that it is one of the most canonical texts of English literature at college and university level. He asks "whether a novel which celebrates this dehumanization, which depersonalizes a portion of the human race, can be called a great work of art," and answers clearly: "No, it cannot" (Achebe 1977, 9). To Achebe the novella is "offensive and totally deplorable" because Africa is turned into a "setting" and "backdrop" without "the African as human factor." He thus reads *Heart of Darkness* as an arrogant metaphysical inquiry which reduces "Africa to the role of props for the breakup of one petty European mind" (Achebe 1977, 11).

Growing up alongside the unnamed narrator is his foil whose name resonates with that of Joseph Conrad: Joseph Countryman. The Rastafarian translates Achebe's critique as follows: "But what 'bout the way he talk 'bout black people?" (Dabydeen 1991a, 97). Although the narrator self-deprecatingly denounces his own reading strategies as "theme-and-imagery spotting" (1991a, 99), while taking seriously his friend's interpretation, the status of Joseph's (and hence Achebe's) inquiry ultimately remains ambiguous. In Joseph's critique of *Heart of Darkness* one can only "glimpse some sense" (1991a, 99); the narrator cannot "answer fully" Joseph's questions—but neither can Joseph entirely answer the narrator.

Achebe's essay has gained quite a reputation and has generated a variety of responses. Wilson Harris (1980), replying to Achebe, criticizes him for being too prescriptive, and finds the charge of racism unfounded. In *Culture and Imperialism,* however, Edward Said suggests that Achebe "does not go far enough" (Said 1993, 200). It seems to me that *The Intended* takes on board the spectrum of responses which *Heart of Darkness* and its critiques and revisions have engendered.

Joseph revises the World Cruise because he "had become discontented with some of the African pictures." Not only does he apply his own paintbrush to "tamp[er] with the landscape," he also introduces Kurtz back into the picture:

> A white man sucking on a bone and firing a gun pointlessly in the air took his place among the native savages. I think he must have been Mr Kurtz. There was also a dead elephant lying on its back, four massive feet stuck in the air like the chimney stacks of Battersea power station which lay just outside the Fun Fair and which provided the model for Joseph's artistry. (Dabydeen 1991a, 112)

Designated as "artistry" as opposed to art, Joseph's unrefined improvements shed some doubt on wrathful rewriting projects. More importantly, his alterations remain confined to the tableaux provided by the Fun Fair sketches. In Achebe's diction, with Conrad turning the Congo into the "backdrop" of a philosophical inquiry, Joseph busies himself by merely redecorating that backdrop. His growth within Dabydeen's novel remains restricted as well. The gifted but untrained artist does not succeed in unfettering himself, but accepts the sketches as a matrix for his own creativity. His films, however, promise greater artistic freedom. He uses South London Park and turns it into the backdrop for an African setting. Yet, tragically, he does not attain artistic freedom and his formation remains incomplete: the videotape inadvertently remains blank, which may accord with Joseph's attraction to nihilism—but it forecloses his project.

■ ■ ■

In *Heart of Darkness*, Marlow realizes that the "conquest of the earth" means expropriation, and is "not a pretty thing." However, "[w]hat redeems it is the idea only" (Conrad 1902, 31–32). His journey is an expression of his will to egress, to leave Europe but still be part of its "idea" of imperialism. Marlow confesses his imperial desires, wanting to fill in the blank spaces on the world map. The fiction of unmarked spaces in want of epistemological, civilizing, governmental, and military "filling in" by European colonial powers is no longer available (although the current Euro-American aggression in the Middle East suggests otherwise). To the growing narrator of *The Intended* who craves fame, imperial grandeur is not obtainable. Instead, he needs to withstand reduction to an entry in the colonialist epistemology as represented at the Battersea Fun Fair. Entertaining and displaying diversity, the World Cruise incorporates scenes from Austria to Zanzibar; but these clichéd symbols of diversity suffer *containment* by being disciplined into alphabetical order.

The will to egress—embodied by Jameson's quest and unattained by Joseph—is paradoxically pursued by the narrator through delivering himself up to ingestion: He is eaten up by a surreal giant black beetle at the close of the novel. Envisaging the narrator inside the belly of the beetle constitutes a reference to Franz Kafka's short story "The Metamorhposis."[25] It also evokes John Newton's image of the overcrowded slave ship which features no empty spaces, merely the confinement between book covers, or in a ship's hold.

The narrator is an immigrant who wants to interrupt the cycle of rebirths to which he feels condemned. His journey from Guyana via London to Oxford is in some respects similar to Lara and Faith's journey that was discussed in chapter 3. Their "return" to parental home countries is followed by a second return to England; the narrator of *The Intended* had also symbolically arrived in Albion before having left Guyana, as has been suggested at the outset of this chapter. His entry into Oxford, the pinnacle of the English education system, then, may also constitute a second return. Studying English, he is to imbibe a version of English culture, as he had already done in some ways in colonial Guyana.

The Intended can be imagined as being voiced from the enclosure of Oxford's Bodleian Library, after the first-person narrator has entered university. The conclusion symbolizes *ingression* (both entry and invasion) and points to agency on the part of the narrator. The former garbage collector may have successfully used Kafka's beetle to transform himself. Previously, his composition of a post-colonial epitaph had been impeded by the belief that Mrs. Ali was an unworthy subject, and, in the Oxford Street cubicle, he had considered himself unworthy of representation. Seeking to become a writer, the narrator—by telling his own story—has already achieved one of his goals.

> I couldn't see, not for years, not until the solitary hours in Oxford University library . . . when Joseph returns to haunt me, and I begin to glimpse some meaning to his outburst. He stalks me even here, within the guarded walls of the library where entry is strictly forbidden to all but a select few, where centuries of tradition, breeding and inter-breeding conspire to keep people of his sort outside the doors. *I am no longer an immigrant here, for I can decipher texts,* I have been exempted from the normal rules of lineage and privilege; yet he, an inveterate criminal, keeps breaking in to the most burglar-proof institutions, reminding me of my dark shadow, drawing me back to my dark self . . . [, to] the condition of blackness. (Dabydeen 1991a, 195–96; my italics)

With a nod to Fanon, this passage reveals an imbricated speaking position: It is not only excessive Anglophilia which marks the narrator's personality. The late Joseph's influence returns from repression to counterbalance the narrator's flirtation with English Heritage. Entry into Oxford, into the "heart of whiteness," has incurred a high price, and certain aspects of the narrator's personality are relegated to his shadow. His "dark self," and his knowledge of the "condition of blackness," appear to have been obliterated upon his entry into university, and it is only the memory of Joseph which can bring them back. His old friend, however, is now experienced as a stalker and burglar; he is not supposed to reinsert "blackness" into the institution which the narrator now inhabits. Given Joseph's suicide, Patel's unappealing career, Nasim's victimization, and the narrator's eradicated selfhood, *The Intended* can be considered a bleak text. Bound to a "burglar-proof" prison house of language, the narrator occupies a library which, in John Newton's image, represents an epistemological order which incorporates and confines colonial subjects.

But the library scene allows another reading; it shows a writer working amid countless volumes, attempting to "master the alien language of medieval alliterative poetry, the sentences wrenched and wrecked by strange consonants, refusing to be smooth and civilised" (Dabydeen 1991a, 195). The writer could well be the author of *Slave Song*, Dabydeen's first poetry collection in Guyanese Creole, which is linked to medieval alliterative poetry in its introduction (1984). In *The Intended* the narrator is struggling to make an alien language his own, but as Dabydeen (1984) explains, medieval English has certain affinities with Guyanese Creole. Previously, the narrator sought to use only words with "status" as opposed to "'black words'" (1991a, 148). But at Oxford he encounters words with status that resemble his native idiom. In some ways, then, Chaucer's English has always already been an aspect of the narrator's own language. A similar observation has been made about his location in England and his intrinsic investment in "English" culture. In a sense, then, the narrator comes to learn a language he already knows, at a place which he has metaphorically always already inhabited. And although not peopling this isle with Calibans it is here that, as a writer, he contributes to the world of texts by adding a volume to the Bodleian's collection.

■ ■ ■

Although Janet is interested, she and the narrator of *The Intended* do not talk about Guyana; instead they talk about the books they read at school. Within the realm of literature they inhabit common ground. That is despite the novel's association of Janet with the Empire and the narrator with a slave on the auction block. Ultimately, by becoming an author, the narrator seizes auctorial control and becomes a more permanent resident in the world of texts which he and Janet previously coinhabited.

The narrator's *logovorous* fantasies evidence an ambivalence about *reading* marks and *leaving* marks. This has been seen in the narrator's relationship to Janet and it also affects his ties to Nasim's family; it has been observed regarding his efforts to compose Mrs. Ali's epitaph, and is pertinent to the composition of his own novel of formation. As a reader he is disdainful of rewriting projects, but as a writer he looks to Milton to write an epitaph. Intertextuality is accepted as a condition of textuality—intertextuality permits no egress.[26] But crucially, as the narrator's example signifies, *ingress* seems possible. The narrator finds expression partly *through other texts*, by reinscribing himself into a literary tradition. *The Intended* is not confined to rewriting *Heart of Darkness*, but is able to enter the debates this novel has engendered. Similarly, the narrator's successful and invasive entry not only entails submission but also textual agency. His book—an emblem of colonial power in Bhabha's framework—becomes emblematic of post-colonial textual agency.

The narrator is not only eaten up by a gigantic beetle, from inside whose belly his voice emits; he has himself become a type of *logovore* as encountered in *Disappearance*. Having literally entered the exclusive archives of "centuries of tradition," settled amid books at the Bodleian Library, the protagonist produces an intertextual narrative, effectively clearing a space for himself and registering his presence. To this aim, the library's volumes are not literally made porous, they are not eaten, they are not destroyed—but some of their contents are recirculated, transposed, and in effect transformed in order to counter elision. The narrator feels no longer an immigrant since he can now decipher texts. Significantly he can also *write* texts, and thereby contribute to the Bodleian's collection, marking his growth with a logovorous novel of transformation.

Conclusion:
Post-colonial Polyphony—
The Construction of a Voice

"The new Zadie Smith"
—(OF HARI KUNZRU, AUTHOR OF *THE IMPRESSIONIST*) [1]

'The new Zadie Smith'
—(OF MONICA ALI, AUTHOR OF *BRICK LANE*) [2]

"Black identity today is autonomous and not tradable."
—(HALL 1997, 127)

There is "virtually no sense of a community (albeit imagined) or tradition (albeit invented) of black British writing," James Procter suggests in his introduction to the anthology *Writing Black Britain* (2000, 6). A certain productive ambiguity results when Procter uses Eric Hobsbawm and Terence Ranger's phrase of the "invented tradition." Either a literary history has not yet been written (but its referent is clearly existent, out there), or an unbroken tradition of black British literature does *itself* not exist, and writers and readers have no sense of it. If the latter is the case, texts are written in the *absence* of a specific tradition and not in its train. Ironically, then, contemporary writers who are placed within such a tradition are so contextualized *before the fact*, that is, before the construction of a genealogy within which they are assumed to practice (and which their practice produces).

I have argued throughout this book for a particular heterogeneity of black British literature, and it is this heterogeneity which may partly account for many critics' difficulty when charting a black British literary history. Given the amorphous shape that characterizes a map of the connections, starting points, and lines of descent, it is understandable that many commentators shy away from drafting such a map *in toto*. It is possible, however, to construct relationships between individual writers and texts, such as between S. I. Martin and Olaudah Equiano, or Salman Rushdie and G. V. Desani, or between David Dabydeen, Wilson Harris, and V. S. Naipaul. Connections like these are the beginnings of the construction of a literary genealogy. A narrative of this sort may indeed constitute one approach to black British literature.

The approach developed here, that of the black British novel of transformation, also points to the existence of a black British literary tradition. The striking preference given to this genre, not only among the younger contemporary writers who are included here, but also its anticipation in earlier texts, points to a continuity that can be seen as a mark of a literary tradition.

I have distinguished between different elements of the black British novel of transformation: intergenerational conflict; the diasporic (reaching across space and time); the postethnic (eroding ethnic divisions); and the logovorous (reaching into other texts). These connections and gestures in time, space, ethnicity, and textuality are enabled by the performative function of the novel of transformation, by its capacity to reach beyond the text. These elements contribute to the transformative potential wielded by the novel, a potential which is indexed by the development of a voice.

A range of novels of transformation having been analyzed, it has emerged that these texts are concerned with the creation of a public sphere and the creation of a voice, a voice which the protagonists and narrators use to make themselves heard. The voice is also a way (a prerequisite even!) of constructing a narrative which can then supplement, revise, confront, and reject other discourses. It is a prerequisite for inventing a tradition and for imagining a community. Dabydeen's unnamed narrator was observed (in chapter 5) not only to craft an epitaph; producing a post-colonial narrative, he also grows into a writer who writes himself into existence. He self-consciously inscribes himself into the tradition of English Letters, and thereby rewrites English literary history by adding to it, and by refracting it.

Finding a voice and inserting a narrative is a key function of the black British novel of transformation. These voices contribute to the heterogenization of stories told in British texts, to polyphony. But the construction of a voice is not merely an outcome of a process of formation, it also points to agency and to the creation of agency. Meena learns to use her voice to confront Sam Lowbridge (Syal 1996); and Angie speaks out for her parents in the NHS hospital (Levy 1994).

Salman Rushdie's controversial novel *The Satanic Verses* pursues related concerns. The Indian immigrant and actor Saladin Chamcha is the bearer of a thousand voices while his English wife is sickened by the single voice she can call her own. With this arrangement the novel mischievously suggests a post-colonial insertion of a multitude of voices into monologic Englishness:

> Pamela Chamcha, née Lovelace, was the possessor of a voice for which, in many ways, the rest of her life had been an effort to compensate. It was a voice composed of tweeds, headscarves, summer pudding, hockey-sticks, thatched houses, saddle-soap, house-parties, nuns, family pews, large dogs and philistinism, and in spite of all her attempts to reduce its volume it was loud as a dinner-jacketed drunk throwing bread rolls in a Club. . . . One of the reasons she had decided to . . . end her marriage . . . was that she had . . . realized that Chamcha was not in love with her at all, but with . . . that hearty, rubicund voice of ye olde dream-England which he so desperately wanted to inhabit. (Rushdie 1988, 179–80)

Chamcha's abundance of voices stands in opposition to his wife's single voice which is "her legacy and curse." It is her parents' voice, an English voice, an Empire voice, a voice which Pamela cannot escape although she tries to all her life. This heritage leads Pamela to reject everything of her parents "that remained within her" (1988, 181). Her opinions and even choice of husband are driven by this rejection. But her husband, Saladin, is on a quest in the opposite direction, and seeks what Pamela tries to exorcise. Despite his thousand voices, he seeks to possess one more, the one "English" voice.

When Pamela realizes that to her husband she personifies the possession he craves, while she is attracted to Saladin precisely through her parents' abhorrent eyes, it dawns upon her that theirs "had been a marriage of crossed purposes." Deciding that he is too much like her parents (1988, 180), she resolves to leave her husband. Bernardine Evaristo shows a related interest in voices in *Lara* (discussed in chapter 3):

> "Oh!" Her cold, egg-sized vowel suspended itself over the table like a full colostomy bag, it was the Oh she'd learnt from the la-di-dahs years ago, omnipotent, it hovered long after the speaker had gone. (Evaristo 1997, 37)

Like Rushdie, Evaristo takes great care to render their linguistic response and the particular quality of their speech, when Lara's grandparents first meet their daughter's Nigerian fiancé, Taiwo. Accent is associated with power, even omnipotence, on the one hand, and with sewage on the other. Once again it is both a legacy and a curse. It lingers, lives on, and is transferred onto posterity.

In both novels the concern with voice, with accent, and with language simultaneously constitutes a concern with the construction of history and the fashioning of tradition: how both "history" and "language" are handed down, and how they remain resonant and effectual "long after the speaker had gone." Like a specter, this discourse endures when its representatives are not present, even when they are deceased. Pamela in rejecting and Saladin in embracing the voice of Englishness are shown to be similarly dependent upon a discourse which allows them to position themselves. They not only position themselves in the discourse of Englishness, they are its bearers and perpetuate it, even though they would both consider themselves unlikely perpetuators. Yet the novels read here are not only perpetuators of Englishness, but conjurers of fresh cultural spaces.

The black British novel of transformation can be considered not only an arena for narrating the construction of a voice; it has also been seen as a transformative genre, one that relates the formation of its protagonists but also describes and induces the transformation of their environs. If the novel of transformation is one of finding a voice to tell of this formation, as well as a forum for achieving it, then it is also a genre for fusing a variety of different voices. What I have termed the performative function of the novel of transformation relies upon vocalizations which strike a chord with a given novel's readership. The image of a concert of voices, which is polyphonic (with distinct melodies side by side; contrapuntal) and not homophonic (subordinate to a dominant melody), also allows us to formalize the notion of connecting and shifting cultural territories—a feature which we have observed about the novel of transformation.

I have argued that the development in Hanif Kureishi's work questions the adequacy of descriptors such as "ethnic," "black British," and "post-colonial" writing. If these categories apply only to some of his work, this indicates that artistic *practice* is decisive and not, or not exclusively, the auctorial position within a culture and society. Kureishi writes texts that can readily be considered from within a post-colonial framework; he also writes texts which are resistant to these frameworks or which are strategically oblivious of them.

While Kureishi has made forays into themes not overtly provoked by his particular ethnic position, white writers such as Marina Warner, Maggie Gee, and Barry Unsworth (today) or Colin MacInnes (in the late 1950s) have also made such forays, if in the opposite direction. This raises the question whether only black and Asian writers' texts can be considered within the framework of black British literature. Why should a white British author's text be excluded point blank? Could not some of Gee, Warner, or Unsworth's work profitably be read alongside that of Caryl Phillips, for example? Warner's *Indigo* (1992) and Unsworth's *Sacred Hunger* (1996) or Gee's *The White Family* (2002) differ decidedly from examples of colonial literature. To some this may seem an obvious point; to others its significance may appear doubtful. Such inclusion would rely not on auctorial ethnicity (once again, it would not exclusively depend upon the author's position in culture and society); rather, *textual practice* would warrant such an inclusion.

The desire to keep separate the former colonizers from the formerly colonized (in terms of cultural production) becomes highly problematic in the case of Britain, where an overlapping space is inhabited by writers who are deemed post-colonial and by writers who are not. The time has come to further differentiate post-coloniality. It is my contention that it will prove productive to open up categories such as black British and post-colonial literature further, so as to include texts from Britain which have hitherto been excluded from these frameworks of reading. This clearly runs counter to any attempts at narrowing down such categories, and at making them more specific and consequently more exclusive.

Although there is surely no strict analogy between British cultural production and that from other parts of the former Empire, considering more parts of British cultural production within the rubric of post-colonial studies is long overdue. By moving beyond the narrowness of "English lit" and at once opening up black British literature, post-colonial British cultural production comes into view more fully, certainly not as a homogenous entity, but as a heterogeneous field of inquiry. The voices of Saladin Chamcha and of Pamela Chamcha, née Lovelace, need to be heard side by side, even if they are in pursuit of radically opposed trajectories. It is true that Rushdie's novel features their divorce, but the voices are at once married between the covers of the same book.

There is quite another way of theorizing the term *voice*; at variance with the notion of post-colonial polyphony is the construction of a recognizable, even iconic voice, one that is homophonic, and stands in for others without being representative. Black British fiction has, perhaps, been transformed most dramatically in one respect, namely the way in which it is now marketed and consumed. Over fifteen years ago, in 1988, Alastair Niven noted that black British literature was going through a "struggle for recognition."[3] At the time, black British literature was far from established, and it was also partly eclipsed by more prominent post-colonial writing from Africa, the Caribbean, and South Asia. Today this judgment no longer holds. Although some black and Asian British writers before her had been eminently successful, the success Zadie Smith has enjoyed with her first novel was still inconceivable in the early and mid-1990s.[4] Her iconic status would seem unprecedented, but what does the nothing but phenomenal success not only of Smith, but also of Hari Kunzru and Monica Ali, say about the "struggle for recognition"? High print runs, huge advances, and prize-winning publicity all seem to point to a *centrality* of black and Asian cultural commodities in today's Britain.[5]

The writers whose successful débuts came in quick succession to *White Teeth* were immediately compared to Smith. Kunzru was literally dubbed "the new Zadie Smith" in 2002. And when Ali was hailed in the same terms the following year, Smith had become a yardstick for assessing new talent.[6] In some ways, "the struggle for recognition" could be considered accomplished once black and Asian writers are not only recognized as a commodity, but recognized on their own terms. For if Smith's name is used to endorse Kunzru and Ali, or Salman Rushdie's to endorse Smith (below), then, arguably, post-colonial writers are no longer measured with an imperial yardstick and the post-colonial yardstick is pulled out instead.

But the yard may yet prove an imperial measure. How representative are these three writers of black and Asian British writers more generally? How representative are their texts? More importantly, how representative are their publishers (Hamish Hamilton, Penguin, and Doubleday) and the size of the allocated marketing budgets? How representative is the resulting exposure and attention the trio have commanded?

I will return to these questions after looking at two visual representations that bear upon this subject.

In a 1932 poster, the well-known logo of the London Underground is reworked into a world-tube map (fig. 2). Around the tip of St. Paul's, and before a sun that never set, we have a sequence of concentric circles with Britain's string of colonial possessions draped along the perimeter. The innermost circle is filled by a globe that has colonial territory marked out in bright red. The silhouettes of St. Paul's and Piccadilly

FIGURE 2
Visit the Empire, *by Michael Dinkel (1932).* © *TfL Reproduced courtesy of London's Transport Museum.*

FIGURE 3.
Shopping by Tube and Bus, *by Christopher Corr (1998).* © *TfL Reproduced courtesy of London's Transport Museum.*

Circus are grouped together with those of many other buildings, forming a composite citadel. These smoke-grey and black metropolitan structures stand in a stark contrast to the surrounding colorful wreathed vignettes from Australia, Asia, and Africa (the Caribbean is left out). Here imperial possessions are not merely exhibited and mapped onto a metropolitan network: in Dinkel's image the colonial world, the "Wealth, Romance and Beauty of the Empire," is lined up for metropolitan consumption. The motley of "animals of the Empire" at the top of the image concedes the fancifulness involved in this projection and reveals an exoticizing impetus. Turning the globe into a suburban backwater accessible to the English commuter, the interdependence of Metropolis and Empire could hardly have been drawn more blatantly. A pallid yet powerful center is irradiated by an electrifying collection of countries offered up to Londoners on their doorsteps.

Six decades later, Christopher Corr, who also designed the book cover for Salman Rushdie's *East West*, presents a commissioned painting that thematizes consumption more emphatically (fig. 3).

At first, Corr's series of rectangular frames strikes the viewer as conjuring fast-paced and colorful metropolitan life. Alongside the well-known tube and the red double-decker bus, iconic buildings from different eras, such as Big Ben and Canary Wharf, are cited. Significantly, the different-colored tableaux represent an emphatically multiethnic metropolis, in which black and Asian Britons sport hip shirts, voguish trainers, and spiky haircuts. By comparison, many of the white youths appear quite plain and unadorned, but there are those whose haircuts or dress-sense has been influenced by black youth culture.

There is an incongruity about the individual scenes in *Shopping* (1998). They are stills which somehow don't seem to belong in the same film. Unlike Dinkel's composition which produced an interconnected whole by way of inserting circles into each other, Corr's numbered tableaux are serialized, approximating a comic strip aesthetic. They are also marked by flatness and a sterile frontal perspective. Of the smaller scenes, few spill over into outdoor life. Therefore these frames not only echo the windows of a bus which is an underlying pattern: they also stand for interiority and for containment,[7] as well as for the chance groupings of passengers and their cultures on the same bus—combinations which might not last beyond the next stop. Significantly, apart from one scene in a small restaurant, dialogue is not foregrounded. There is no community, there is no public sphere in Corr's London, and there is certainly no black public sphere, to borrow Arjun Appadurai's term (1994). There are only shiny surfaces enticing to shop, surfaces which are juxtaposed with monochrome interiors designed to trigger the same impulse.

Corr's work not only seeks to make shopping in London appealing; it also illustrates the commodification of cultural difference, or, as Graham Huggan would have it, "the postcolonial exotic." While Dinkel clearly projected an imperial geography inward, onto London, his work remained legible as such a projection. With Corr the Empire has truly come home to the center. Its peoples now not only complement the iconography of the metropolis, they have indeed been incorporated, absorbed. However, the depicted contiguity of a range of ethnicities completely belies the tensions and the violence that also characterizes multiethnic London. Instead, there is an impulse to parade London's multiethnic composition much in the way its wares are displayed. This seems to lend the painting credibility, authenticity, and a particular *hipness*. Stuart Hall speaks of an "enforced glamour" with which black and Asian bodies are charged in such representations which reveals them as "the host culture['s] . . . object of desire" (1997, 128). In Corr's tableaux, black and Asian Londoners have undergone an aestheticizing process: They are not only consumers, they are at once there to be consumed. Difference is sublimated into congenial diversity, while the range of ethnicities serves as an analogue to the product range offered in the capital.

In some ways, the corporate publishing world's celebration of hybridity by way of a small group of writers relates to the shopping oasis created by Corr. Ali Nobil Ahmad's piercing complaint about the "naivety of intellectuals and artists who are celebrating their racial otherness, degrading themselves with multicultural exoticism and feeding their bodies and cultures to the gluttonous mainstream beasts" (Ahmad 2001, 84), is relevant here. For Ahmad, hybridity (or "champagne hybridity," as he dubs it) is complicit with late capitalism and globalized commodity culture inasmuch as the concept reads out class, nation, and politics; he also accuses it of perpetuating nineteenth-century biologism (Ahmad 82). While in itself this is neither a very new critique of the paradigm or an entirely convincing one for that matter, it is interesting that Ahmad considers the impact of academic trends (via the concept of hybridity) on the broader issue of the representation of black and Asian Britons.[8] His notion of a white "gluttonous mainstream beast" consuming "racial otherness" is unconvincing because it presupposes a *homogenous mainstream* culture alongside intellectuals and artists who primarily define—and indeed sell—themselves in terms of race. Despite this oversimplification, it is feasible to ask how far Ahmad's critique of Stuart Hall, Homi Bhabha, and Paul Gilroy can be transposed to successful young writers of black British literature. How much are they responsible for having "racial otherness" and "multicultural exoticism" celebrated in their name? Have they been absorbed into corporate publishing as icons of racial and cultural otherness? Have writers like Zadie Smith, Monica Ali, and Hari Kunzru been co-opted or are they indeed actively colluding in this scenario? Do their texts conjure up worlds akin to Corr's London? Or do they, instead, offer resistance to corporate versions of the metropolis? How does Smith's take on multiethnic London, which publishers quickly recognized as a valuable commodity and snapped up at auction, fit into this?

In his wide-ranging article on *White Teeth*, Dominic Head also considers how the novel was and continues to be marketed. Comparing two photographs of the author, one from the hardback edition, the other from the paperback, he notes that Smith was first promoted as a woman with a "mixed-race identity" while sporting "an Asian look" a year later (2003, 106). Head is careful not to berate the representation of Smith as false or misleading but suggests that the author's purported "indeterminate ethnicity" facilitates such a shift in representation—a shift he in fact considers appropriate to the novel's thematics. Certainly the second point is credible; the *represented* indeterminacy is a felicitous feature, given *White Teeth*'s ethos. But Head associates Smith with the capacity to don different ethnic "guises" from which he concludes a "substantive hybridized identity" which exceeds "the more cynical marketing objectives" (Head 2003, 106). I would suggest, however, that we cannot glean information on Smith's ethnic *identity* from the photographs staged and chosen for Hamish Hamilton and Penguin. Neither do we know it to be Smith herself who is adopting different ethnic guises, or whether it is not in fact the publicists who determine which image is projected at what stage of their campaign. The dissemination of images of the author and prepublication publicity are the responsibility of media departments and the publicist in the case of established presses. It is therefore crucial to acknowledge the narrow limits within which authors (especially first-time authors) have a bearing on the ways in which their work is marketed.

In the case of the 2004 Black Swan paperback edition of *Brick Lane* by Monica Ali, great care seems to have been taken to select a "balanced" series of endorsements, so that on the front cover the *Sunday Times* is cited alongside Meera Syal. When the acclaimed literary journalist Maya Jaggi planned to write a profile for the *Guardian*, she requested to meet the then little-known Ali. But the exclusive interview was vetoed on the grounds of Jaggi's ethnicity. The publicist wrote that, given Jaggi and Ali's shared British Asian background, the book might get locked into a corner of the market; therefore a white male journalist seemed preferable to the press.[9] Ali has distanced herself somewhat from her publicist's statement, asserting that she had not been consulted about Jaggi's request, and her publishers have sent an explanation to the paper concerned (H. Lane 2003). Despite the publishers backtracking in this case, the incident raises not only the question whether a less influential journalist would have achieved this turnaround; it also illustrates how carefully—and to what extent—the public persona of sacrosanct writers is controlled by the publishing machine.

White Teeth, too, was launched with a high measure of publicity and marketing support. Publicist Charlotte Greig's campaign for the hardcover edition was even honored with a Publishers' Publicity Circle Award.[10] By the time Smith's book appeared in the shops in 2000, it had been preceded by several years' worth of publicity. Details about the auction of the author's copyrights and a sizeable advance, appraisals of her prodigious talent, her family background, her days in Cambridge, and her good looks were disseminated by way of newspaper profiles, articles, photographs, radio talk shows, television, and web sites. Excerpts from the manuscript had been contained in *Granta* and the *New Yorker*'s millennial fiction issue (Z. Smith 1999a, 1999b). As a result, reviewers were not only aware of the publicity but also considered it in their assessment. A "prodigious novel," judged Ali Smith, adding that it "would have to be . . . , just to live up to the . . . hype this first novel has already had" (A. Smith 2000). Likewise, many of her future readers will also have been aware of Zadie Smith's reputation before a single copy of the book had been distributed. When readers finally held their copy in hand, they were immediately faced with an acknowledgment that had already set the tone for Smith's reception.

■ ■ ■

An astonishingly assured début, funny and serious . . . it has bite.—Salman Rushdie

Right across the front page of the British first edition of *White Teeth* looms a raving endorsement (above) by that doyen of black British letters. In large highlighted pink caps his name—Salman Rushdie—takes a central position on this blockbuster, neatly separating the author's two-inch name from her equally tall title. And the back cover of *White*

Teeth is entirely devoted to him, featuring the abbreviated quotation from the front at full length.[11] Such a process of legitimization is not unusual, tagging the book with a recognized authority so that some of their cachet might rub off onto the new product. This is a way of branding a book, affiliating it with concerns or a particular aesthetics, and with "literary legitimacy."[12] "The consecrated writer," says Pierre Bourdieu, "is the one who has the power to consecrate and to win assent when he or she consecrates an author or a work—with a preface, a favourable review, a prize, etc." (quoted in Huggan 2001, 5). Rushdie's verdict turns himself into one of Smith's subjects, the novel being "about how *we* all got here" (my italics). He thereby transfers even more of his authority to Smith, subjecting himself to her voice, but not without reinscribing his own authority in the process. Not only are customers animated to purchase the latest commodity, the bearer of cultural capital has also reinforced his own position. What is unusual is the blatant prominence given to Rushdie on Smith's cover page, the way in which his pronouncement and name are wedged in between the author's own name and book title, with the brand-name "Rushdie" authenticating the marketed product.

Huggan's *The Postcolonial Exotic: Marketing the Margins* has broken new ground pursuing the question of how far the cultural capital of post-colonial literatures is "bound up in a system of cultural translation operating under the sign of the *exotic*" (2001, viii). In this context I'm interested here specifically in who endorses and authenticates whose voice and how these positions develop. Such is the impact of black British literature that there are now a range of black and Asian British authors who are sanctioned to underwrite fresh work. It is striking that today young black and Asian writers in fact *can* have their voices authenticated in this fashion. This not only bespeaks transformed economic conditions (and conditions of reception); it also bespeaks the radically increased cultural capital held by black and Asian British producers of symbolic goods.[13] The writers who had migrated from the West Indies in the 1950s did not have a preceding generation of authenticating, endorsing gatekeepers whose cultural backgrounds they shared. If and when they were "consecrated" by other writers, then, almost by default, these were white.

Today, black British literature is not only sufficiently established so as to be authenticated and endorsed by black and Asian writers. With Rushdie authenticating Smith's voice (granting it "real writerly idiosyncrasy"), who in turn has authenticated Kunzru and Ali, it is in fact possible to speak of *circuits* of authorization, circuits which accumulate and control cultural capital (Bourdieu's term), and which monopolize "the power to consecrate producers or products" (quoted in Huggan 2001, 5). We need to note two things; first, these circuits of authorization are not bounded by ethnicity. Instead, such endorsements occur across ethnicities, as in the examples cited here. Second, authentication does not come solely from within the black and Asian communities, for black British literature is by no means wholly apart from other British literatures. If anything, black and white British literatures are slowly becoming more entangled.

Sustained media attention has on the one hand brought a handful of black and Asian British writers to the attention of a very wide cross section of consumers, both nationally and internationally. Given the "enforced glamour" projected onto black and Asian Britons, black British literature has also become an object of desire. But if Corr's tube advert can be read as a self-congratulatory celebration of a rebranded New Britain, projecting an inclusive and multicultural image, then the scramble for black British literature may fulfill an equivalent function. In celebrating black and Asian writers, Britain also celebrates its own "official" multiculturalism and in this way affiliates itself with diversity. With the British Council, for example, supporting a range of British writers from ethnic minorities, alongside writers from the Commonwealth, the image of an open, tolerant, and quintessentially mixed society is exported. However, the narrow focus and the disproportionate attention on a few young celebrities (not in the Council's work, but in parts of the media, the book trade, etc.) in fact belie the breadth and heterogeneity of black British cultural production which characterizes the south of Britain and, increasingly, other areas as well. The virtually exclusive focus on the novel, at the expense of drama and poetry, exacerbates this effect. This tendency entails once more the occlusion of writing which does not match the stencil created for and also by the novels at the center of the hype. The effect can be considered one of containment: By concentrating disproportionally on a small number of recognizable voices, post-colonial polyphony is in danger of being muffled (or transposed into homophony), with many writers being confined to the margin. Paradoxically, this is a marginalization that occurs under the sign of celebrating diversity.

Notes on Writers
compiled by Nilüfer Caglayan

The year of first publication is mentioned in the text; the author bibliographies mention available editions wherever possible.

- **Diran Adebayo**

A is of Nigerian descent and was born in London in 1968. He studied law at Oxford University and, after finishing his degree, worked as a journalist for television and newspapers. A's first novel, *Some Kind of Black* (1996), is about a black student at Oxford University who inhabits various identities and who is led to consider his black British identity and African background after a racist attack on his sister. This novel won the Saga Prize, a Betty Trask Award, and several other prizes. Part detective story, part science fiction, part fairy tale, *My Once Upon a Time* (2000) is about an investigator trying to find a bride for his wealthy client. A lives in London.

Selected Bibliography

1997. *Some Kind of Black*. London: Abacus.
2000. *My Once Upon a Time*. London: Abacus.

- **John Agard**

The poet, playwright, and editor A was born in Guyana (then British Guyana) in 1949 and moved to Britain in 1977. At a young age A developed a strong interest in poetry and published two collections in Guyana. When he came to England, he became a lecturer at the Commonwealth Institute, touring schools across Britain to promote a deeper understanding of Caribbean culture. He continues to write and perform poetry for adults and children. In 1998 A became the first BBC poet-in-residence and played an important role in the fiftieth anniversary of the arrival of the SS *Empire Windrush*. He lives with his partner, the poet Grace Nichols, in southeast England.

Selected Bibliography

1982. *Man to Pan*. Havana: Casa de las Américas.
1987. *Mangoes and Bullets: Selected and New Poems 1972–1984*. London: Serpent's Tail.

1997. *From the Devil's Pulpit*. Newcastle-upon-Tyne: Bloodaxe Books.
2000. *Weblines*. Newcastle-upon-Tyne: Bloodaxe Books.

- **Monica Ali**

A (1967–) has an English mother and a Bangladeshi father. She was born in Dakha, Bangladesh, where she spent the first few years of her life until the family returned to Bolton, England. After studying at Wadham College, Oxford University, she worked in marketing, publishing, and design before turning to writing. A's first novel, *Brick Lane* (2003), tells the story of Nazneen whose arranged marriage takes her from rural Bangladesh to London's Tower Hamlets. Pursuing a love marriage, her sister Hasina runs away from home at an early age, and by way of her letters to Nazneen the reader follows the stories of both women. A was included on the 2003 *Granta* list "Best of Young British Novelists." She lives in London.

Selected Bibliography

2004. *Brick Lane*. Old Tappan, NJ: Scribner.

- **Biyi Bandele**

B was born in Kafanchan, Nigeria, in 1967. He is a novelist, playwright, and poet. B studied drama at Obafemi Awolowo University, Ile-Ife, and came to London in 1990 where he writes and contributes to BBC productions and periodicals. His writing includes a poetry collection, numerous plays, three novels, and a new stage adaptation of Aphra Behn's *Oroonoko*. Set in multicultural Brixton, his third novel, *The Street*, which he also adapted for the stage, centers on the painter Nehushta and her father, who has recenlty awoken from a fifteen-year coma.

Selected Bibliography

1993. *Marching for Fausa*. Oxford: Amber Lane Press.
1993. *The Sympathetic Undertaker and Other Dreams*. Oxford: Heineman.
1994. *Two Horsemen*. Charlbury: Amber Lane Press.
1999. *Aphra Behn's* Oroonoko *in a New Adaptation by 'Biyi Bandele*. Oxford: Amber Lane Press.
1999. *The Street*. London: Picador.

- **Amit Chaudhuri**

C was born in Calcutta, India, in 1962 and grew up in Bombay. He studied English at University College London and completed his doctoral dissertation on D. H. Lawrence at Balliol College, Oxford University. C is the author of four novels and has contributed to journals such as *Granta, London Review of Books, Times Literary Supplement*, and the *New Yorker*. He is the editor of *The Picador Book of Modern Indian Literature* (2001). C's first novel, *A Strange and Sublime Address* (1991), consisting of a novella and numerous short stories, won the Betty Trask Award, and a Commonwealth Writers Prize. His second novel, *Afternoon Raag* (1993), uses the metaphor of Indian classical music, the *raag*, in order to show the emotions of a young Indian studying at Oxford University. This novel won the Southern Arts Literature Prize and the Encore Award. The following novel, *Freedom Song* (1998), is set in Calcutta in 1992–93 and deals with the growing political and religious tensions between Hindus and Muslims. The American edition of *Freedom Song* received the *Los Angeles Times* Book Prize in 2000. His fourth novel, *A New World* (2000), tells the story of an Indian writer living in America, who travels with his son to his elderly parents in Calcutta. *Real Time* (2002) comprises short stories situated in Calcutta and Bombay. The author and his family live in Calcutta.

Selected Bibliography

1991. *A Strange and Sublime Address.* London: Picador.
1993. *Afternoon Raag.* London: Picador.
1998. *Freedom Song.* London: Picador.
2000. *A New World.* London: Picador.
2000. Ed. *The Picador Book of Modern Indian Literature.* London: Picador.
2002. *Real Time.* London: Picador.
2003. *D. H. Lawrence and 'Difference': Post-coloniality and the Poetry of the Present.* Oxford: Oxford University Press.

▪ David Dabydeen

D has published poetry, prose, and academic texts on literature and art. Born in Guyana (then British Guyana) in 1955, he moved to England in 1969. D studied English literature at Cambridge University and received his doctorate from University College London. He has lectured at the University of Warwick for many years, where he is a professor at the Centre for Caribbean Studies. D has published four novels and three poetry collections as well as seminal texts on black British literature. *Slave Song* (1984), D's first collection of poems, won the Commonwealth Poetry Prize and is noted for its use of Creole. His third novel, *The Counting House* (1996), is set in the Caribbean, while *The Intended* (1991), *Disappearance* (1993), and *A Harlot's Progress* (1999) are set in Britain. The latter is in dialogue with Hogarth's title-giving series of prints. His long poem *Turner* revisits William Turner's painting *The Slave Ship.* D is currently coediting the *Oxford Companion to Black British History.*

Selected Bibliography

1984. *Slave Song.* Coventry: Dangaroo Press.
1985. Ed. *The Black Presence in English Literature.* Manchester: Manchester University Press.
1985. *Hogarth's Blacks: Images of Blacks in Eighteenth Century English Arts.* Mundelstrup: Dangaroo.
1991. *The Intended.* London: Secker and Warburg.
1993. *Disappearance.* Secker and Warburg.
1994. *Turner: New and Selected Poems.* London: Cape.
1996. *The Counting House.* London: Cape.
1999. *A Harlot's Progress.* London: Cape.

▪ G. V. Desani

D (1909–2001) was born in Nairobi, Kenya, and died in Dallas, Texas. He grew up in India, where he was privately educated, and left for England at eighteen. In his twenties he became a journalist and returned to the subcontinent. Between 1939 and 1952, back in London, D wrote his main work, *All about Mr. Hatterr* (1948) as well as the play *Hali* (1950) and essays, short fiction, parodies, and sketches. *All about Mr. Hatterr* has been extensively revised several times. D uses colloquialisms of London and Delhi speech in order to represent India and Britain. Amitov Ghosh and Salman Rushdie have acknowledged the influence of D on their work. D returned to India and then immigrated to the United States in 1968, where he was appointed professor of philosophy in 1970 at the University of Texas at Austin.

Selected Bibliography

1948. *All About Mr. Hatterr, a Gesture.* London: Francis Aldor.
1991. *Hali and Collected Stories.* Kingston, NY: McPherson.

- **Farrukh Dhondy**

D was born in Poona, India, in 1944. He came to England in the 1960s and studied English literature at Cambridge University. D became a political activist, working with the Indian Workers Association, the Black Panther Movement, and *Race Today*. In this context he started to write novels and short stories, mainly for children. His first novel for adults, *Bombay Duck* (1990), features two protagonists based in London and Bombay, wherein the text seesaws between two consciousnesses and two worlds. D has also adapted some of his own short stories for television and has written numerous screenplays for the BBC. As Commissioning Editor for Multicultural Programmes at Channel 4 until 1997, he was able to implement more inclusive programming.

Selected Bibliography

1976. *East End at Your Feet.* London: Macmillan.
1978. *Come to Mecca.* London: Collins/Fontana.
1990. *Bombay Duck.* London: Picador.

- **Olaudah Equiano (Gustavus Vassa)**

E (1745–1797) was born in what is today southeast Nigeria according to his autobiography. When about eleven years old he was kidnapped, taken first to the West Indies and then to Virginia, where he was sold to a planter. This biographical information has been questioned by critics such as S. E. Ogude and Vincent Carretta. Carretta has presented evidence suggesting that E was born in the Carolinas. E was later resold, taken to London, and renamed Gustavus Vassa, a name he continued to use even after he was able to buy his freedom. E then served as a seaman and also worked as a buyer and overseer of slaves, resigning from this position after becoming an abolitionist. The autobiography *The Interesting Narrative* was published in 1789 and appeared in nine British and one American edition, as well as in translations into Dutch, German, and Russian during the author's lifetime. Today the narrative is again very popular and available in many editions and abridged versions.

Selected Bibliography

Carretta, Vincent, ed. and intr. 2003. *The Interesting Narrative and Other Writings.* 2d. rev. ed. Harmondsworth: Penguin. (Based on the 9th ed.)
Sollors, Werner, ed. 2001. *The Interesting Narrative of the Life of Olaudah Equiano, or*

Gustavus Vassa, The African, Written by Himself. New York: Norton. (Based on the 1st ed.)

▪ Bernardine Evaristo

E (1959–) was born in Eltham, London, the fourth of eight children, to a Nigerian father and an English mother. She trained to be an actress at Rose Bruford College of Speech and Drama (1979–82). She writes poetry, novels, plays, and radio plays. Her first novel, *Lara* (1997), won the EMMA Best Novel Award in 1999. Like *Lara*, her second novel, *The Emperor's Babe* (2001), is a novel-in-verse. It narrates the romance between a Sudanese girl and a senator in a reinvented Roman London. In her forthcoming novel, *Soul Tourists,* two travelers traverse Europe, meeting the ghosts of black people who have played their part in the continent's history. Her research and writing on unrecorded aspects of black history "in places where you wouldn't expect to find them" is supported by a three-year NESTA Award which she has held since 2003. She lives in London.

Selected Bibliography

1994. *Island of Abraham*. Leeds: Peepal Tree.
1997. *Lara*. Tunbridge Wells, Kent: Angela Royal.
2001. *The Emperor's Babe*. London: Penguin.

▪ Maggie Gee

G was born in Poole, Dorset, to white English parents in 1948 and studied English at Somerset College, Oxford University. She worked as an editor and held a research post at Wolverhampton Polytechnic, where she completed her PhD. G has written eight novels, and was included on the 1983 *Granta* list "Best of Young British Novelists." In *Dying, in Other Words* (1981), G's first novel, a woman who is supposed to be dead retells the story of her own death. Her subsequent novels deal with various issues such as families torn apart by war, homeless children, British politics, and responsibility in relationships. Set in an ice age in 2050, the dystopian novel *The Ice People* (1998) has its biracial protagonist migrate from Britain to Africa, where he survives as a storyteller. Her latest novel, *The White Family* (2002), is a careful exploration of racism and its impact in contemporary Britain. G is a Teaching Fellow at Sussex University and lives in London with her family.

Selected Bibliography

1994. *Lost Children*. London: Flamingo.
1998. *The Ice People*. London: Richard Cohen Books.
2002. *The White Family*. London. Saqi Books.

▪ Abdulrazak Gurnah

Novelist G was born in 1948 in Zanzibar, Tanzania. He first came to Britain as a student in 1968 and is now a senior lecturer in English at the University of Kent. G was also editor of Heinemann's African Writer's Series and is now associate editor of the journal *Wasafiri*. His first three novels, *Memory of Departure* (1987), *Pilgrims Way* (1988), and *Dottie* (1990), deal with immigration experiences in present-day Britain using numerous points of view and focusing on notions of identity effacement and displacement. His fourth novel, *Paradise* (1994), short-listed for the Booker

Prize for Fiction and the Whitbread Prize, is set in colonial East Africa during World War I. *Admiring Silence* (1996) narrates the life of a man who leaves Zanzibar for Britain where he becomes a teacher and gets married. *Bye the Sea* (2001), G's most recent novel, is set in an English seaside town where two men who left Zanzibar meet up again.

Selected Bibliography

1987. *Memory of Departure*. London: Cape.
1988. *Pilgrims Way*. London: Cape.
1994. *Paradise*. Middlesex: Penguin Books.
1996. *Admiring Silence*. Middlesex: Penguin Books.
2001. *By the Sea*. London: Bloomsbury.

- **Jackie Kay**

K was born in Edinburgh in 1961 to a Scottish mother and a Nigerian father. At birth she was adopted by a white couple and grew up in Glasgow, where she later studied at the Royal Scottish Academy of Music and Drama. She also studied English literature at Stirling University. K is a playwright, poet, novelist, and short story writer. Written between 1980 and 1990, her first poetry collection, *The Adoption Papers* (1991), was inspired by her biography; from three different perspectives it narrates the story of a black girl who is adopted by white Scottish parents. The collection was critically acclaimed and won a Scottish Arts Council Book Award and the Saltire Society First Book of the Year Award. It was also broadcast on BBC 3 radio. One of her subsequent poetry collections, *Other Lovers* (1993), won a Somerset Maugham Award. K's first novel, *Trumpet* (1999), tells the story of a Scottish jazz trumpeter who lived his life as a man, but whose death reveals the body of a woman. The story is told from the perspectives of several people, including his wife, his adopted son, and a tabloid journalist. *Trumpet* was awarded the *Guardian* Fiction Prize. K lives in Manchester with her son and her partner, the poet Carol Ann Duffy.

Selected Bibliography

1987. "Chiaroscuro." In *Lesbian Plays*. Edited by J. Davis. London: Methuen.
1991. *The Adoption Papers*. Newcastle-upon-Tyne: Bloodaxe Books.
1993. *Other Lovers*. Newcastle-upon-Tyne: Bloodaxe Books.
1998. *Off Colour*. Newcastle-upon-Tyne: Bloodaxe Books.
1999. *Trumpet*. London: Picador.
2002. *Why Don't You Stop Talking?* London: Picador.

- **Hari Kunzru**

K, novelist, short story writer, journalist, and editor, was born in London in 1969. He studied English literature at Oxford University and philosophy at Warwick University. While writing his first novel, K worked as a journalist and became the *Observer*'s Young Travel Writer of the Year in 1999. K has published a number of short stories as well as *The Impressionist* (2002), which was short-listed for the Whitbread First Novel Award in 2002. He was also included on the 2003 *Granta* list "Best of Young British Novelists." *The Impressionist* is the story of the light-skinned outcast Pran Nath, who navigates colonial India, travels to Oxford, and finally to the imaginary "Fotseland" in Africa in an exploration of his own identity and Empire.

Selected Bibliography

2002. *The Impressionist*. London. Hamish Hamilton.

▪ Hanif Kureishi

K (1954–) was born south of London to an English mother and a Pakistani father. He studied philosophy at King's College London and had his early plays produced at the Royal Court Theatre where he was writer-in-residence in 1982. He is well known for his novels, short stories, and films. K's early work has influenced many younger black and Asian writers today. His screenplay *My Beautiful Laundrette* (1984) received an Oscar nomination and made K and the director, Stephen Frears, known internationally. It is a film about a love affair between two men from different cultural backgrounds. His first novel, *The Buddha of Suburbia* (1990), was rewarded with the Whitbread Prize for Best First Novel and adapted for television in 1993. While many of K's novels portray British and British-Asian adolescence (*The Buddha of Suburbia*, *The Black Album* [1995], and *Gabriel's Gift* [2001]), both *Intimacy* (1998) and *The Body* (2002), as well as many of his more recent short stories, are introspective tales of middle-aged men, frequently of indeterminate ethnicity. In 1999, his play *Sleep with Me*, an exploration of masculinity, opened in London. His film *The Mother* (2003) broaches female sexuality in late life. K also edited, with Jon Savage, *The Faber Book of Pop* in 1995. He lives in London.

Selected Bibliography

1990. *The Buddha of Suburbia*. London: Faber.
1997. *Love in a Blue Time*. London: Faber.
2002. *The Body*. London: Faber.

Selected Filmography

1985. *My Beautiful Laundrette*, director Stephen Frears.
1987. *Sammy and Rosie Get Laid*, director Stephen Frears.
1991. *London Kills Me*, director Hanif Kureishi.
1993. *The Buddha of Surburbia*, director Roger Mitchell.
1998. *My Son the Fanatic*, director Udayan Prasad.
2003. *The Mother*, director Roger Michell.

▪ George Lamming

The novelist L (1927–) was born in Barbados and lived there until he left for Trinidad in 1946, where he became a teacher. L moved to London in 1950 and worked as a BBC broadcaster to finance his writing career. His first novel, *In the Castle of My Skin* (1953), is regarded as a classic of Caribbean literature. His novel *The Emigrants* (1954) and his essay collection *The Pleasures of Exile* (1960) are important works in the context of both black British literature and Caribbean literature. L has received prestigious awards such as the Somerset Maugham Award for Literature, a Guggenheim Fellowship, and an honorary doctorate from the University of the West Indies. He has also been an academic, lecturing at a variety of universities around the world. He now lives in Barbados and still travels frequently outside the Caribbean.

Selected Bibliography

1991. *In the Castle of My Skin.* Ann Arbor: University of Michigan Press.
1992. *The Pleasures of Exile.* Ann Arbor: University of Michigan Press.
1993. *Natives of My Person.* Ann Arbor: University of Michigan Press.
1994. *The Emigrants.* Ann Arbor: University of Michigan Press.

▪ Andrea Levy

L was born in London in 1956 to Jamaican parents. Her father came to Britain from Jamaica on the *Empire Windrush* in 1948. L is the author of three semi-autobiograhical novels dealing with conflicts involving racism and passing. They also reflect problems around children who define themselves as British and are growing up to migrant parents. In her first novel, *Every Light in the House Burnin'* (1994), the protagonist, Angie, wants to be successful in the arts in 1960s London but feels held back by her Jamaican family and the racism she encounters. Her second novel, *Never Far from Nowhere* (1996), contrasts the growing up of two sisters, one of whom can pass as white while the other has darker skin. L's third novel, *Fruit of the Lemon,* centers on a protagonist who, after being disillusioned in Britain, travels to Jamaica, where her parents were born. Her fourth novel, *Small Island,* won the Orange Prize for Fiction; it tells of the interwoven lives of two families, one black, one white, in 1948 London. L lives with her partner in London.

Selected Bibliography

1994. *Every Light in the House Burnin'.* London: Headline Review.
1996. *Never Far from Nowhere.* London: Headline Review.
1999. *Fruit of the Lemon.* London: Headline Review.
2004. *Small Island.* London: Headline Review.

▪ S. I. Martin

M, novelist, music promoter, and journalist, was born in Bedford, England, in 1959. His novel *Incomparable World* (1996) is a historical thriller set in the eighteenth century, just after the American War of Independence. The protagonist is a former slave who gains his freedom by fighting on the British side and manages to make his way to London. The novel describes "multicultural" life, focusing on crime-related issues and the threat of reenslavement. In addition, the novel revisits the beginnings of black British literature with the protagonist meeting Olaudah Equiano and Ottobah Cugoano. M lives in London.

Selected Bibliography

1996. *Incomparable World.* London: Quartet Books.

▪ V. S. Naipaul

N was born in Chaguanas, Trinidad, in 1932. Winning a government scholarship, he studied English literature at University College, Oxford. He is an internationally acclaimed writer of many novels and travelogues; he received the Nobel Prize for Literature in 2001; his novel *In a Free State* won the Booker Prize in 1971, and he was knighted in Britain in 1989. His books on the Caribbean, such as *A*

House for Mr. Biswas (1961) or *The Suffrage of Elvira* (1958); on India, such as *India: An Area of Darkness* (1964) or *India: A Wounded Civilization* (1964); and on Africa, such as *A Congo Diary* (1980) or *A Bend in the River* (1979), have been criticized for passing harsh judgments on post-colonial societies. N has also written on Britain (e.g., *The Enigma of Arrival*, 1987) and the United States (*A Turn in the South*, 1989), casting an ironic and critical eye on metropolitan societies. In 1958 *The Mystic Masseur* (1957) won the *Mail on Sunday*/ John Llewellyn Rhys Prize and in 2001 it was turned into a film with a screenplay by Caryl Phillips. N lives in Wiltshire.

Selected Bibliography

1959. *Miguel Street*. London: André Deutsch.
1961. *A House for Mr. Biswas*. London: André Deutsch.
1962. *The Middle Passage*. London: André Deutsch.
1964. *An Area of Darkness*. London: André Deutsch.
1967. *The Mimic Men*. London: André Deutsch.
1971. *In a Free State*. London: André Deutsch.
1977. *India: A Wounded Civilization*. London: André Deutsch.
1979. *A Bend in the River*. London: André Deutsch.
1981. *Among the Believers: An Islamic Journey*. London: André Deutsch.
1990. *India: A Million Mutinies Now*. Oxford: Heinemann.
1994. *A Way in the World*. Oxford: Heinemann.
1998. *Beyond Belief: Islamic Excursions*. London: Little, Brown.
2001. *Half a Life*. London: Picador.

■ Courttia Newland

N, novelist and playwright, was born in London in 1973. *The Scholar* (1997) and *Society Within* (1999) are both set on the fictitious West London Greenside Housing Estate and in a world of violence, drugs, and gang warfare. *Snakeskin* (2002) is a thriller about the investigation into the murder of a black politician's daughter. N has coedited a collection of black British writing.

Selected Bibliography

1997. *The Scholar: A West Side Story*. London: Abacus.
1999. *Society Within*. London: Abacus.
2000. Ed. with K. Sesay. *IC3: The Penguin Book of New Black Writing in Britain*. London: Penguin.
2002. *Snakeskin*. London: Abacus.

■ Grace Nichols

N was born in Guyana (then British Guyana) in 1950. Before coming to Britain in 1977, she worked as a teacher and a journalist. She has published poetry and a novel, and has written and edited children's literature. Her first poetry collection *i is a long memoried woman* (1983) develops a historical memory of Caribbean women in slavery; it won the Commonwealth Poetry Prize. This book was also adapted for television and radio. Her subsequent collections, *The Fat Black Woman's Poems* (1984) and *Lazy Thoughts of a Lazy Woman* (1989), are concerned with issues of black identity and gender. Her novel *Whole of a Morning Sky* (1986) narrates a Guyanese childhood in times of political instability. N lives with the poet John Agard and two daughters in southeast England.

Selected Bibliography

1983. *i is a long memoried woman.* London: Karnak House.
1984. *The Fat Black Woman's Poems.* London: Virago Press.
1986. *Whole of a Morning Sky.* London: Virago Press.
1989. *Lazy Thoughts of a Lazy Woman.* London: Virago Press.

▪ Ben Okri

O, poet and novelist (1959–), was born in Nigeria and lived in London until 1968, when he returned to Nigeria with his family. A grant from the Nigerian government enabled him to go back in 1978 to Britain, where he studied comparative literature at Essex University. O's narrative is strongly influenced by the violence he experienced during the Nigerian civil war. His first two novels, *Flowers and Shadows* (1980) and *The Landscapes Within* (1981), are set in Nigeria, focusing on the country's chaos and disintegration. O's subsequent works, such as the short story collections *Incidents at the Shrine* (1986) and *Stars of the New Curfew* (1988), are characterized by experimentalism in which O fuses (post)modernist writing with post-colonial political issues. O has won a number of prestigious literary prizes such as the Booker Prize for Fiction (1991) for his best-known novel *The Famished Road* and was included on the 1993 *Granta* list "Best of Young British Novelists." He is an active member of PEN and lives in London.

Selected Bibliography

1980. *Flowers and Shadows.* London: Longman.
1993. *The Famished Road.* Anchor.
1999. *Infinite Riches.* London: Phoenix.
1999. *Mental Fight.* London: Phoenix.

▪ Caryl Phillips

P (1958–), novelist, scriptwriter, and editor, was born in St. Kitts, grew up in Leeds, England, and studied English literature at Queen's College, Oxford University. He has written six novels, a number of nonfiction and travel books, and scripts for television and theater. His work has often centered on the slave trade and experiences of migration. In 1998 P was appointed Henry R. Luce Professor of Migration and Social Order at Barnard College in New York. He is editor of the Faber Caribbean Series. He was included on the 1993 *Granta* list "Best of Young British Novelists." His novel *A Distant Shore* (2003) has won the 2004 Commonwealth Writers Prize.

Selected Bibliography

1993. *Cambridge.* New York: Vintage.
1998. *The Nature of Blood.* New York: Vintage.
1997. *Extravagant Strangers: A Literature of Belonging.* London: Faber.
2000. *The Atlantic Sound.* London: Faber.
2002. *A New World Order.* New York: Vintage.

▪ Mary Prince

P was born a slave in Bermuda in 1788. She worked in numerous Caribbean islands, was baptized in 1817, and got married in 1826. Two years later, her owners brought her to London. With the help of the Moravian church and the Anti-Slavery Society, P tried to gain her freedom. Her attempts were unsuccessful as her owners refused her liberty, even though Thomas Pringle, for whom she worked as a servant, also tried to buy her freedom. Therefore, P could not rejoin her husband in the West Indies and remained in London, pleading her case. P's autobiography, *The History of Mary Prince, A West Indian Slave* (1831), was dictated to the Anti-Slavery Society's Susanna Strickland and edited by Pringle. This was the first published narrative by a female slave; it became very successful, achieving three editions in the first year of publication and also sparking a public debate on slavery. Despite her activism, P remained a slave until the abolition of slavery in the British colonies in 1833–34.

Selected Bibliography

Salih, Sara, ed. 2000. *The History of Mary Prince, A West Indian Slave.* Harmondsworth: Penguin.

- **Ravinder Randhawa**

The writer and activist R was born in India in 1952 and grew up in Warwickshire. She was the cofounder of the Asian Women Writers' Collective. R is the author of two novels, both dealing with race, class, and gender issues. Characteristic of her novels is the mixture of colloquial English and Hindi slang which reflects the hybrid identities of her characters.

Selected Bibliography

1987. *A Wicked Old Woman.* London: Women's Press.
1992. *Hari-Jan.* London: Mantra.

- **Joan Riley**

R was born in St. Mary, Jamaica, in 1958. She left her home country as a young woman and studied at Sussex and London Universities and has since worked for a drugs advisory agency. Her first three novels focus on a variety of themes around black British women; the fourth one is set in St. Mary, Jamaica. *The Unbelonging* (1985) relates the story of an eleven-year-old girl who has to leave Jamaica for Britain where she encounters racism at school and domestic violence. Her second novel, *Waiting in the Twilight* (1987), is the story of an elderly woman coming from the Caribbean to Britain where she experiences numerous social setbacks and struggles against racism. Her third novel, *Romance* (1988), tells the story of two Jamaican sisters and the cultural heritage that they were granted by their grandmother. R was awarded the *Voice* Award for Literary Excellence in 1992 and became the *Voice* Literary Figure of the Decade. *A Kindness to the Children* won the Mind Book of the Year Award in 1993.

Selected Bibliography

1985. *The Unbelonging.* London: Women's Press.
1987. *Waiting in the Twilight.* London: Women's Press.
1988. *Romance.* London: Women's Press.
1992. *A Kindness to the Children.* London: Women's Press.

▪ Salman Rushdie

R (1947–) was born in Bombay (now Mumbai) one month before India's independence from Britain and partition, and was sent to school in Rugby, England. He studied history at King's College, Cambridge University, where he joined the Cambridge Footlights theater company. After finishing his degree, R went to Pakistan, where his family had relocated, and worked for television. When returning to England he took up a copywriting job with an advertising company and then published his first novel, *Grimus*, in 1975. By 1983 he was included on the *Granta* list "Best of Young British Novelists." His second novel, *Midnight's Children* (1981), won the Booker Prize in 1981 and was adapted for the stage in 2003. The novel constructs a history of the subcontinent by focusing on the fate of two "midnight's children" born on the day India proclaimed its independence. *The Satanic Verses* (1988), R's fourth novel, faced severe criticism from Muslim communities around the world, leading to protest by Islamic groups and the novel's ban in many Muslim countries. When the Iranian Ayatollah Khomeini declared a *fatwa* (death sentence) in 1989, R was effectively forced into hiding for almost a decade. R continued to write, publishing numerous award-winning novels, including a children's book, *Haroun and the Sea of Stories*, about the dangers of storytelling. He is an honorary professor at the Massachusetts Institute of Technology as well as a fellow of the Royal Society of Literature. He lives in New York.

Selected Bibliography

1975. *Grimus*. London: Gollancz.
1981. *Midnight's Children*. London: Cape.
1983. *Shame*. London: Cape.
1988. *The Satanic Verses*. London: Viking/Penguin.
1990. *Haroun and the Sea of Stories*. London: Granta.
1990. *In Good Faith*. London: Granta.
1995. *East, West*. New York: Vintage.
1997. *The Vintage Book of Indian Writing*. London: Vintage.
1999. *The Ground beneath Her Feet*. London: Cape.
2001. *Fury*. London: Cape.
2003. *Midnight's Children: The Play*. London: Vintage.

▪ Mary Seacole

S (1805–1884) was born a free black woman in Jamaica, the daughter of a Scottish army officer and a free black woman. She worked as a doctor and nurse, and also as a hotelier in Jamaica, Panama, and Colombia. During the Crimean War she worked as a nurse and was recognized alongside Florence Nightingale. Her autobiography was published in 1857.

Selected Bibliography

1857. *The Wonderful Adventures of Mrs. Seacole in Many Lands*. London: James Blackwood.
Gates, Henry L., ed. 1988. *The Wonderful Adventures of Mrs. Seacole in Many Lands*. Oxford: Oxford University Press.
Alexander, Z., and A. Dewjee, eds. 1984. *The Wonderful Adventures of Mrs. Seacole in Many Lands*. Bristol: Falling Wall Press.

- **Samuel Selvon**

S (1923–1994) was born and died in Trinidad. He was the son of an Indian father and an Indian-Scottish mother. He graduated from San Fernando's Naparima College in 1938 and began writing fiction and poetry while serving in the Royal Navy during World War II. He worked as the fiction editor of the *Trinidad Guardian*'s literary magazine until he moved to Britain in 1950 where he worked at the BBC. He moved to Canada in 1978. Arriving in London, his short stories and poetry were published in various journals and newspapers, such as the *London Magazine, New Statesman,* and the *Nation*. He also wrote a variety of radio programs and a film adaptation of the *Lonely Londoners,* his major novel. A distinguishing feature of his work is the use of Caribbean Creole not only in dialogue but also for the narrative voice. S's work has influenced the next generation of black British writers.

Selected Bibliography

1956. *The Lonely Londoners.* London: Allan Wingate.
1957. *Ways of Sunlight.* London: MacGibbon & Kee.
1975. *Moses Ascending.* London: Davis-Poynter.
1988. *Eldorado West One.* Leeds: Peepal Tree Press.
1991. *Highway in the Sun: And Other Plays.* Leeds: Peepal Tree Press.
1992. *Moses Migrating.* Harlow: Longman, 1983; Washington, DC: Three Continents Press.
2002. *A Brighter Sun.* Harlow: Longman.

- **Ambalavaner Sivanandan**

S (1923–) was born in Sri Lanka and came to the United Kingdom in 1958, shortly after the riots in Notting Hill. He is a political activist fighting for black issues not only in Britain but also in the United States, South America, and Sri Lanka. He is the founder and director of the Institute of Race Relations, which established the journal *Race and Class,* in which S's early writings were published. His collected essays, *A Different Hunger* (1982) and *Communities of Resistance* (1990), are significant documents in black British politics.

Selected Bibliography

1982. *A Different Hunger: Writings on Black Resistance.* London: Pluto.
1990. *Communities of Resistance: Writings on Black Struggles for Socialism.* London: Verso.

- **Zadie Smith**

S was born in North London in 1975 to a white English father and a black Jamaican mother. S studied English literature at King's College, Cambridge University, and wrote *White Teeth,* her first novel, in her senior year before graduating in 1997. *White Teeth* (2000) was widely acclaimed and won a number of prestigious literary awards, including the *Guardian* First Book Award, the Orange Prize for Fiction, the Whitbread First Novel Award, the Commonwealth Writers Prize, and was shortlisted for the Booker Prize. *White Teeth* explores multicultural London from the perspective of three families belonging to different ethnic backgrounds. An exploration of fame and the ephemeral, *The Autograph Man* (2002), which won the *Jewish Quarterly* Literary Prize for Fiction, has its eponymous hero pursue an elusive autograph by a 1940s movie actress. Alex-Li Tandem, the Jewish-Chinese protagonist, buys, sells, and sometimes forges autographs. S was included on the 2003 *Granta* list "Best of Young British Novelists."

Selected Bibliography

2001. Ed. *Piece of Flesh*. London: ICA.
2001. *White Teeth*. London: Penguin.
2003. *The Autograph Man*. London: Penguin.

▪ Atima Srivastava

S was born in Mumbai, India, in 1961, moved to Britain at the age of eight, and has been living in North London since then. She studied at Essex University and, after finishing her degree in English literature, she worked as a researcher, editor, and director in television. She was writer-in-residence at several universities in Europe and Asia. S is the author of two novels, *Transmission* (1992) and *Looking for Maya* (1999). *Transmission* centers on a young Indian TV researcher working on a documentary about an HIV-positive friend. Her second novel deals with a young graduate falling in love with an older man while her boyfriend is traveling to India. S has also written a number of screenplays and an opera libretto.

Selected Bibliography

1992. *Transmission*. London: Serpent's Tail.
1999. *Looking for Maya*. London: Quartet Books.

▪ Meera Syal

S was born in Essington, near Wolverhampton, in 1963. She studied English literature and drama at Manchester University and now works as a novelist and actress. She writes regularly for the *Guardian* newspaper and is the author of the acclaimed screenplay *Bhaji on the Beach*. She is also coauthor and cast member of the popular BBC sitcom *Goodness Gracious Me*, acted in *The Kumars at No. 42*, and has written the script for the musical *Bombay Dreams* (2002). Her first novel, *Anita and Me* (1996), was influenced by S's personal experiences. Set in a small mining village near Birmingham, it deals with a girl trying to cope with her traditional Punjabi background and her white friends. The book won a Betty Trask Award and was short-listed for the *Guardian* Fiction Prize. Her second novel, *Life Isn't All Ha Ha Hee Hee* (1999), centers on the lives of three Asian women in Britain sharing common memories of the past. She lives in London.

Selected Bibliography

1996. *Anita and Me*. London: Flamingo.
1999. *Life Isn't All Ha Ha Hee Hee*. London: Doubleday.
Syal, Meera, and G. Chadha. 1994. *Bhaji on the Beach*. London: Umbi.

Further Reading

As early as 1986 Guptara[1] compiled a bibliography of black British literature which extended over 160 pages. A current bibliography, if based on Guptara's criteria, would easily run to three times the size. However, Guptara's bibliography also includes texts about black Britons or those which have black characters. His bibliography constitutes a survey of black British literature until the mid-1980s. Another bibliographic work is David Dabydeen and Nana Wilson-Tagoe's *A Reader's Guide to Westindian and Black British Literature* (1987, reprint 1998) in which, among other things, central motifs of these literatures are described and the representation of black people in British texts is investigated. The four anthologies edited by Dennis and Khan (2000), Newland and Sesay (2000), Owusu (2000), and Procter (2000) also contain useful bibliographies and offer introductions into black British writing, or aspects of it. Alison Donnell's 2002 *Companion to Contemporary Black British Culture* is a wide-ranging research tool for literary and cultural studies. For resources on black and Asian British history, see the studies by Fryer (1984), Visram (1986), Myers (1996), and Ramdin (1999).

Up to the late 1990s, black British literature had only been covered by few panoptic studies, on drama (e.g., Joseph 1993; Dahl 1995), poetry (e.g., D'Aguiar 1993b), film (e.g., Mercer 1988; Joseph 1993), and, to a larger extent, the literature of women (e.g., Grewal 1988; Wisker 1993; Bryce and Darko 1993)[2] and early black British literature (Edwards and Dabydeen 1991, Gerzina 1995, and, on Ignatius Sancho: King 1997). Tim Brennan's special issue of the *Literary Review* (1990) on "Writing from Black Britain" also falls into this realm, as do the later special issues of *Kunapipi* (Dabydeen 1998; McLeod 1999) and *Wasafiri* (Nasta 1999). A. Robert Lee's essay collection *Other Britain, Other British: Contemporary Multicultural Fiction* (1995a) gathers several voices on various writers and groups of writers in Britain. Finally there are quite a number of monographs on well-known male authors such as Salman Rushdie, V. S. Naipaul, George Lamming, Timothy Mo, Kazuo Ishiguro, and Hanif Kureishi,[3] which, however, do not necessarily situate their texts in a black British context.

Scholarly articles on black British literature have been appearing in collections such as Maggie Butcher's *Tibisiri*, Susheila Nasta's *Motherlands*, and in journals such as *Journal of Commonwealth Literature, Kunapipi, Moving Worlds, Third Text*, and *Wasafiri* dealing with black British novels,[4] theater,[5] film,[6] music,[7] and poetry.[8] From the mid- to late 1990s onward, black British literature itself has grown exponentially; this is reflected by the growth in studies on the field. There are a number of studies which contextualize parts of black British literature in different frameworks of research, such as Gikandi (1996), Bromley (2000), Blake (2001), and R. Lane (2003). There are also essay collections by Rushdie (1991, 2002), C. Phillips (2001), and Kureishi (2002a). Monographs on the literature in its entirety have now begun to appear, as, for example, Roy Sommer's study of "intercultural" British novels (2001), Susheila Nasta's wide-ranging study of South Asian writers in Britain (2002), Lyn Innes's comprehensive literary history of black and Asian writers (2002), Susanne Reichl's work on *Cultures in the Contact Zone* (2002), James Procter's study of *Dwelling Places* (2003), and Sukhdev Sandhu's comprehensive history of black and Asian writing on London (2003).

Notes

Notes to Introduction

1. Note the markers of time such as "midnight," "late," and "still" in this passage. It is only late in the twentieth century that the amalgamation celebrated by *White Teeth* has "finally" come about; those who are fighting against processes of cultural transformation are "still" doing so, but, as the passage suggests hopefully, their days have gone.

2. Chapter 1 provides further detail; for a full account see Fryer 1984 and Ramdin 1999.
   Bibliographic references are given parenthetically in the main body of the text. They contain only the author's last name, year of first publication, and page number. The bibliography provides full details of the editions used.

3. Salman Rushdie winning not only the prestigious Booker Prize (in 1981) but also the Booker of Bookers (in 1993) for his novel *Midnight's Children* and V. S. Naipaul receiving the Nobel Prize for Literature in 2001 might be good examples of this.

4. In their 1987 guide to black British literature, Dabydeen and Wilson-Tagoe focused almost exclusively on poetry, noting that just a "few novels are beginning to appear" which, however, had not "as yet made any significant innovative impact on the language or form of the novel" (Dabydeen and Wilson-Tagoe, 84f). Whether this was an entirely accurate observation at the time (*Midnight's Children* had, for example, already been published) is one thing; certainly today this situation has changed dramatically with novels such as *The Buddha of Suburbia*, *Lara*, or *White Teeth* expanding the novel form and creating a black British literary language. So much so, that, as the conclusion deplores, other genres are being sidelined by the novel genre and the attention it achieves.

5. Post-colonial literatures can be defined as those europhone literatures that have arisen in the wake of European colonialism. But the term *post-colonial* is highly contested, both from inside the field of Post-colonial Studies and from the outside. One area of debate is whether post-colonial is a marker of temporality, marking a particular historical phase, or whether it suggests an ideological position, as in "anticolonial." Can the paradigm be accused of neglecting present-day

neocolonial realities by implicitly relegating colonialism to the past (cf. Ashcroft et al. 1989; Shohat 1992; Hall 1996)? Another area of concern is in whose interest post-colonial theory works; are Eurocentric bodies of thought once more inflicted upon non-European cultures? Can the "Subaltern" speak, be theorized, and, indeed, be read (cf. Parry 1987; Spivak 1988; Döring et al. 1996)? In the context of this study I use *post-colonial* as a term of convenience to refer to cultural production which continues to negotiate the impact of European colonialism.

6. The *Wasafiri* editorial uses "black British" to reference South Asian, African, and Caribbean British cultural production alongside each other (Nasta 1999), as do Mirza's *Black British Feminism* (1997), Donnell's *Companion to Black British Culture* (2002), and Procter's anthology *Writing Black Britain* (2000), for example. On the other hand, while both Innes (2002) and Sandhu (2003) read British-based black and South Asian writing alongside each other, they do so without resorting to an overarching term. And in *Black British Culture & Society,* the term *black British* predominantly refers to Britain's African Caribbean and African cultural production (Owusu 2000).

7. The work of Caryl Phillips or David Dabydeen, for example, is sometimes considered as black British and sometimes as Caribbean literature. Due to its references to distinct cultural traditions, black British literature partakes of different literatures and is in turn claimed for various bodies of literature. This is not only a question of reception but also one of production; economic conditions have meant that many post-colonial texts were and are published in London. In his 1969 introduction to C. L. R. James's *Minty Alley,* Kenneth Ramchand notes that the West Indian "literary capital" then was London (Ramchand 1971, 5).

The fact that London plays this pivotal role for Caribbean literature (but also for many African literatures) makes it especially difficult to ascertain where to place migrant writers who have spent time in London and then return or move on (see chapter 3).

Notes to Chapter 1

1. Timothy Brennan has referred to this as "a now fairly well-known tale about the Moorish soldiers of Hadrian's army" (Brennan, ed. 1990, 7).

2. See Lyn Innes's work on these and more eighteenth- and nineteenth-century writers (2002), and also Sandhu (2003) and Fryer (1984).

3. On the fiftieth anniversary of the arrival of the *Empire Windrush,* several publications dealing with this event have appeared: e.g., Mike and Trevor Phillips (1998), David Dabydeen (1998), Tony Sewell (1998), and Onyekatchi Wambu (1998).

4. I use the term *Windrush generation* to differentiate between those migrant writers who started to write in the 1940s and 1950s, and those younger "post-*Windrush*" writers who did not migrate to Britain but were born in the country.

5. It is common to mention only the 492 West Indian migrants who came on board the *Windrush.* However, in June 1948, the SS *Empire Windrush* docked at Tilbury with 1,024 passengers. The passenger list (held at the Public Record Office) and displayed at the Museum of London in the 1998 exhibition Windrush-Sea Change hints at a network of migrant workers not only from the Caribbean.

The history of twenty Polish citizens, for example, relocating from Mexico to Britain, is regularly overlooked in accounts of the *Windrush*.

6. The text was first published as *Old Man Trouble* in 1975.

7. Interview with Cecil Holness (Phillips and Phillips 1998, 81).

8. "By the end of 1958 there were in this country about 55,000 Indians and Pakistanis. All these West Indians and Asians were British citizens. The 1948 Nationality Act had granted United Kingdom citizenship to citizens of Britain's colonies and former colonies. Their British passports gave them the right to come to Britain and stay here for the rest of their lives" (Fryer 1984, 373).

9. "The notion of migration as a form of rebirth is one whose truths many migrants will recognize. Instantly recognizable, too, and often very moving, is the sense of a writer feeling obliged to bring his new world into being by an act of pure will, the sense that if the world is not described into existence in the most minute detail, then it won't be there. The immigrant must invent the earth beneath his feet" (Rushdie 1991, 149).

10. Samuel Selvon worked in his native Trinidad until 1950 when, at the age of twenty-seven, he came to London. During the twenty-eight years of his stay in Britain he gained an international reputation as a writer. In 1978, he left for Canada where he spent the rest of his life, until he died in Trinidad during a visit in 1994.

11. This is by no means a new constellation. Comparing the situations of the contemporaries Ignatius Sancho and Olaudah Equiano, we note that the former grew up in England from the age of two while the latter arrived as an adult, after the experience of slavery and at the end of extended travels. Again, the two writers may not differ in terms of "generation," but their affiliations with English culture are quite distinct.

12. See (Stein 1995); note that Dabydeen speaks of "rituals of ancestry" which emphasize *practice* rather then *essence* in the construction of ancestry; I will return to this quotation later (Dabydeen 1989b, 134).

13. Enoch Powell was one of the foremost and most influential postwar racist politicians in Britain. His 1968 speech, which cost him his position as an MP, is reprinted in *Freedom and Reality* (Powell 1969, 281–90).

14. This is a reference to Derek Walcott's poem "The Schooner *Flight*" about the "red nigger" Shabine who sets out to travel as a seaman through the Caribbean islands. In the third section, "Shabine Leaves the Republic," the speaker says: "I had no nation now but the imagination./ After the white man, the niggers didn't want me/ when the power swing to their side" (Walcott 1986, 350).

15. The case of Stephen Lawrence, the south London teenager who was murdered by white racists in 1993, is relevant in this context; Lawrence has now the status of an icon among black youths of differing backgrounds.

16. Hall's essay revisits an important debate between Salman Rusdhie, Darcus Howe, and himself about the 1987 film *Handsworth Songs*; this debate is reprinted as "The Hansworth Songs Letters" in Procter 2000.

17. Hall 1988; cf. Young 1995; Grewal 1988. Note that Hall has revised his position in his 1997 interview "Frontlines and Backyards: The Terms of Change." In the context of black British "confidence beyond its own measure," Hall notes that blackness "is not necessarily any longer a counter identity, a source of resistance" (Hall 1997, 127; cf. the vehement critique by A. Sivanandan 2000).

18. This imbrication applies to *all* of what D'Aguiar calls the "usual variants of class, sex, race, time and place" (1989, 106).

19. The formulation "new British" seeks to stress the ongoing process of negotiation as to who is and what is "British," a process which of course dates back farther than migration from the former colonies to Britain.

20. This quotation is taken from the entry form which contains the "Saga Prize 1996 Rules."

21. The prize was only awarded for a few years and the company now has a new literary award, the Saga Prize for Wit and Humour.

22. The Asian Women Writers' Workshop was later renamed Asian Women Writers' Collective. It has published two remarkable anthologies of short stories. The novelist Ravinder Randhawa, who initiated the collective, has left the group and also distanced herself from its exclusive policy.

23. These issues are addressed by Ng and Malique (1993).

24. Commenting on the irreconcilability between hybridity and particularism, Bart Moore-Gilbert has described this "dilemma between respect for difference and the desire to stress points of connection and to make common cause" as "two apparently incompatible models of cultural identity and political positioning in postcolonial studies" (Moore-Gilbert 1997, 190).

25. Hannerz has salvaged and resuscitated the term *ecumene* from 1940s anthropology, a concept which unfortunately belies the radically uneven distribution of power among the global ecumene he perceives (Hannerz 1996, 7).

26. See, for example, Bhatnagar (1980), Jusdanis (1995), and Hannerz (1996).

27. Gayatri Chakravorty Spivak describes her new book, *A Critique of Postcolonial Reason*, as "chart[ing] a practitioner's progress from colonial discourse studies to transnational cultural studies" (Spivak 1999, ix–x).

28. Themes such as traveling, the Middle Passage, growing up abroad, and also re-memory projects are found in African American literature, Caribbean literature, and black British literature.

29. This seems corroborated also by what might be a growing tendency of black British texts, which are increasingly ethnically "unmarked" and thus not easily placed within the confines of black British literature. I'm thinking of some of the stories in Kureishi's *Love in a Blue Time* (1997), his recent novel *Intimacy* (1998), and also of Bidisha's first novel, *Seahorses* (1997).

30. Selvon's Canadian or West Indian contexts could obviously be further subdivided, e.g., into Trinidadian and Indo-Trinidadian writing.

31. Cited in Jaggi (1996, 64). This is reminiscent of a comment made by Hanif Kureishi a few years previously which is cited below as an epigraph to part III of this chapter (Kureishi 1986, 38).

32. For the term *third space*, see Bhabha (1990a, 211 et passim).

33. The incongruity of "Yardmen," the signifier pointing to the culture of tenement yards in Jamaica on the one hand, and Nigeria on the other, will be dealt with later.

34. These are the protagonists of novels by Levy (1994), Adebayo (1996a), Randhawa (1992), Kureishi (1990), Kureishi (1995), Gurnah (1990), Srivastava (1992), Syal (1996), Riley (1985), and Carr (1998), respectively.

35. Cf. the following studies of the last twenty years that focus on the bildungsroman: Randolph P. Shaffner, *The Apprenticeship Novel: A Study of the Bildungsroman as a Regulative Type in Western Literature* (1984); Esther Kleinbord

Labovitz, *The Myth of the Heroine: The Female Bildungsroman in the Twentieth Century: Dorothy Richardson, Simone De Beauvoir, Doris Lessing, Christa Wolf* (1987); Franco Moretti, *The Way of the World: The Bildungsroman in European Culture* (1987); Susan Ashley Gohlman, *Starting Over: The Task of the Protagonist in the Contemporary Bildungsroman* (1990); James Hardin, ed., *Reflection and Action: Essays on the Bildungsroman* (1991); Todd Curtis Kontje, *Private Lives in the Public Sphere: The German Bildungsroman as Metafiction* (1992); Jack Hendriksen, *This Side of Paradise as a Bildungsroman* (1993); Todd [Curtis] Kontje, *The German Bildungsroman: History of a National Genre* (1993); Geta LeSeur, *Ten Is the Age of Darkness: The Black Bildungsroman* (1995); Wangari Wa Nyatetu-Waigwa, *The Liminal Novel: Studies in the Francophone-African Novel as Bildungsroman* (1996); Michael R. Minden, *German Bildungsroman: Incest and Inheritance* (1997); Pin-Chia Feng, *The Female Bildungsroman by Toni Morrison and Maxine Hong Kingston: A Postmodern Reading* (1998); Julia Alexis Kushigian, *Reconstructing Childhood: Strategies of Reading for Culture and Gender in the Spanish American Bildungsroman* (2003); see also Laura Sue Fuderer, *The Female Bildungsroman in English: An Annotated Bibliography of Criticism* (1990).

36. Yet Fritz Martini has found Karl Morgenstern discussing the bildungsroman in lectures as early as 1820 (Martini 1961, 44 et passim). Nevertheless: "Mit Wilhelm Dilthey (1833–1911) beginnt die eigentliche Geschichte der Bildungsroman-Forschung" (Selbmann 1988, 20).

37. Redfield's title echoes Jeffrey Sammons, who speaks of the bildungsroman as a phantom genre in "The Mystery of the Missing Bildungsroman" (Sammons 1981).

38. Jerome Buckley Hamilton takes this position, cf. below.

39. Cf. Jeffrey Sammons (1981, 232).

40. Cf. Bidisha's *Seahorses* for a single father, Kureishi's *Black Album* for an absent father but an extended family, Dabydeen's *The Intended* for a protagonist without family in Britain.

41. These elements Buckley sums up as: "childhood, the conflict of generations, provinciality, the larger society, self-education, alienation, ordeal of love, the search for a vocation and a working philosophy" (Buckley 1974, 18).

42. The bildungsroman lends itself to the investigation into generational tensions; these figure prominently in black British literature (see chapter 3).

43. Dele is keenly aware of the fact that he has few peers as well as fewer role models.

44. *The Enigma of Arrival* comes to mind, while the earlier *Mr. Stone and the Knight's Companion* (1963) is often overlooked; *The Mimic Men* (1967) has a narrator located in Britain and while part of the narrative is set here, the novels looks to the Caribbean. These three novels, however, cannot be formalized as bildungsromane.

45. These are the protagonists of Kureishi's (1990), Adebayo's (1996a), and Levy's (1994) novels discussed in this chapter.

Notes to Chapter 2

1. Ultimately, texts are part of what makes up culture, and the distinction

between text and culture used here serves only to make clear and overstate the nonidentity between these categories.

2. The plural form "British cultures" is used advisedly; given the heterogeneity of Britain it would be misleading to speak of *one* British culture only. The plural form may, however, also be misleading if it is taken to signify cultures which are sealed off from each other. Instead, the notion of overlapping spheres of permeable cultures is most appropriate here.

3. Historiographical fiction and re-memory projects are, next to the bildungsroman, an important feature of black British literature. Novels such as Caryl Phillips's *Cambridge* and *The Nature of Blood* or David Dabydeen's *A Harlot's Progress*, like their African American counterparts best embodied by Toni Morrison's *Beloved*, are concerned with the retrieval of lost histories, the rewriting of recorded history, and the bestowing of agency on under- and unrepresented groups.

4. Chaudhuri's novel differs from the others considered here. Most black British novels that are novels of transformation feature a protagonist born in Britain, growing up with both backgrounds, her/his parents' and that of Britain. Chaudhuri's text constitutes an *Entwicklungsroman*, a novel of development, which covers one year of the protagonist's study at Oxford. At the same time, a much longer period is covered through flashbacks; moreover, there is the context of other characters at different stages of maturing. Although his parents, in contradistinction to those in other texts, don't live in Britain but in India, his time at university is connected to theirs. His parents also studied in England, where the couple met. So there is a continuity of a different sort, a tradition of studying abroad to return. The experience becomes not only formative for the student but formative for universities also, as *Afternoon Raag* indicates, featuring many students from the Indian diaspora and elsewhere. This text, then, indicates that not only immigration changes the face of a culture, but also the passing through of people with distinct cultural backgrounds, a phenomenon which is not at all recent.

5. See also Gurnah's novel *Dottie*, which paints a bleak picture of Britain, with Dottie's colleagues being marked out by their coarseness. The male workers are constantly groping the women, and their exchanges always contain sexual innuendo. Racism is ubiquitous and Dottie is often afraid. Andreas, the Cypriot slum landlord, is an example of a species of immigrant who thrives on the misery of fellow immigrants. One can't help but assume, however, that his stay in Britain has contributed to this.

6. The tinned-milk label depicting a well-kept cow is reminiscent of the Czech dramatist and novelist Karel P. Čapek's inquiry into Englishness. He began "one of his last chapters in his *Letters from England* with the remark: 'In England I should like to be a cow or a baby'" (Briggs 1991, 190). An article in the *Guardian* also indicates the significance that cows have to visitors of Britain, reporting on tourists complaining that they miss "the odd herd of Friesians grazing in [England's] lush green fields" (Ahuja 1994, 26).

7. Srivastava (1992), Randhawa (1995), and Bidisha (1997) provide further examples of the issues of class and gender.

8. See chapter 4 for a discussion and comment on the concept of passing.

9. The term *dual bildungsroman* is used to describe a bildungsroman in which

the bildungs-hero is contrasted with a second character as his or her foil; the term *multiple bildungsroman* expands this conception.

10. Fanon modifies later that it was "no longer a question of being aware of my body in the third person but in a triple person. . . . I was responsible at the same time for my body, for my race, for my ancestors" (1952, 112).

11. But there are ways of dealing with this burden as Hanif Kureishi's texts show. In his novel *The Buddha of Suburbia* (1990) and in his screenplay *My Beautiful Laundrette* (1986) he satirizes the Pakistani community of London. Omar's homosexual relationship with Johnny, a skinhead and former National Front member, was quite unpalatable to some viewers.

Adebayo's novel *Some Kind of Black* is also unwilling to make concessions to his different readerships. On the one hand, a scene of police violence which leaves the protagonist's sister in a coma for most of the novel is of key importance to the text. Criticism of the racist police officers is quite explicit and insulated neither by humor nor in any other way. On the other hand, this beating is explicitly related to the protagonist's Nigerian father, who apparently beat his children too. The novel thus makes no bones about being critical in two directions. Parts of both the white society and the Nigerian community are denounced in many ways.

12. This subversive class of literature, that Bhabha (with convenient vagueness) terms *colonial fantasy*, resists being integrated into the "Great Tradition of literary Realism" by using the "uncanny" as its "mode of address" (1984, 115), and therefore requires "another kind of reading, another gaze" (1984, 119).

13. The debate between Fredric Jameson (1987) and Aijaz Ahmad (1992, 95–122) is relevant here, as is Neil Lazarus's (2003) measured defense of Jameson's position.

Notes to Chapter 3

1. Vera Mihailovich-Dickman's edited collection *"Return" in Post-Colonial Writing: A Cultural Labyrinth* follows this theme through a large number of post-colonial texts.

2. Cf. Stuart Hall (1990), Paul Gilroy (1993a, 1993b), Alasdair Pettinger (1998), Caryl Phillips (ed., 1997), and Onyekachi Wambu (1998). Hall and Gilroy speak of black Britain more generally; the remaining three authors refer to black British writing more specifically.

3. Stephen Castles and Mark J. Miller thus describe our age in their study of population movements (1993).

4. See Hortense Spillers's comment: "Those African persons in 'Middle Passage' were literally suspended in the 'oceanic,' if we think of the latter in its Freudian orientation as an analogy for undifferentiated identity: removed from the indigenous land and culture, and not-yet 'American' either, these captive persons, without names that their captors would recognize, were in movement across the Atlantic, but they were also *nowhere* at all. Inasmuch as, on a given day, we might imagine, the captive personality did not know where s/he was, we could say that they were the culturally 'unmade,' thrown in the midst of a figurative darkness that 'exposed' their destinies to an unknown course" (Spillers 1987, 72).

5. Both, what has been called "systematic mingling" and "actual physical injuries," are well illustrated by two edicts in the Trinidadian writer Marlene Nourbese Philip's poem "Discourse on the Logic of Language" (1989):

> Edict I Every owner of slaves shall, wherever possible, ensure that his slaves belong to as many ethno-linguistic groups as possible. If they cannot speak to each other, they cannot then foment rebellion and revolution. . . .

> Edict II Every slave caught speaking his native language shall be severely punished. Where necessary, removal of the tongue is recommended. The offending organ, when removed, should be hung on high in a central place, so that all may see and tremble.

6. While "epilogue" is divided into five lines in *i is a long-memoried woman*, it has four lines only in *The Fat Black Woman's Poems*. As the earlier version has been identified as a printer's error by Grace Nichols (in a private conversation), I refer to the four-line version as authoritative.

7. This ongoing project involves many writers in compatible situations within black British, West Indian, and African American literature. (Cf. the following texts, all published in the same decade as *i is:* Toni Morrison, *Beloved;* Shirley Anne Williams, *Dessa Rose;* Charles Johnson, *The Middle Passage;* Michelle Cliff, *Abeng;* David Dabydeen, *Slave Song;* and Patrick Chamoiseau, *Texaco*).

8. Scarce use of punctuation and the virtual omission of the full stop characterize the entire collection, and inscribe defiance to English linguistic convention.

9. The poems cover the cathartic process of remembering the various stages of history, such as: *preslavery* (e.g., in "Taint," "Sacred Flame," and "Like Clamouring Ghosts"), the *Middle Passage* (in "One Continent/to Another" or "Eulogy"), *slavery* (in "Waterpot" or "Ala"), *encountering South American cultures* (in "Of Golden Gods" or "I Will Enter"), and *resistance* (in "I Coming Back," "Blow Winds Blow," or "This Kingdom"). While Nichols looks at the specific history of Caribbean peoples, she does so from women's perspectives, developing a vision encompassing women's experience in different phases of history. This entails criticism of European and African patriarchy as well as of colonialism.

10. Whether disarticulation was attempted rather than achieved (or a bit of both) is a crucial question which cannot be resolved on a generalized level. In "Can the Subaltern Speak?" Gayatri Spivak has famously answered in the negative the question her title poses, a position that has been challenged by Benita Parry and others (Spivak 1988; Parry 1987). With reference to the black British context, Helen Thomas rightly argues that neither Equiano nor Sancho or Gronniosaw are "the 'historically-muted subject' defined by Spivak's thesis" (Thomas 1999, 6).

11. Fred D'Aguiar's poem "Home," in his 1993 collection *British Subjects*, describes the immigration procedure at Heathrow Airport which leads the lyrical I to conclude that "home is always elsewhere" (D'Aguiar 1993a, 14).

12. The term *diaspora* originates in Deuteronomy 28:25 according to the *OED*: "thou shalt be a diaspora (or dispersion) in all kingdoms of the earth."

13. As a young girl, Lara does have contact to "Daddy People" who she imagines are speaking to her.

14. As I am writing, Sir William Macpherson's investigation into the murder of black teenager Stephen Lawrence has accused London's Metropolitan Police of *institutional racism.*

15. The *OED* suggests that *Columbia* (q.v. Columbine) is the poetic name for America and also allows us to read Faith's unusual middle name as "pertaining to a dove." By name, then, the central character is marked as a traveler, as seafaring and sea-crossing. In view of this, it is ironic that Faith claims at one point that it is an "old family name" (Levy 1999, 103).

16. Faith has elected to live with her parents during her studies. However, she does not perceive *her* part in this decision but blames others: "The grant authority had ummed and ahhed for months before they decided that my parents didn't live far enough away from the college to warrant them giving me independent status. And for four years I had had to juggle late-night parties, sit-ins and randy boyfriends, with 1940s Caribbean strictures" (Levy 1999, 16). Faith relies on others to confer her "independent status"—her parents and government agencies—and complains about the "demanding lifestyle" of university and its clash with her parents' values. The novel thus portrays with irony Faith's protracted struggle for independence, and her biased perception of her proactive parents as docile.

17. The intention to return is harbored by many migrants; Ferdinand Dennis's *The Last Blues Dance* is a popular novel that captures well the panache of Boswell Anderson as his West Indian friends and customers leave one after another for their island home until Anderson feels isolated in London. This is in many ways an untypical story, however; the *unrealized return* is a more prominent motif (see Phillips 1986).

18. *OED* q.v. "homesickness."

19. See, for example, the scenes in the country pub, buying a car, at the BBC, and with Carl's girlfriend.

20. Note the sound-bite quality of the phrase "If Englishness doesn't define me, then redefine Englishness" (Jaggi 1996, 64), a phrase which has been endlessly quoted (my work not excluded) since being brought into circulation by *Guardian* journalist Maya Jaggi in the bookseller Waterstone's magazine and the Web version of her essay.

21. The US-based Jamaican novelist Orlando Patterson explores the dynamics of Garveyism and Rastafarianism in his novel *The Children of Sisyphus* (1964).

22. Cf. the house motif in V. S. Naipaul's classic *A House of Mr. Biswas.* Decomposing structures, for example, are employed as extended metaphors in the following texts: Naipaul's *The Enigma of Arrival* is full of decaying structures, and David Dabydeen's *Disappearance* boasts Jack's leaning shack as well as the crumbling coast of England.

23. See "Of Mimicry and Men" in *The Location of Culture* (Bhabha 1994, 85–92).

24. Why her English father Edmund Noble does not clarify the confusion remains unclear.

25. The novel's title echoes a Caribbean folk song which accompanied West Indian migrants from the 1950s onward. It was popularized in Europe by Sandie Shaw, Lonne Donegan, Trini Lopez, and The Seekers.

26. Selvon's parks, Naipaul's Salisbury Plains in Wiltshire, and Dabydeen's Dunsmere come to mind. "Country breaks" are taken in Adebayo's *Some Kind of*

Black just as in *The Black Album*. Indeed, most of Kureishi's works play out the tension between "the garden of England" (Kent) and London. See also Stein (1995).

27. Lara's grandmother Edith came to London from Birr in southern Ireland in 1888 (Evaristo 1997, 11).

28. Lara's relationship to her mother is also inflected by differences in their bodies, as becomes clear when Ellen is unable to appreciate her daughter's fascination with having a suntan: "'Look, I've a suntan!'/ 'Don't be silly, dear.' Ellen mumbled, rolling thick pastry" (Evaristo 1997, 60). Ellen also does not provide her daughter with hair oil and skin cream (1997, 76).

29. Lara tries out various disguises until "she was now a blonde," covering her hair with her mother's yellow cardigan (Evaristo 1997, 64). This is reminiscent of Faith covering the mirrors in her room in an attempt not to be confronted with her own image. Lara is at ease in Turkey where her phenotype is not considered (see below).

30. See also Traynor (1997).

31. The birth metaphor corresponds to Levy's motif of houses, and other such structures.

32. Gilroy made the statement "Colonial history is allocated to its victims" at the conference "London: Post-Colonial City," organized by the Architectural Association and the London Consortium, March 12–13, 1999.

33. One example of the revisionary historiography which Rushdie seems to call for is the "alternative discourse" of the Subaltern Studies Group formed by the Indian historian Ranajit Guha (Guha and Spivak 1988).

34. *Lara* is one of the few books which tell the story of the freed Brazilian slaves returning to Nigeria, the *Agudas*; it is quite precise about the privileged social position often enjoyed by this group.

35. Raleigh traveled up the Orinoco in 1595 and a second, fatal expedition followed in 1617. See his *The Discoverie of the lovlie, rich and beautiful Empyre of Guiana [. . .]* (London, 1596).

36. Miles has suggested that the Picaro is "the nondeveloping hero, the unselfconscious adventurer or man of action" (Miles 1974, 980).

37. According to Stuart Hall, cultural identity " . . . is a matter of 'becoming' as well as of 'being.' It belongs to the future as much as to the past" (Hall 1990, 225).

38. The essay has been reprinted in Phillips's recent collection (2001); my citations are from the original publication.

39. On this point, see also Donald Hind, *Journey to an Illusion*.

The specific reasons for the migration of the West Indian writers, who were published in Britain between 1948 and 1958, were not necessarily the same as those which swayed the economic migrants. George Lamming addresses this question in *The Pleasures of Exile*. He speaks of West Indian societies as a "lonely desert of mass indifference, and educated middle-class treachery." Consequently, the writers "simply wanted *to get out* of the place where they were born . . . in the hope that a change of climate might bring a change of luck" (1960, 41).

40. The quotation is taken from the anonymous introduction to Caryl Phillips's article "Following On" (1999, 34).

41. In his "Minute on Indian Education," Thomas Macaulay lays out the following task: "We must at present do our best to form a class who may be interpreters between us and the millions whom we govern; a class of persons, Indian in blood and colour, but English in taste, in opinions, in morals and in intellect"

(Macaulay 1835, 729). See also Gauri Viswanathan's *Masks of Conquest: Literary-Study and British Rule in India* (1989); Sara Suleri, *The Rhetoric of English India* (1992); and Homi Bhabha, "Of Mimicry and Men" (in Bhabha 1994).

42. Gandhi, who studied law in London from 1888 to 1891, comes to mind.

43. Evaristo's Taiwo comes to study in England in 1949. Soyinka, Naipaul, Ngũgĩ wa Thiong'o, and Rushdie all studied in England, and Achebe went to University College of Ibadan, then a constituent college of the University of London founded in 1948; Walcott studied at a the University College of the West Indies in Mona, an institution then likewise tied to London.

44. Grace Nichols echoes this dictum in her collection *Lazy Thoughts of a Lazy Woman*, where she asserts: "Wherever I hang me knickers—that's my home" (10).

45. Lamming and Selvon of course mediated return with hindsight already; see the account by Aimé Césaire (*Notebook of a Return to the Native Land*, 1939).

46. Cf. his first two novels, *The Final Passage* (1985) and *A State of Independence* (1986).

47. June 27, 1998, Royal Festival Hall, South Bank Centre, London.

48. Alan Rice's wide-ranging *Radical Narratives of the Black Atlantic* gives a more extensive reading of this image of Johnson (Rice 2003, 206–10).

49. Manchester, for example, was dubbed "Britain's Bronx" in 1999, when three fatal shootings occurred in sixteen days. Harlesden, in West London, was also notorious in 1999 for gang violence. See also Back 1996.

Notes to Chapter 4

1. The exhibition (May 25–June 24, 1999) was curated by Bashir Ahmed and held at his "One Gallery," Brick Lane, Whitechapel, London.

2. I take this phrase from Tobias Döring's critique of post-colonial reading practices, an essay that informs this chapter on postethnicity (Döring 1996a, 91).

3. Kureishi's work also addresses transgressive sexualities, aging, and the body.

4. The prefix *post* does actually constitute an obsolete form of *posed*, the past participle of the verb *pose* (*OED*).

5. Schoene–Harwood has suggested that "like Hanif Kureishi in *The Buddha of Suburbia*, Meera Syal experiments with alternative, expressly anti-*Bildung* modes of hybrid self-authentication" (Schoene-Harwood 160). See also Marc Porée's treatment of the question in which ways *The Buddha of Suburbia* can be considered a bildungsroman (Porée 52–63).

6. With reference to *My Beautiful Laundrette*, Mahmood Jamal has accused Kureishi of "reinforc[ing] stereotypes of [his] own people for a few cheap laughs" (Jamal 21).

Alamgir Hashmi relates that some critics read *My Beautiful Laundrette* as suggesting that "all Pakistanis are taken to be homosexual" (89). The feminist critic bell hooks angrily speaks of "stylish nihilism" with reference to the films *London Kills Me* and *Sammy and Rosie Get Laid* (163).

7. A son not understanding Urdu appears not only in *The Buddha of Suburbia*, but also in *My Beautiful Laundrette* and in the short story "We're Not Jews" (*Love in a Blue Time*).

8. *Midnight's Children*, which first made Rushdie famous, is referred to explicitly in *The Black Album*. *The Satanic Verses* attains an indirect but significant presence: "But this time he has gone too far" (*Album* 9). Hence—and although neither Rushdie nor his most controversial novel are named—*The Black Album* relates directly to issues brought to the fore by the publication of *The Satanic Verses* and the fatwa against its author.

9. In her recent study *Postcolonial Contraventions,* Laura Chrisman has suggested that the "Rushdie Affair" "risks obscuring other important dynamics of 1980s Englishness" (2003, 9). See also Brennan 1989, Gikandi 1996, Baucom 1999, and Rushdie 2002.

10. This theme has also been dealt with in Hanif Kureishi's short story "My Son the Fanatic," and its film adaptation. The short story appears in *Love in a Blue Time* (1997a), and the BBC film was released in Britain in 1997 and in 1999 in the United States.

11. The topic of transracial adoptions is explored in Jackie Kay's collection of poetry *The Adoption Papers* and in Yinka Sunmonu's *Cherish* (2003).

12. In her comprehensive study of Hanif Kureishi, Sri Lankan critic Ruvani Ranasinha reads Kureishi's work from *Love in a Blue Time* onward as privileging individualism (Ranasinha, 2002, 102–20).

13. In his book-length study of *The Buddha of Suburbia,* Marc Porée (58) has suggested, however, that the spirit of this novel, its emphatic individualism, is in tune with the Thatcherite era, with whose ominous beginning the novel ends.

14. This can also be seen in his short stories and in *The Body.*

15. The reader could speculate on this question. Jay has an uncle in Lahore, for example. His name, if rendered simply as the letter *J*, may in fact be the inconspicuous version of another name, possibly acquired during school days. Arjun Sankaramangalam, a character in Meena Alexander's *Manhattan Music,* for example, uses the name Jay instead of his own. Susanne Reichl, however, suggests that "the protagonist has Asian ancestry" (Reichl 2002, 116).

16. The narrator is drinking alcohol and smoking cannabis; this may be a mundane explanation to the blinding whiteness of Nina and Susan.

17. Kureishi's former partner identified *Intimacy* as being based on her separation from Kureishi; her attack seems to have given the book added publicity. For a concise account of this see Ranasinha 2002, 113f.

18. I'm thinking of the following stories: "In a Blue Time," "D'accord, Baby," "Blue, Blue Pictures of You," "The Tale of the Turd," "Nightlight," "Lately," and "The Flies."

19. For a different reading of Kureishi's texts, see Graham Huggan's *The Postcolonial Exotic* (2001), where Kureishi is positioned alongside Rushdie and Naipaul. Here Kureishi is accused of "fashionable provocation" and the critical potential of his work is considered secondary to his "highly stylised, ultimately self-ingratiating narrative of mildly anti-social capers" (94).

Notes to Chapter 5

1. The *OED* defines the verb "undo" in two principal ways: "To unfasten and open" and "To annul, cancel . . . ; to reduce to the condition of not having been

done." Both senses of reversing and unfixing are noted by the dictionary.

2. This recipe from 1932 was published by the Empire Marketing Board, which existed between 1926 and 1933 to promote imperial produce. While the colonies demanded lower taxation for exports within the British Empire in order to sell more of their own goods, the board found it expedient to opt for advertising, and produced this recipe book in response to their request.

3. The National Maritime Museum has radically changed its face over the last few years, and has developed into a site for the critical investigation of the nation's naval and imperial history. I am focusing upon the Wolfson Gallery of Trade and Empire, which seems to have elicited the most criticism. It has attracted not only new visitors in large numbers, but also numerous critics within and outside the museum since it was opened in May 1999.

4. "Cultural work" is a category employed by Jane Tompkins (1985) in her study *Sensational Designs: The Cultural Work of American Fiction 1790–1860*.

5. See "Heroes No More" (James 1999), "With No Added Salts" (Purves 1999), "Was Britain's Empire so Evil?" (Pocock 1999a), and "Our Glorious Naval Past, Summed Up in a Greenpeace Protest Pod" (Benham 1999); see also Pocock (1999b), Ormond (1999), and Couper (1999).

6. This could be read as a reference to The Other Story, the important 1980 art exhibition of postwar British-based artists with African, Asian, and Caribbean origins, which was curated by artist and activist Rasheed Araeen for the Hayward Gallery. See Araeen (1989, 9–15, 100–103); cf. Mercer (1994, 233–36).

7. In his early work, Bhabha stresses that "the practices and discourses of revolutionary struggle" are not "the under/other side of 'colonial discourse.'" He adds that "Anti-colonialist discourse requires an alternative set of questions, techniques and strategies in order to construct it" (Bhabha 1983, 198). This assessment is absent in subsequent versions of "The Other Question."

8. Albion is a poetic name for Britain; it derives from the Latin word for white, *albus*, and refers to the white cliffs of Dover.

9. The reference is to Dabydeen (1985, 1987).

10. See the interviews with Dabydeen by Wolfgang Binder, Frank Birbalsingh, and Kwame Dawes: Dabydeen (1989b, 168); Dabydeen (1991b, 184–85); Dabydeen (1994a, 220).

11. In the interview with Kwame Dawes his skepticism concerning viable connections between the Caribbean or Black Britain on the one side, and Africa or the subcontinent on the other, becomes clear. Without romanticizing it, he emphasizes the "epistemological freedom" this situation entails (Dabydeen 1994a, 206 et passim).

12. See Dabydeen 1984, 1989a, 1994a, 1991a, 1993.

13. See also Dabydeen's remarks on the relationship between his absent mother and creativity in the interview with Kwame Dawes (Dabydeen 1994a, 220); *Turner* (1994b) is dedicated to Dabydeen's mother.

14. I call the mode of reading which is embodied by the narrating engineer *logovorous* (*logos* [word, reason] + *vorous* [eating, devouring]) in order to denote a reading practice which is at once consumptive and reconstitutive of the processed text. It thus entails both, a destruction/erasure and a transformation/transposition.

15. Another scene involving racialized and repressed sexuality involves the daughter of Mrs. Khan. When his *surrogate mother* "stretched out her arms in

welcome," the narrator feels "guilty" that he had been "lusting after her daughter," Rashida. He feels that his desires can be guiltlessly directed at Janet or Monica, "but not an Asian girl." However, it is not only Rashida who "looked so vulnerable"; the narrator by extension considers the "whole sitting-room," including "the brown dolls . . . all vulnerable to being smashed up, vulgarised. I knew that we had to look after each other" (Dabydeen 1991a, 212). Growing up in an orphanage, the boy is very much attracted to Rashida's family life, and yet barred from it, and therefore he harbors violent instincts toward the family's home, wanting to destroy what he cannot share in. In concurrence with the designs of the bildungsroman, the narrator envisages rebellion against parents and the class they represent to him.

16. The narrator has internalized racist views: visiting his friend Nasim in the hospital after a racist attack, for example, he muses that Nasim's family "presented a right sight to the white patients and guests" (Dabydeen 1991a, 15). From this internalized racist perspective the narrator desires invisibility (15). However, at the novel's close the narrator explicitly desires visibility but cannot bear the glaring light into which he puts himself (Dabydeen 1991a, 246).

17. Tobias Döring reads *The Intended* as a text which "question[s] the institutional frameworks and cultural traditions in which [it] operate[s] and to which [it] seek[s] affiliation" (Döring 2001, 113). Engaging with critiques of the novel by Parry and Grant, his chapter on the "Remapping" of the mother country argues persuasively that Dabydeen seeks to intertextually "entomb" his Conradian and Naipaulian intertexts (136).

18. This is noteworthy since the narrator confesses toward the end of the novel that he has "forgotten what my mother looks like. There are no clever cameras in the place to fix time" (Dabydeen 1991a, 214); cf. Dabydeen's point on the absence of a Caribbean visual memory (Dabydeen 1994a).

19. My point is not that Guyanese peasant life is glorified in the novel; on the contrary, the scenes of Albion village are shot through with poverty, alcoholism, and wife battering.

20. *The Empire Writes Back* is a prime example of this view (Ashcroft et al. 1989).

21. See Ashcroft, Griffiths, and Tiffin (1989); cf. Rose (1993); Hutcheon (1985); Tiffin (1987).

22. The narrator's search for literary exemplars takes him high and low in the world of texts. He turns not only to Conrad, Blake, and Milton; moved by the blurb on a sex toy, his ambition becomes to "write like that" (1991a, 175). The mixture of incongruous source texts which are openly employed by the narrator—note the novel's impudent opening paragraph—strongly suggests that he is not as enthralled by his sources as it sometimes would appear. The narrator's excessive Anglophilia is at once displayed and kept in check in the course of the novel.

23. The post-colonial trio took the phrase from Salman Rushdie's 1982 essay "The Empire Writes Back with a Vengeance." Rushdie had been inspired by the publication *The Empire Strikes Back* (Centre for Contemporary Cultural Studies, 1982), and this in turn pointed to George Lucas's 1980 sci-fi blockbuster of the same title. Up to a point, the convoluted chain of references commanded by this title itself exemplifies the notion of writing back.

24. Such readings have already been suggested and performed; see the articles by Benita Parry, Margery Fee, and Mark McWatt collected in Grant (1997).

25. The image can also be related to George Orwell's essay "Inside the Whale," and Salman Rushdie's response in *Imaginary Homelands*.

26. By default, texts are *dialogic* and talk to each other, according to Mikhail Bakhtin (Bakhtin 1975). Moreover, all texts are marked by intertextuality, if we follow Kristeva or Roland Barthes's developments of Bakhtin's work. According to Julia Kristeva, a text is "a permutation of texts, an intertextuality" where "several utterances, taken from other texts, intersect and neutralize one another" (Kristeva 1977, 36). Barthes goes as far as seeing intertextuality as "the condition of any text whatsoever" (Barthes 1981, 39).

Notes to Conclusion

1. For example, Nadine O'Regan (2002) in the *Business Post*.
2. For example, Fiachra Gibbons (2003) in the *Guardian*.
3. See (Niven 1990, 326); his paper is discussed in chapter 1.
4. Smith received a high number of awards for *White Teeth*, among them the James Tait Black Memorial Prize for Fiction 2001, the Whitbread Award for First Novel, the Guardian First Book Award 2000, the WH Smith Book Award for New Talent, the Frankfurt eBook Award for Best Fiction Work Originally Published in 2000, and both the Commonwealth Writers First Book Award and the Overall Commonwealth Writers Prize. She was nominated for the Whitbread Book of the Year 2000, the South Bank Show Award for Literature 2001, and shortlisted for the Orange Prize 2000.
5. Stephanie Merritt noted that Smith, at the age of twenty-one, earned an unconfirmed advance of £250,000 for *White Teeth*, or rather for the eighty pages she had finished when leaving Cambridge University in 1997 (Merritt 2000). Her novel was published in 2000 and has since been turned into a four-hour series for Channel Four television. Nadine O'Regan reports that Kunzru's two-book deal earned him "one of the highest advances ever paid to an unknown debut novelist—an estimated stg£1.25 million" (O'Regan 2002). Harriet Lane's article in the *Observer* is a good example of how Ali's début was reviewed in close association with the preceding spate of PR and a keen awareness of how the book was marketed. Lane notes gratingly that Ali "was voted one the UK's best young novelists" when her "first book was only a manuscript. Now she's being hailed as a new Zadie Smith" (Lane 2003).
6. Monica Ali was from the onset "labouring under the tag of the 'new Zadie Smith'" (Gibbons 2003). Kunzru responded to the label with sarcasm, suggesting that he was "doomed to be the new Zadie Smith . . . I'm under 35, brown-skinned and able to write a sentence" (O'Regan 2002).
7. Similar to the Marxist notion of incorporation, containment denotes a strategy of maintaining the status quo by neutralizing subversion.
8. Ahmad's critique is reminiscent of the debate about Ofili's work discussed in chapter 4.
9. Apparently speaking in Ali's name, the publicist informed Jaggi that the author "feels that black and Asian writers are often talked about and presented solely in terms of their race, whereas she would like to be seen as a writer who is naturally concerned about issues surrounding race, but who would also just like

to be seen and judged as an interesting writer too" (Jaggi 2003; cf. H. Lane 2003).

10. Greig won the Publishers' Publicity Circle Award for hardback fiction in 2001. <http://www.penguin.co.uk/static/packages/uk/articles/smith/smith4.html> (accessed October 15, 2003).

11. Susanne Reichl has referred to this type of endorsement as "a case of postcolonial marketing cross-fertilisation" (2002, 63). For an incisive analysis of the pre-reception process with respect to Black British literature, see her comprehensive chapter "Ethnic Semiosis in Depth" (112–207).

12. The phenomenon is not entirely new. Equiano had a long list of subscribers who not only bought a copy of his book; they also lent their name to Equiano's cause, the abolition of the slave trade. Having highly respected names on the subscription list (which was reproduced in the book) enhanced the book and the author's status. And it allowed subscribers to be seen as supporting him. Equiano's success certainly cannot be measured just in material terms, but the fact that he left his daughter a considerable inheritance and died a gentleman underscores the success of his publishing and book-selling venture.

13. Cf. chapter 2 on the representation, exertion, and normalization of black British cultural authority.

Notes to Further Readings

1. All references in this short survey are to the main bibliography.

2. Bryce, Grewal, and Wisker do not exclusively focus on black British women writers.

3. The study on Joan Riley by Gohrisch (1994) seems an early exception to the rule. See U. Parameswaran (1988) and T. Brennan (1989) for Rushdie; J. Levy (1995), J. Thieme (1987), and P. Hughes (1988) for Naipaul; S. Pouchet Paquet (1982) for Lamming; E. Ho (2000) for Mo; B. Ledent (2002), K. Kaleta (1998), B. Moore-Gilbert (2001,) and R. Ranasinha (2002) for Kureishi.

4. Cf. articles by Ash (1995), Ball (1996), Bharucha (1995), Döring (1998), Hand (1995), Ho (1995), Hussein (1994), Ilona (1995), Michel (1997), Nowak (1998), and Stein (1998b).

5. Cf. articles by Dahl (1995), Joseph (1993), and Stone (1994).

6. E.g., Spivak (1993b) on Kureishi.

7. Cf. articles by Back (1995–96) and Sharma (1996).

8. D'Aguiar (1993b), Easton (1994), and Berry (1998).

Bibliography

Abrams, M. H. 1993. *A Glossary of Literary Terms*. 6th ed. Fort Worth: Harcourt Brace Jovanovich.
Achebe, Chinua. 1977. "An Image of Africa: Racism in Conrad's *Heart of Darkness*." *Research in African Literatures* 9, no. 1 (1978): 1–15.
Adair, Gilbert. 1990. "The Skin Game." Review of *The Buddha of Suburbia*, by Hanif Kureishi. *New Statesman and Society* 94: 34.
Adebayo, Diran. 1996a. *Some Kind of Black*. London: Virago.
———. 1996b. Interview. *Bookseller* 7 (June): 27.
———. 2000. *My Once Upon a Time*. London: Abacus.
Agard, John. 1998. *Remember the Ship*. In Procter 2000, 258–59.
Ahmad, Aijaz. 1992. *In Theory: Classes, Nations, Literatures*. London: Verso, 1994.
Ahmad, Ali Nobil. 2001. "Whose Underground? Asian Cool and the Poverty of Hybridity." *Third Text* (Spring 2001): 71–84.
Ahmad, Rukhsana, and Rahila Gupta. 1994. Foreword. "The Asian Women Writers' Collective." In *Flaming Spirit: Stories from the Asian Women Writer's Collective*, edited by Rukhsana Ahmad and Rahila Gupta, vii-viii. London: Virago.
Ahuja, Anjana. 1994. "Tourists Yearning for Cows to Come Home." London *Guardian*, April 19, 26.
Alberge, Dalya. 1998. "Turner Shortlist Shows How Modern Art Is Dung." London *Times*, July 2, 6.
Alexander, Claire. 1996. *The Art of Being Black: The Creation of Black British Youth Identities*. Oxford: Clarendon.
Ali, Monica. 2003. *Brick Lane*. London: Doubleday.
Alibhai-Brown, Yasmin. 1995. *No Place Like Home*. London: Virago.
———, and Anne Montague. 1992. *The Colour of Love: Mixed Race Relationships*. London: Virago.
Anderson, Benedict. 1991. *Imagined Communities: Reflections on the Origin and Spread of Nationalism*. Rev. ed. London: Verso.
Anim-Addo, Joan, ed. 1996. *Framing the Word: Gender and Genre in Caribbean Women's Writing*. London: Whiting and Birch.

Appadurai, Arjun, et al., eds. 1994. "On Thinking the Black Public Sphere." Editorial Comment. *Public Culture* 7: xi–xiv.
Araeen, Rasheed. 1978. "Preliminary Notes for a Black Manifesto." *Black Phoenix* 1: 3–12.
———. 1989. *The Other Story: Afro Asian Artists in Post-War Britain*. London: South Bank Centre.
Ash, Ranjana Sidhanta. 1995. "Writers of the South Asian Diaspora in Britain: A Survey of Post-War Fiction in English." *Wasafiri* 21: 47–49.
Ashcroft, Bill. 2001. *Post-Colonial Transformation*. London: Routledge.
———, Gareth Griffiths, and Helen Tiffin. 1989. *The Empire Writes Back: Theory and Practice in Post-Colonial Literatures*. 2d ed. London: Routledge, 2002.
———. 1998. *Key Concepts in Post-Colonial Studies*. London: Routledge.
Asian Women Writers' Workshop. 1988. Introduction to *Right of Way*, 1–6. London: Women's Press.
Back, Les. 1995–96. "X Amount of Sat Siri Akal! Apache Indian, Reggae Music and the Cultural Intermezzo." *New Formations* 27: 128–47.
———. 1996. *New Ethnicities and Urban Culture: Racism and Multiculture in Young Lives*. London: UCL Press.
Baker, Houston A., Jr., Manthia Diawara, and Ruth H. Lindeborg, eds. 1996. *Black British Cultural Studies: A Reader*. Chicago: University of Chicago Press.
Bakhtin, Mikhail. 1975. "From the Prehistory of Novelistic Discourse." In *The Dialogic Imagination: Four Essays by M. M. Bakhtin*, edited by Michael Holquist, translated by Caryl Emerson and Michael Holquist, 61–83. Austin: University of Texas Press, 1981.
Baldick, Chris, ed. 1990. *The Concise Oxford Dictionary of Literary Terms*. Oxford: Oxford University Press.
Balibar, Etienne, and Pierre Macherey. 1978. "Literature as an Ideological Form." Translated by Ian McLeod, John Whitehead, and Ann Wordsworth. *Oxford Literary Review* 3, no. 1: 4–12.
Ball, John Clement. 1996. "The Semi-Detached Metropolis: Hanif Kureishi's London." *Ariel* 27, no. 4: 7–27.
Barthes, Roland. 1973. *S/Z*. Translated by Richard Miller. Oxford: Blackwell, 1990.
———. 1981. "Theory of the Text." In *Untying the Text: A Post-structuralist Reader*, edited by Robert Young, translated by Ian McLeod, 31–47. Boston: Routledge and Kegan Paul.
Baucom, Ian. 1999. *Out of Place: Englishness, Empire and the Locations of Identity*. Princeton, NJ: Princeton University Press.
Benham, Mark. 1999. "Our Glorious Naval Past, Summed Up in a Greenpeace Protest Pod." *Evening Standard*, April 26, 21.
Bennett, Louise. 1982. "Colonization in Reverse." In *Selected Poems*, edited and introduced by Mervyn Morris, 106–7. Kingston: Sangster 1983.
Benson, Eugene, and L. W. Conolly, eds. 1994. *Encyclopedia of Post-Colonial Literatures in English*. London: Routledge.
Bhabha, Homi. 1983. "Difference, Discrimination and the Discourse of Colonialism." In *The Politics of Theory: Proceedings of the Essex Conference on the Sociology of Literature, July 1982*, edited by Francis Barker et al., 194–211. Colchester: University of Essex.
———. 1984. "Representation and the Colonial Text: A Critical Exploration of

Some Forms of Mimeticism." In *The Theory of Reading*, edited by Frank Gloversmith, 93–122. Brighton: Harvester.

———. 1987. "Interrogating Identity." In *The Real Me: Post-Modernism and the Question of Identity: ICA Documents 6*, edited by Lisa Appignanesi, 5–11. London: Institute of Contemporary Arts.

———. 1990a. "The Third Space: Interview with Homi Bhabha." In *Identity: Community, Culture, Difference*, edited by Jonathan Rutherford, 207–21. London: Lawrence and Wishart.

———. 1990b. *Nation and Narration*. London: Routledge.

———. 1994. *The Location of Culture*. London: Routledge.

———. 1996. "Aura and Agora: On Negotiating Rapture and Speaking Between." In *Negotiating Rapture: The Power of Art to Transform Lives*, edited by Sue Taylor, 8–17. Chicago: Museum of Contemporary Art.

Bharucha, Nilufer E. 1995. "The Floodgates Are Open: Recent Fiction from the Indian Sub-Continent." *Wasafiri* 21: 72–74.

Bhatnagar, O. P. 1980. "Literature in National and Transnational Contexts." *Journal of English Studies* (Nagercoil, India): 3: 1–12.

Bidisha. 1997. *Seahorses*. London: Flamingo.

Blake, Ann, et al., eds. 2001. *England through Colonial Eyes in Twentieth-Century Fiction*. Houndmills: Palgrave.

Boehmer, Elleke. 1995. *Colonial and Postcolonial Literature: Migrant Metaphors*. Oxford: Oxford University Press.

Boelhower, William. 1998. "Enchanted Sites: Remembering the Caribbean as Autobiographical Tactics." In *Postcolonialism & Autobiography: Michelle Cliff, David Dabydeen, Opal Palmer Adisa*, edited by Alfred Hornung and Ernstpeter Ruhe, 115–33. Amsterdam: Rodopi.

Borgmann, Ulrike, ed. 1999. *From Empire to Multicultural Society: Cultural and Institutional Changes in Britain. Proceedings of the 9th British Cultural Studies Conference, Würzburg 1998*. Trier [Germany]: WVT Wissenschaftlicher Verlag.

Brah, Avtar. 1996. *Cartographies of Diaspora: Contesting Identities*. London: Routledge.

Brennan, Timothy. 1989. *Salman Rushdie and the Third World: Myths of the Nation*. Houndmills: Macmillan.

———. 1997. *At Home in the World: Cosmopolitanism Now*. Cambridge, MA: Harvard University Press.

Brennan, Timothy, ed. 1990. "Writing from Black Britain." *Literary Review* 34, no. 1: 5–11.

Briggs, Asa. 1991. "The English: How the Nation Sees Itself." In *Literature in the Modern World: Critical Essays and Documents*, edited by Dennis Walder, 189–94. Oxford: Oxford University Press.

Bromley, Roger. 2000. *Narratives for a New Belonging: Diasporic Cultural Fictions*. Edinburgh: Edinburgh University Press.

Brooke, Rupert. 1915. "The Soldier." In *The Nation's Favourite Poems*, edited by Griff Rhys Jones, 44. London: BBC 1996.

Brown, Stewart. 1988. "James Berry–Celebration Songs." *Kunapipi* 20, no. 1: 45–56.

———. 1999. Review of *Lara*, by Bernardine Evaristo. *Wasafiri* 29: 83–84.

Bryan, Judith. 1998. *Bernard and the Cloth Monkey*. Flamingo.

Bryce, Jane, and Kari Darko. 1993. "Textual Deviancy and Cultural Syncretism: Romantic Fiction as a Subversive Strain in Black Women's Writing." *Wasafiri* 17: 10–14.
Brydon, Diana. 1994. "Criticism (Overview)." In *Encyclopedia of Post-Colonial Literatures in English*, edited by Eugene Benson and L. W. Conolly, 282–84. London: Routledge.
Buck, Louisa. 1996. "Fever Pitch [Chris Ofili]." *Artforum* 35, no. 2: 35–37.
———. 1997. "Openings: Chris Ofili." *Artforum* 36, no. 1: 112–13.
Buckley, Jerome Hamilton. 1974. *Season of Youth: The Bildungsroman from Dickens to Golding*. Cambridge, MA: Harvard Unversity Press.
Butcher, Maggie, ed. 1989. *Tibisiri. Caribbean Writers and Critics*. Sydney: Dangaroo Press.
Butcher, Margaret K. 1982. "From *Maurice Guest* to *Martha Quest*: The Female Bildungsroman in Commonwealth Literature." *World Literature Written in English* 21: 254–62.
Byatt, A[ntonia] S. 1998. Introduction. In *The Oxford Book of English Short Stories*, edited by Antonia S. Byatt, xv–xxx. Oxford: Oxford University Press, 1999.
Carr, Rocky. 1998. *Brixton Bwoy*. London: Fourth Estate.
Castles, Stephen, and Mark J. Miller. 1993. *The Age of Migration*. London: Macmillan.
Centre for Contemporary Cultural Studies [University of Birmingham]. 1982. *The Empire Strikes Back: Race and Racism in 70s Britain*. London: Hutchinson.
Chambers, Iain, and Lidia Curti, eds. 1996. *The Post-Colonial Question: Common Skies, Divided Horizons*. London and New York: Routledge.
Chaudhuri, Amit. 1993. *Afternoon Raag*. London: Heinemann. London: Minerva, 1994.
Chew, Shirley, Lars Jensen, and Anna Rutherford, eds. 1994. *Into the Nineties: Post-Colonial Writing*. Armidale, New South Wales: Dangaroo.
Cheyette, Bryan. 1996. "'Ineffable and Usable': Towards a Diasporic British-Jewish Writing." *Textual Practice* 10: 295–313.
Cheyette, Bryan, ed. 1996. *Between 'Race' and Culture: Representations of 'the Jew' in English and American Literature*. Stanford, CA: Stanford University Press.
Chow, Rey. 1993. *Writing Diaspora: Tactics of Intervention in Contemporary Cultural Studies*. Bloomington: Indiana University Press.
Chrisman, Laura. 2003. *Postcolonial Contraventions: Cultural Readings of Race, Imperialism, and Transnationalism*. Manchester: Manchester University Press.
Clifford, James. 1997. *Routes: Travel and Translation in the Late Twentieth Century*. Cambridge, MA: Harvard University Press.
Cohen, Robin. 1995. "Fuzzy Frontiers of Identity: The British Case." *Social Identities* 1, no. 1: 35–62.
Connor, Steven. 1996. *The English Novel in History: 1950–1995*. London: Routledge.
Conrad, Joseph. 1902. *Heart of Darkness*. Case Studies in Contemporary Criticism. 2d ed. Edited by Ross C. Murfin. Boston: Bedford, 1996.
Couper, Alastair. 1999. Letter. London *Guardian* Rev. sec., p. 12.
Cudjoe, Selwyn R[eginald]. 1988. *V. S. Naipaul: A Materialist Reading*. Amherst: University of Massachusetts Press.
Dabydeen, David. 1984. *Slave Song*. Sydney: Dangaroo.
———. 1985. *Hogarth's Blacks: Images of Blacks in Eighteenth Century English Arts*.

Mundelstrup: Dangaroo.
———. 1987. *Hogarth, Walpole and Commercial Britain*. London: Hansib.
———. 1988a. *Coolie Odyssey*. London: Hansib.
———. 1988b. "From Care to Cambridge." In Holst Petersen and Rutherford 1988, 137–41.
———. 1989a. Interview with Wolfgang Binder. In Grant 1997, 159–76.
———. 1989b. "On Not Being Milton: Nigger Talk in England Today." In Butcher 1989, 121–35.
———. 1991a. *The Intended*. London: Minerva, 1992.
———. 1991b. Interview with Frank Birbalsingh. In Grant 1997, 177–98.
———. 1993. *Disappearance*. London: Secker and Warburg.
———. 1994a. Interview with Kwame Dawes. In Grant 1997, 199–221.
———. 1994b. *Turner: New and Selected Poems*. London: Cape.
———. 1999a. *A Harlot's Progress*. London: Cape.
———. 1999b. Interview with Mark Stein. *Wasafiri* 29: 27–29.
———, ed. 1998. "West Indians in Britain: 1948–1998: The *Windrush* Commemorative Issue." *Kunapipi* 20, no. 1.
———, and Nana Wilson-Tagoe. 1987. *A Reader's Guide to Westindian and Black British Literature*. London: Hansib, 1998.
D'Aguiar, Fred. 1989. "Against Black British Literature." In Butcher 1989, 106–14.
———. 1993a. *British Subjects*. Newcastle-upon-Tyne: Bloodaxe.
———. 1993b. "Have You Been Here Long? Black Poetry in Britain." In *New British Poetries: The Scope of the Possible,* edited by Robert Hampson and Peter Barry, 51–71. Manchester: Manchester University Press.
Dahl, Mary Karen. 1995. "Post-colonial British Theatre." In *Imperialism and Theatre,* edited by J. Ellen Gainor, 38–56. London: Routledge.
Dasenbrock, Reed Way. 1992. Review of *London Kills Me: 3 Screenplays and 4 Essays,* by Hanif Kureishi. *World Literature Today* 66: 724.
Davey, Kevin. 1999. "David Dabydeen: Coolie Lessons for Cool Britannia." In *English Imaginaries: Six Studies in Anglo-British Modernity,* 139–70. London: Lawrence and Wishart.
Davis, Thadious M. 1997. Introduction to *Passing,* by Nella Larsen, edited by Davis, vii–xxxv. New York: Penguin.
Dawes, Kwame. 1999. "Negotiating the Ship on the Head: Black British Fiction." *Wasafiri* 29: 18–24.
Deleuze, Gilles, and Félix Guattari. 1986. "What Is a Minor Literature?" In *Out There: Marginalization and Contemporary Cultures,* edited by Russell Ferguson, 59–69. New York: New Museum of Contemporary Art, 1990.
Dennis, Ferdinand. 1998. *The Duppy Conqueror*. London: Flamingo.
Dennis, Ferdinand, and Naseem Khan, eds. 2000. *Voices of the Crossing: The Impact of Britain on Writers from Asia, the Caribbean and Africa*. London: Serpent's Tail.
Desai, Anita. 1985. *Bye-Bye Black Bird*. Delhi: Orient.
Desani, G. V. 1948. *All About H. Hatterr*. New Delhi: Gulab Vazirani, 1972.
Dhillon-Kashyap, Perminder. 1988. "Locating the Asian Experience." *Screen* 29, no. 4: 120–26.
Dhondy, Farrukh. 1976. *East End at Your Feet*. Houndmills: Macmillan.
———. 1978. *Come to Mecca and Other Stories*. London: Fontana and Collins.
———. 1990. *Bombay Duck*. London: Cape.

Dodd, Philip. 1991. "Requiem for a Rave." *Sight and Sound*, n.s., 1, no. 5: 9–13.
Donnell, Alison J., ed. 2002. *Routledge Companion to Black British Culture*. London: Routledge.
Döring, Tobias. 1996a. "Reading for Transparency? Rereading the Obscure." In Döring et al. 1996, 90–101.
———. 1996b. "A Battle Between Opposing Forces and a Plea for Pluralization." Review of *The Black Album*, by Hanif Kureishi. *Hard Times* 56: 18–20.
———. 1998. "The Passage of the Eye/I: David Dabydeen, V. S. Naipaul and the Tombstones of Parabiography." In *Postcolonialism & Autobiography: Michelle Cliff, David Dabydeen, Opal Palmer Adisa*, edited by Alfred Hornung and Ernstpeter Ruhe, 149–66. Amsterdam: Rodopi.
———. 2002. *Caribbean-English Passages: Intertextuality in a Postcolonial Tradition*. London: Routledge.
———, and Heike Härting. 1995. "Amphibian Hermaphrodites: A Dialogue with Marina Warner and David Dabydeen." *Third Text* 30: 39–45.
———, Uwe Schäfer, and Mark Stein, eds. 1996. *Can "The Subaltern" Be Read? Acolit Sonderheft* 2. Frankfurt: Institut für England- und Amerikastudien.
Driver, Felix, and David Gilbert. 1999. "Imperial Cities: Overlapping Territories, Intertwined Histories." In *Imperial Cities: Landscape, Display and Identity*, edited by Felix Driver and David Gilbert, 1–17. Manchester: Manchester University Press.
Duncker, Patricia. 1996. *Hallucinating Foucault*. London: Serpent's Tail.
Dyer, Richard. 1997. *White*. London: Routledge.
Dyer, Richard. 1999. Review of Chris Ofili's Exhibition, Serpentine Gallery, London, September 30–November 1, 1998. *Wasafiri* 29: 79–80.
Easton, Alison. 1994. "The Body as History and 'Writing the Body': The Example of Grace Nichols." *Journal of Gender Studies* 3, no. 1: 55–67.
Edwards, Paul. 1967. Introduction. *Equiano's Travels*, by Olaudah Equiano. Ed. Edwards, vii–xix. London: Heinemann.
———, and David Dabydeen, eds. 1991. *Black Writers in Britain: 1760–1890*. Edinburgh: Edinburgh University Press.
Eliot, T. S. 1948. *Notes towards the Definition of Culture*. London: Faber.
Equiano, Olaudah. [1789] 1995. *The Interesting Narrative and Other Writings*. Rev. ed. Edited by Vincent Carretta. New York: Penguin, 2003.
Evaristo, Bernardine. 1997. *Lara*. Tunbridge Wells: Angela Royal.
———. 1999. "Bernardine Evaristo." *Wasafiri* 29: 49.
———. 2001. *The Emperor's Babe: A Novel*. London: Hamish.
Fanon, Frantz. 1952. *Black Skin, White Masks*. Translated by Charles Lam Markmann. London: Pluto, 1986.
Feaver, William. 1998. "Chris Ofili, Serpentine, London." *Artnews* 97, no. 11: 159.
Felski, Rita. 1986. "The Novel of Self-Discovery: A Necessary Fiction?" *Southern Review* (Adelaide) 19, no. 2: 131–48.
Feng, Pin-Chia. 1998. *The Female Bildungsroman by Toni Morrison and Maxine Hong Kingston: A Postmodern Reading*. New York: Modern American Literature.
Ferguson, Russell, Martha Gever, Trinh T. Minh-ha, and Cornel West, eds. 1990. *Out There: Marginalization and Contemporary Cultures*. New York: New Museum of Contemporary Art.

Fhlathúin, Máire ní. 1999. "The Location of Childhood: 'Great Expectations' in Post-Colonial London." *Kunapipi* 21, no. 2: 86–92.
Flint, Kate. 1998. "Looking Backward? The Relevance of Britishness." *Unity in Diversity Revisited? British Literature and Culture in the 1990s.* In Korte and Müller 1998, 35–50.
Foucault, Michel. 1999. "Space, Power and Knowledge." Interview with Paul Rabinow. *The Cultural Studies Reader,* 2d ed., edited by Simon During, 134–41.
Fryer, Peter. 1984. *Staying Power: The History of Black People in Britain.* London: Pluto Press.
———. 1985. "Black British Literature." *Times Literary Supplement* 4284: 521.
Fuderer, Laura Sue. 1990. *The Female Bildungsroman in English: An Annotated Bibliography of Criticism.* New York: MLA.
Gee, Maggie. 2002. *The White Family.* London: Saqi.
George, Rosemary Marangoly. 1996. *The Politics of Home: Postcolonial Relocations and Twentieth-Century Fiction.* Cambridge: Cambridge University Press.
Gerzina, Gretchen. 1995. *Black England: Life before Emancipation.* London: Murray.
Ghose, Sudhindra Nath. 1949. *And Gazelles Leaping.* London: Michael Joseph.
Gibbons, Fiachra. 2003. "Obscure Unpublished Novelist Joins the Elite." London *Guardian,* January 6, 2003, http://books.guardian.co.uk/print/0,3858,4577307–103690,00.html (September 3, 2003).
Gikandi, Simon. 1996. *The Maps of Englishness: Writing Identity in the Culture of Colonialism.* New York: Columbia University Press.
Gilroy, Beryl. 1996. *Inkle & Yarico.* Leeds: Peepal.
Gilroy, Paul. 1987. *There Ain't No Black in the Union Jack: The Cultural Politics of Race and Nation.* London: Routledge, 1992.
———. 1993a. *Small Acts: Thoughts on the Politics of Black Cultures.* London: Serpent's Tail.
———. 1993b. *The Black Atlantic: Modernity and Double Consciousness.* London: Verso.
———. 1995. *The Status of Difference: From Epidermalisation to Nano-politics.* London: Goldsmiths College.
———. 1997. *Between Camps: Race and Culture in Postmodernity.* London: Goldsmiths College.
Giovanni, June I. 1992. *Black Film and Video List.* London: BFI Education.
Glage, Liselotte, and Martina Michel, eds. 1993. *Postkoloniale Literaturen: Peripherien oder neue Zentren?* Gulliver. Deutsch-Englische Jahrbücher 33. Hamburg: Argument.
Godfrey, Tony. 1998. "Recent Painting [Chris Ofili]." *Burlington Magazine* 140 (September 1998): 633–35.
Gohrisch, Jana. 1994. *(Un)Belonging? Geschlecht, Klasse, Rasse und Ethnizität in der Britischen Gegenwartsliteratur: Joan Rileys Romane.* Frankfurt: Lang.
Grant, Kevin, ed. 1997. *The Art of David Dabydeen.* Leeds: Peepal Tree.
Grewal, Shabnam, et al., eds. 1988. *Charting the Journey: Writings by Black and Third World Women.* London: Sheba.
Guha, Ranajit, and Gayatri Chakravorty Spivak. 1988. *Selected Subaltern Studies.* New York: Oxford University Press.
Guptara, Prahbu. 1986. *Black British Literature: An Annotated Bibliography.* Sydney: Dangaroo.

Gurnah, Abdulrazak. 1990. *Dottie*. London: Cape.
Hall, Catherine. 1996. "Histories, Empires and the Post-colonial Moment." In *The Post-Colonial Question: Common Skies, Divided Horizons*, edited by Iain Chambers and Lidia Curti, 65–77. London: Routledge.
Hall, Stuart. 1987. "Minimal Selves." In *The Real Me: Post-Modernism and the Question of Identity: ICA Documents* 6, edited by Lisa Appignanesi, 44–46. London: Institute of Contemporary Arts.
———. 1988. "New Ethnicities." In *Black Film, British Cinema: ICA Documents* 7, edited by Kobena Mercer, 27–31. London: Institute of Contemporary Arts.
———.1990. "Cultural Identity and Diaspora." In *Identity, Community, Culture, Difference*, edited by Jonathan Rutherford, 222–37. London: Lawrence and Wishart.
———. 1991a. "The Local and the Global: Globalization and Ethnicity." In *Culture, Globalization and the World-System: Contemporary Conditions for the Representation of Identity*, edited by Anthony D. King, 19–39. Houndsmills: Macmillan.
———. 1991b. "Old and New Identities, Old and New Ethnicities." In *Culture, Globalization and the World-System: Contemporary Conditions for the Representation of Identity*, edited by Anthony D. King, 41–68. Houndsmills: Macmillan.
———. 1992. "The Question of Cultural Identity." In *Modernity and Its Futures*, edited by Stuart Hall, David Held, and Tony McGrew, 274–316. Cambridge: Polity.
———. 1996. "When Was the Post-Colonial?" In *The Post-Colonial Question: Common Skies, Divided Horizons*, edited by Ian Chambers and Lidia Curti, 242–59. London: Routledge.
———. 1997. "Frontlines and Backyards." In Owusu 2000, 127–29.
———. 1999. "Stuart Hall Opens the Discussion." *Wasafiri* 29: 37–38.
Hamner, Robert. 1977. *Critical Perspectives on V. S. Naipaul*. Washington: Three Continents.
Hand, Felicity. 1995. "How British are the Asians?" *Wasafiri* 21: 9–13.
Hannerz, Ulf. 1996. *Transnational Connections: Culture, People, Places*. London: Routledge.
Harris, Margaret Ann. 1998. "Writers' Moment." *Sunday Advocate* (Bridgetown, Barbados), April 19, 23.
Harris, Wilson. 1980. "The Frontier on which *Heart of Darkness* Stands." *Explorations: A Selection of Talks and Articles 1966–1981*, edited by Hena Maes-Jelinek, 134–41. Mundelstrup: Dangaroo 1981.
Hashmi, Alamgir. 1992. "Hanif Kureishi and the Tradition of the Novel." *International Fiction Review* 19, no. 2: 88–95.
Hawthorn, Jeremy. 1994. *A Concise Glossary of Contemporary Literary Theory*. 2d ed. London: Edward Arnold.
Head, Dominic. 2003. "Zadie Smith's *White Teeth*." In R. Lane 2003, 106–19.
Headly, Victor. 1992. *Yardie*. London: X Press, 1993.
Hiro, Dilip. 1969. *A Triangular View*. Delhi: Hind, 1973.
———. 1971. *Black British, White British: A History of Race Relations in Britain*. London: Grafton, 1991.
Ho, Elaine Yee Lin. 1995. "Of Laundries and Restaurants: Fictions of Ethnic Space." *Wasafiri* 21: 16–19.

———. 2000. *Timothy Mo.* Manchester: Manchester University Press.
Hollinger, David. 1995. *Postethnic America: Beyond Multiculturalism.* New York: BasicBooks.
Holst Petersen, Kirsten, and Anna Rutherford, eds. 1988. *Displaced Persons.* Sydney: Dangaroo.
hooks, bell. 1991. "Stylish Nihilism: Race, Sex, and Class at the Movies." In *Yearning: Race, Gender, and Cultural Politics,* 155–63. London: Turnaround.
Hosain, Attia. 1961. *Sunlight on a Broken Column.* London: Chatto.
Huggan, Graham. 2001. *The Postcolonial Exotic: Marketing the Margins.* London: Routledge.
Hughes, Peter. 1988. *V. S. Naipaul.* London and New York: Routledge.
Hulme, Peter. 1986. *The Colonial Encounter: Europe and the Native Caribbean, 1492–1797.* London: Methuen.
———. 1995. "Including America." *Ariel* 26, no. 1: 117–23.
Hussein, Aamer. 1994. "Changing Seasons: Post-colonial or 'Other' Writing in Britain Today." *Wasafiri* 20: 16–18.
———. 2000. Review of *A Strange and Sublime Address* by Amit Chaudhuri. London *Independent,* June 10. http://enjoyment.independent.co.uk/books/interviews/story.jsp?story=45523 (acc.3.5.2004)
Hutcheon, Linda. 1985. *A Theory of Parody: The Teachings of Twentieth-Century Art Forms.* New York: Routledge, 1991.
Ilona, Anthony. 1995. "Crossing the River: A Chronicle of the Black Diaspora." *Wasafiri* 22: 3–9.
———. 2003. "Hanif Kureishi's *The Buddha of Suburbia:* 'A New Way of Being British.'" In Lane 2003, 87–105.
Innes, C. L[yn]. 1995. "Wintering: Making a Home in Britain." In Lee 1995a, 21–34.
———. 2002. *A History of Black and Asian Writing in Britain, 1700–2000.* Cambridge: Cambridge University Press.
Jacobs, Jürgen, and Markus Krause. 1989. *Der deutsche Bildungsroman: Gattungsgeschichte vom 18. bis zum 20. Jahrhundert.* Munich: Beck.
Jaggi, Maya. 1996. "Redefining Englishness." *Waterstone's Magazine* 6: 62–69.
———. 2003. "Colour Bind." Manchester *Guardian,* February 7 http://www.guardian.co.uk/race/story/0,11374,890859,00.html (September 3, 2003).
Jamal, Mahmood. [1987] 1988. "Dirty Linen." In *Black Film, British Cinema: ICA Documents 7,* edited by Kobena Mercer, 21–22. London: Institute of Contemporary Arts.
James, C. L. R. 1936. *Minty Alley.* London: New Beacon, 1971.
James, Lawrence. 1999. "Heroes No More." London: *Daily Mail* April 3, 12–13.
James, Winston, and Clive Harris. 1993. Introduction to *Inside Babylon: The Caribbean Diaspora in Britain,* edited by James and Harris, 1–8. London: Verso.
Jameson, Fredric. 1987. "Third World Literature in the Era of Multinational Capitalism." *Social Text* 17: 3–25.
———. 1991. *Postmodernism or, the Cultural Logic of Late Capitalism.* London: Verso.
JanMohamed, Abdul R. 1992. "Worldliness-without-World, Homelessness-as-Home: Toward a Definition of the Secular Border Intellectual." In *Edward Said: A Critical Reader,* edited by Michael Sprinker, 96–120. Oxford: Blackwell.
———, and David Lloyd. 1987. Introduction. "Minority Discourse–What Is to Be Done?" *Cultural Critique* 7: 5–17.

Joseph, May-Rosalind. 1993. *Black British Theatre and Film as Postcolonial Discourse*. Ann Arbor, MI: DAI.
Joyce, James. 1922. *Ulysses*. London: Bodley Head, 1992.
Jusdanis, Gregory. 1995. "Beyond National Culture?" *Boundary 2*, 22, no. 1: 23–60.
Jussawalla, Feroza. 1988. "Chiffon Saris: The Plight of South Asian Immigrants in the New World." *Massachusetts Review* 29: 583–95.
Kaleta, Kenneth C. 1998. *Hanif Kureishi: Postcolonial Storyteller*. Austin: University of Texas Press.
Kay, Jackie. 1999. Interview with Maya Jaggi. *Wasafiri* 29: 53–56.
———. 1998. *The Trumpet*. London: Picador, 1999.
Kellaway, Kate. 1995. "The Undiscovered Country." *Observer*, August 13, 6.
Khan, Almas. 1993. *Chapati and Chips*. Castleford: Springboard.
King, Reyahn, et al., eds. 1997. *Ignatius Sancho: An African Man of Letters*. London: National Portrait Gallery.
Korte, Barbara, and Klaus Peter Müller, eds. 1998. *Unity in Diversity Revisited? British Literature and Culture in the 1990s*. Tübingen: Narr.
Kramer, Jürgen. 1997. *British Cultural Studies*. Munich: Fink.
Kristeva, Julia. 1977. *Desire in Language: A Semiotic Approach to Literature and Art*, edited by Leon S. Roudiez, translated by Thomas Gora, Alice Jardine, and Leon S. Roudiez. Oxford: Blackwell, 1980.
———. 1987. "On the Melancholic Imaginary." In *Discourse in Psychoanalysis and Literature*, edited by Shlomith Rimmon-Kenan, 104–23. London: Methuen.
Kunzru, Hari. 2002. *The Impressionist*. London: Penguin, 2003.
Kureishi, Hanif. 1986. "The Rainbow Sign." In *My Beautiful Laundrette and The Rainbow Sign*, 7–38. London: Faber.
———. 1989. "London and Karachi." In *Patriotism: The Making and Unmaking of British National Identity*, edited by Raphael Samuel, 270–87. London: Routledge.
———. 1990. *The Buddha of Suburbia*. London: Faber, 1991.
———. 1992. Introduction. *Plays One*, by Kureishi, vii–xx. London: Faber, 1999.
———. 1995. *The Black Album*. London: Faber, 1996.
———. 1997a. *Love in a Blue Time*. London: Faber.
———. 1997b. *My Son the Fanatic*. London: Faber.
———. 1998. *Intimacy*. London: Faber.
———. 1999a. "London in Hanif Kureishi's Films: Hanif Kureishi in Interview." *Kunapipi* 21, no. 2: 5–14.
———. 1999b. *Midnight All Day*. London: Faber.
———. 2001. *Gabriel's Gift*. London: Faber.
———. 2002a. *Dreaming and Scheming: Reflections on Writing and Politics*. London: Faber.
———. 2002b. *The Body: And Seven Stories*. London: Faber, 2002.
Kureishi, Hanif, and Jon Savage. 1995. *The Faber Book of Pop*. London: Faber.
Lamming, George. 1960. *The Pleasures of Exile*. Ann Arbor: University of Michigan Press, 1992.
Lane, Harriet. 2003. "Ali's in Wonderland." London *Observer*, June 1, 2003 http://observer.guardian.co.uk/review/story/0,6903,967705,00.html (August 7, 2003).
Lane, Richard J., et al., eds. 2003. *Contemporary British Fiction*. Cambridge: Polity.

Lawson Welsh, Sarah. 1998. "Critical Myopia and Black British Literature: Reassessing the Literary Contribution of the Post-Windrush Generation(s)." *Kunapipi* 20, no. 1: 132–42.
Lazarus, Neil. 2003. "Fredric Jameson and Third World Literature: A Qualified Defence." Paper presented at *Colloquium on Connecting Cultures,* University of Kent at Canterbury, March 15, 2003.
Ledent, Bénédicte. 2002. *Caryl Phillips.* Manchester: Manchester University Press.
Lee, A. Robert, ed. 1995a. *Other Britain, Other British: Contemporary Multicultural Fiction.* London: Pluto.
———. 1995b. "Changing the Script: Sex Lies and Videotapes in Hanif Kureishi, David Dabydeen and Mike Phillips." In Lee 1995a, 69–89.
LeSeur, Geta J. 1986. "One Mother, Two Daughters: The Afro-American and Afro-Caribbean Female Bildungsroman." *Black Scholar* 17, no. 2: 26–33.
———. 1995. *Ten Is the Age of Darkness: The Black Bildungsroman.* Columbia: University of Missouri Press.
Levy, Andrea. 1994. *Every Light in the House Burnin'.* London: Headline Review.
———. 1996. *Never Far from Nowhere.* London: Headline.
———. 1999. *Fruit of the Lemon.* London: Headline.
Levy, Judith. 1995. *V. S. Naipaul: Displacement and Autobiography.* New York: Garland.
Lima, Maria Helena. 1993. "Revolutionary Developments: Michelle Cliff's *No Telephone to Heaven* and Merle Collins's *Angel.*" *Ariel* 24, no. 1: 35–56.
Lively, Adam. 1998. *Masks: Blackness, Race and the Imagination.* London: Chatto and Windus.
Lloyd, David. 1994. "Ethnic Cultures, Minority Discourse and the State." In *Colonial Discourse/Postcolonial Theory,* edited by Francis Barker, Peter Hulme, and Margaret Iversen, 221–38. Manchester: Manchester University Press.
Loomba, Ania. 1998. *Colonialism/Postcolonialism.* London: Routledge.
Macaulay, Thomas Babington. 1835. "Indian Education. Minute on the 2d of February, 1835." In *Macaulay: Poetry & Prose,* edited by G. M. Young, 719–30. London: Hart-Davis 1952.
MacInnes, Colin. 1957. *City of Spades.* London: Allison & Busby, 1980.
Mackenthun, Gesa. 1996. "*E Pluribus Unum*? Die Position der USA im Postkolonialen Diskurs." *Argument* 215: 373–79.
Maes-Jelinek, Hena, ed. 1991. *Wilson Harris: The Uncompromising Imagination.* Sydney: Dangaroo.
Mahomet, Sake Dean. 1794. *The Travels of Dean Mahomet, a Native of Patna in Bengal Through Several Parts of India, While in the Service of the Honourable East India Company, Written by Himself, in a Series of Letters to a Friend, In Two Volumes.* Cork.
Markandaya, Kamala. 1972. *The Nowhere Man.* London: Allen Lane, 1973.
Marke, Ernest. 1975. *In Troubled Waters: Memoirs of Seventy Years in England.* London: Karia, 1986.
Martin, S. I. 1996. *Incomparable World.* London: Quartet.
Martini, Fritz. 1961. "Der Bildungsroman: Zur Geschichte des Wortes und der Theorie." *Deutsche Vierteljahresschrift* 35: 44–63.
McIntyre, Karen. 1996. "'A Different Kind of Book': Literary Decolonization in David Dabydeen's *The Intended.*" *Ariel* 27, no. 2: 151–75.

McLeod, John. 1999. "Laughing in the Storm: Representations of Post-Colonial London." *Kunapipi* 21, no. 2: vi–viii.
McWatt, Mark. 1997. "'Self-Consciously Post-Colonial': The Fiction of David Dabydeen." In Grant 1997, 111–22.
Mehmood, Tariq. 1983. *Hand on the Sun*. Harmondsworth: Penguin.
Melville, Pauline. 1990. *Shape-Shifter*. London: Picador, 1991.
Mercer, Kobena. 1990. "Black Art and the Burden of Representation." *Third Text* 10: 61–78.
——— 1994. *Welcome to the Jungle: New Positions in Black Cultural Studies*. New York: Routledge.
———. 1998. "Intermezzo Worlds." *Art Journal* 57, no. 4: 43–45.
———, ed. 1988. *Black Film British Cinema: ICA Documents* 7. London: Institute of Contemporary Arts.
Merritt, Stephanie. 2000. "She's Young, Black, British—and the First Publishing Sensation of the Millennium." *Observer*, January 16, 2000, http://books.guardian.co.uk/departments/generalfiction/story/0,6000,122817,00.html (September 3, 2003).
Michel, Martina. 1997. "Un(der)-Cover: Ravinder Randhawa's *A Wicked Old Woman*." In *(Sub)Versions of Realism—Recent Women's Fiction in Britain. Anglistik & Englischunterricht* 60, edited by Irmgard Maassen and Anna Maria Stuby, 143–57.
Mihailovich-Dickman, Vera. 1994. *"Return" in Post-Colonial Writing: A Cultural Labyrinth*. Amsterdam: Rodopi.
Miles, David H. 1974. "The Picaro's Journey to the Confessional: The Changing Image of the Hero in the German Bildungsroman." *PMLA* 89: 980–92.
Minden, Michael R. 1997. *The German Bildungsroman: Incest and Inheritance*. Cambridge: Cambridge University Press.
Mirza, Heide Safia, ed. 1997. *Black British Feminism: A Reader*. London: Routledge.
Moore-Gilbert, Bart. 1997. *Postcolonial Theory: Contexts, Practices, Politics*. London: Verso.
———. 2001. *Hanif Kureishi*. Manchester: Manchester University Press.
Moretti, Franco. 1987. *The Way of the World: The Bildungsroman in European Culture*. London: Verso.
Morgan, Ellen. 1972. "Humanbecoming: Form and Focus in the Neo-Feminist Novel." In *Images of Women in Fiction: Feminist Perspectives*, edited by Susan Koppelman Cornillon, 183–205. Bowling Green: Bowling Green University Popular Press.
Morley, David, and Kuan-Hsing Chen, eds. 1996. *Stuart Hall: Critical Dialogues in Cultural Studies*. London: Routledge.
Morrison, Toni. 1992. *Playing in the Dark: Whiteness and the Literary Imagination*. New York: Vintage, 1993.
Mühleisen, Susanne. 2002. "Black British Englishes (Languages)." In Donnell 2002, 42–44.
Murray, Patricia. 1999. "Stories Told and Untold: Post-Colonial London in Bernardine Evaristo's Lara." *Kunapipi* 21, no. 2: 38–46.
Myers, Norma. 1996. *Reconstructing the Black Past: Blacks in Britain, 1780–1830*. London: Frank Cass.
Naipaul, V. S. 1963. *Mr. Stone and the Knight's Companion*. London: Four Square, 1966.

———. 1967. *The Mimic Men.* London: Deutsch.
———. 1987. *The Enigma of Arrival: A Novel in Five Sections.* London: Penguin.
Nasta, Susheila. 1995. "Setting Up Home in a City of Words: Sam Selvon's London Novels." In Lee 1995a, 48–68.
———. 2002. *Home Truths: Fictions of the South Asian Diaspora in Britain.* Houndmills: Palgrave.
Nasta, Susheila, ed. 1991. *Motherlands: Black Women's Writing from Africa, the Caribbean and South Asia.* London: Women's Press.
———. 1999. "Taking the Cake: Black Writing in Britain." *Wasafiri* 29: 3–4.
Newland, Courttia. 1997. *The Scholar: A West Side Story.* London: Abacus, 1998.
———, and Kadija Sesay, eds. 2000. *IC3: New Black Writing in Britain.* London: Hamish Hamilton.
Newman, Judie. 1995. *The Ballistic Bard: Postcolonial Fictions.* London: Arnold.
Newton, John. 1788. *Thoughts Upon the African Slave-Trade.* 2d ed. London: J. Buckland & J. Johnson.
Ng, Siu Won, and Jahanara A Malique. 1993. "Asian Women Writers' Collective: Women Who Define Themselves and Who Define Writing." In Glage and Michel 1993, 105–8.
Nichols, Grace. 1983. *i is a long memoried woman.* London: Karnak House.
———. 1984. *The Fat Black Woman's Poems.* London: Virago.
———. 1989. *Lazy Thoughts of a Lazy Woman.* London: Virago.
———. 1990. "The Battle with Language." In *Caribbean Women Writers: Essays from the First International Conference,* edited by Selwyn R. Cudjoe, 283–89. Wellesley, MA: Calaloux.
———. 1994. Personal Interview. May 28.
Niven, Alastair. 1990. "Black British Writing: The Struggle for Recognition." In *Crisis and Creativity in the New Literatures in English,* edited by Geoffrey Davis and Hena Maes-Jelinek, 325–32. Amsterdam: Rodopi.
Nixon, Rob. 1992. *London Calling: V. S. Naipaul, Postcolonial Mandarin.* Oxford: Oxford University Press.
Nowak, Helge. 1998. "Black British Literature—Unity or Diversity?" In Korte and Müller 1998, 71–87.
Nyatetu-Waigwa, Wangari Wa. 1996. *The Liminal Novel: Studies in the Francophone-African Novel as Bildungsroman.* New York: Peter Lang.
Omotoso, Kole. 1971. *The Edifice.* London: Heinemann.
O'Regan, Nadine. 2002. "Seeking Self amid the Feeding Frenzy." *Sunday Business Post Online,* April 14, 2002, http://archives.tcm.ie/businesspost/2002/04/14/story317716.asp (September 3, 2003).
Ormond, Richard. 1999. Letter. *Daily Telegraph,* August 20, 20.
Owusu, Kwesi, ed. 2000. *Black British Culture & Society: A Text Reader.* London: Routledge.
Papastergiadis, Nikos. 1998. *Dialogues in the Diasporas: Essays and Conversations on Cultural Identity.* London: Rivers Oram Press.
Parameswaran, Uma. 1988. *The Perforated Sheet: Essays on Salman Rushdie's Art.* New Delhi: Affiliated East-West Press.
Parry, Benita. 1987. "Problems in Current Theories of Colonial Discourse." *Oxford Literary Review* 9, nos. 1–2: 27–58.
Patterson, Orlando. 1964. *The Children of Sisyphus.* Burnt Mill: Longman, 1994.

Paul, Heike. 1999. *Mapping Migration.* Heidelberg: Winter.
Perera, Shyama. 1999. *Haven't Stopped Dancing Yet.* London: Sceptre.
Pettinger, Alasdair. 1998. *Always Elsewhere: Travels of the Black Atlantic.* London: Cassell.
Philip, Marlene Nourbese. 1989. "Discourse on the Logic of Language." In Nasta 1991, xi–xii.
Phillips, A. A. 1958. "The Cultural Cringe." In *The Australian Tradition: Studies in a Colonial Culture,* 112–17. Melbourne: Lansdowne, 1966.
Phillips, Caryl. 1985. *The Final Passage.* London: Faber.
———. 1986. *A State of Independence.* London: Picador, 1995.
———. 1987. *The European Tribe.* London: Picador, 1993.
———. 1988. Interview with Frank Birbalsingh. In Holst Petersen and Rutherford 1988, 145–51.
———. 1989. *Higher Ground: A Novel in Three Parts.* London: Picador, 1993.
———. 1991. *Cambridge.* London: Picador, 1992.
———. 1994. *Crossing the River.* New York: Knopf.
———. 1997. *The Nature of Blood.* London: Faber.
———. 1999. "Following On: The Legacy of Lamming and Selvon." *Wasafiri* 29: 34–36.
———. 2000. "Mixed and Matched." *Observer,* January 9, Rev. sec., 11.
———. 2001. *A New World Order: Selected Essays.* London: Vintage, 2002.
———. 2003. *A Distant Shore.* London: Vintage, 2004.
Phillips, Caryl, ed. 1997. *Extravagant Strangers: A Literature of Belonging.* London: Faber, 1998.
Phillips, Mike. 1997. *The Dancing Face.* London: HarperCollins.
———, and Trevor Phillips. 1998. Windrush: *The Irresistible Rise of Multi-Racial Britain.* London: HarperCollins.
Pocock, Tom. 1999a. "Was Britain's Empire so Evil?" *Mail on Sunday,* August 29, 55.
———. 1999b. Letter. *Daily Telegraph,* August 18, 19.
Porée, Marc. 1997. *Hanif Kureishi: The Buddha of Suburbia.* Paris: Didier Erudition.
Pouchet, Sandra Paquet. 1982. *The Novels of George Lamming.* London: Heinemann.
Powell, Enoch. 1969. *Freedom & Reality,* edited by John Wood, 281–90. London: Paperfront.
Pratt, Mary Louise. *Imperial Eyes: Studies in Travel Writing and Transculturation.* London: Routledge, 1992.
Prescod, Colin. 1998. "Dealing with Difference beyond Ethnicity." In *Empire Windrush: Fifty Years of Writing about Black Britain,* edited by Onyekachi Wambu, 406–12. London: Gollancz.
Prince, Mary. 1831. *The History of Mary Prince, a West Indian Slave Related by Herself.* Edited by M. Ferguson. London: Pandora, 1987.
Procter, James. 2003. *Dwelling Places: Postwar Black British Writing.* Manchester: Manchester University Press.
Procter, James, ed. 2000. *Writing Black Britain, 1948–1998: An Interdisciplinary Anthology.* Manchester: Manchester University Press.
"Profile [of Hanif Kureishi]." 1988. *Times,* May 10, Rev. sec., 3.
Purves, Libby. 1999. "With No Added Salts." *Sunday Times,* May 11, 20.

Ramchand, Kenneth. 1970. *The West Indian Novel and Its Background*. London: Faber.
———. 1971. Introduction to *Minty Alley*, by C. L. R. James, 5–15. London: New Beacon.
———. 1985. Introduction to *The Lonely Londoners*, by Samuel Selvon, 3–21. London: Longman.
Ramdin, Ron. 1999. *Reimaging Britain: Five Hundred Years of Black and Asian History*. London: Pluto.
Ranasinha, Ruvani. 2002. *Hanif Kureishi*. Plymouth: Northcote.
Randhawa, Ravinder. 1987. *A Wicked Old Woman*. London: Women's Press.
———. 1992. *Hari-Jan*. London: Mantra, 1995.
Redfield, Marc. 1996. *Phantom Formations: Aesthetic Ideology and the Bildungsroman*. Ithaca: Cornell University Press.
Reichl, Susanne. 2002. *Cultures in the Contact Zone: Ethnic Semiosis in Black British Literature*. Trier: WVT Wissenschaftlicher Verlag.
Riemenschneider, Dieter, ed. 1983. *The History and Historiography of Commonwealth Literature*. Tübingen: Gunter Narr.
Riley, Joan. 1985. *The Unbelonging*. London: Women's Press.
Rose, Margaret. 1993. *Parody: Ancient, Modern, and Post-Modern*. Cambridge: Cambridge University Press.
Ross, Leone. 1996. *All the Blood Is Red*. London: Angela Royal.
Rushdie, Salman. 1983. *Shame*. London: Vintage, 1995.
———. 1988. *The Satanic Verses*. New York: Penguin, 1989.
———. 1991. *Imaginary Homelands: Essays and Criticism 1981–1991*. London: Granta, 1992.
———. 1994. *East, West*. London: Cape.
———. 1999. Reading from *The Ground beneath Her Feet*. Conference on London: Post-Colonial City, Architectural Association, London, March 12–13, 1999.
———. 2002. *Step across This Line: Collected Non-Fiction 1992–2002*. London: Cape.
Said, Edward. 1978. *Orientalism: Western Concepts of the Orient*. London: Routledge & Kegan Paul.
———. 1983. *The World, the Text, and the Critic*. Cambridge, MA: Harvard University Press.
———. 1992. Interview by Jennifer Wicke and Michael Sprinker. In *Edward Said: A Critical Reader*, 221–64. Edited by Michael Sprinker. Oxford: Blackwell.
———. 1993. *Culture and Imperialism*. London: Vintage, 1994.
———. 1998. "In Conversation with Neeladri Bhattacharya, Suvir Kaul and Ania Loomba." *Interventions* 1, no. 1: 81–96.
———. 1999. *Out of Place: A Memoir*. London: Granta.
Sammons, Jeffrey L. 1981. "The Mystery of the Missing Bildungsroman." *Genre* 14: 229–46.
Sancho, Ignatius. 1994. *The Letters of Ignatius Sancho*. Edited by Paul Edwards and Polly Rewt. Edinburgh: Edinburgh University Press.
Sandhu, Sukhdev. 2003. *London Calling: How Black and Asian Writers Imagined a City*. London: HarperCollins.
Schäfer, Jürgen. 1981. "Sprache oder Nation: Zum Problem einer englischen Nationalliteratur." In *Commonwealth Literatur*, 12–28. Düsseldorf: August Bagel.

Schäffner, Raimund. 1998. "'Identity Is Not in the Past to Be Found, but in the Future to Be Constructed': History and Identity in Caryl Phillips's Novels." In Korte and Müller 1998, 107–26.

Schoene-Harwood, Berthold. 1999. "Beyond (T)race: *Bildung* and *Proprioception* in Meera Syal's *Anita and Me*." *Journal of Commonwealth Literature* 34, no. 1: 159–68.

Seacole, Mary. 1857. *Wonderful Adventures of Mrs Seacole in Many Lands*. Edited by Ziggi Alexander and Audrey Dewjee. Bristol: Falling Wall Press, 1984.

Searle, Adrian. 1998. "Top Plop." London *Guardian*, April 21, 10.

Segal, Ronald. 1995. *The Black Diaspora*. London: Faber.

Selbmann, Rolf, ed. 1988. Einleitung. *Zur Geschichte des deutschen Bildungsromans*, 1–44. Darmstadt: Wissenschaftliche Buchgesellschaft.

Selvon, Samuel. 1956. *The Lonely Londoners*. Harlow: Longman, 1985.

———. 1957. *Ways of Sunlight*. Harlow: Longman, 1979.

———. 1988. "Finding West Indian Identity in London." In Holst Petersen and Rutherford 1988, 122–25.

Sen, Sudeep. 1995. Foreword. *Wasafiri* 21: 3–4.

Sewell, Tony. 1998. *Keep on Moving*. London: Voice.

Shakespeare, William. 1623. *The Tempest*. Edited by Frank Kermode. London: Methuen, 1958.

Shamsie, Kamila. 2000. *Salt and Saffron*. London: Bloomsbury, 2001.

Sharma, Sanjay, John Hutnyk, and Ashwani Sharma. 1996. Introduction to *Dis-Orienting Rhythms: The Politics of the New Asian Dance Music*, edited by Sharma, Hutnyk and Sharma, 1–11. London: Zed.

Sheikh, Farhana. 1991. *The Red Box*. London: Women's Press.

Shohat, Ella. 1992. "Notes on the 'Post-Colonial.'" *Social Text* 31–32: 99–113.

Shohat, Ella, and Robert Stam. 1994. *Unthinking Eurocentrism: Multiculturalism and the State*. London: Routledge.

Sissay, Lemn, ed. *The Fire People*. Edinburgh: Payback Press, 1998.

Sivanandan, A. "The Struggle for a Radical Black Political Culture: An Interview." In Owusu 2000, 416–24.

Smith, Ali. 2000. "Saga That Goes Straight to the Heart of the Century." *Scotsman* (January 15, 2000).

Smith, Zadie. 1999a. "The Waiter's Wife." *Granta* 67 (Autumn 1999): 127–42.

———. 1999b. "Stuart." *New Yorker*, December 20, 1999 and January 3, 2000, 60–67.

———. 2000. *White Teeth*. London: Hamish Hamilton.

Sollors, Werner. 1986. *Beyond Ethnicity: Consent and Descent in American Culture*. New York: Oxford University Press.

Sollors, Werner, ed. 1989. *The Invention of Ethnicity*. New York: Oxford University Press.

Sommer, Roy. 2001. *Fictions of Migration: Ein Beitrag zur Theorie und Gattungstypologie des zeitgenössischen interkulturellen Romans in Großbritannien*. Trier: WVT Wissenschaftlicher Verlag.

Soyinka, Wole. 1984. "On Barthes and Other Mythologies." In *Black Literature and Literary Theory*, edited by Henry Louis Gates Jr., 27–57. New York: Methuen.

Spillers, Hortense J. 1987. "Mama's Baby, Papa's Maybe: An American Grammar Book." *Diacritics* 17, no. 2: 65–81.

Spivak, Gayatri Chakravorty. 1987. *In Other Worlds: Essays in Cultural Politics*. New York: Routledge, 1988.

———. 1988. "Can the Subaltern Speak?" In *Marxism and the Interpretation of Culture*, edited by Cary Nelson and Lawrence Grossberg, 271–313. Chicago: University of Illinois Press.
———. 1993a. *Outside in the Teaching Machine*. New York: Routledge.
———. 1993b. "Sammy and Rosie Get Laid." In *Outside in the Teaching Machine*, 243–54. New York: Routledge.
———. 1999. *A Critique of Postcolonial Reason: Toward a History of the Vanishing Present*. Cambridge, MA: Harvard University Press.
Srivastava, Atima. 1992. *Transmission*. London: Serpent's Tail.
Stein, Mark. 1995. "The Perception of Landscape and Architecture in V. S. Naipaul's *The Enigma of Arrival* and David Dabydeen's *Disappearance*." *Acolit Sonderheft* 1, edited by Dieter Riemenschneider and Frank Schulze-Engler, 15–29.
———. 1996. "Retrospective Resistance: Homi Bhabha's Mimicry." In Döring et al. 1996, 41–49.
———. 1998a. "The Black British *Bildungsroman* and the Transformation of Britain: Connectedness across Difference." In Korte and Müller 1998, 89–105.
———. 1998b. "Cultures of Hybridity: Reading Black British Literature." *Kunapipi* 20, no. 2: 76–89.
———. 2000a. "Posed Ethnicity and the Postethnic: Hanif Kureishi's Novels." In *English Literatures in International Contexts*, edited by Heinz Antor and Klaus Stierstorfer, 119–39. Heidelberg: C. Winter.
———. 2000b. "Undoing Empire: Work and Leisure in the Gallery of Trade and Empire." *Journal for the Study of British Culture* 7, no. 2: 153–67.
———. 2001. "Black City of Words: London in the Popular Novel." In *Anglistentag 2000 Berlin: Proceedings*, edited by Peter Lucko and Jürgen Schlaeger, 155–65. Trier: Wissenschaftlicher Verlag.
———. 2002. "Globe-Trotting and Geo-Ethnic Entertainments: Thoughts on a Black Artist in a British Museum." Edited by Tobias Döring. *Matatu* 25–26: 125–132.
Stone, Judy S. J. 1994. "Black British Theatre. The Theatre of Exile: Edgar White, Mustapha Matura, Caryl Phillips." In *Theatre*, 161–79. London: Macmillan Caribbean.
Suleri, Sara. 1989. *Meatless Days*. Chicago: University of Chicago Press.
———. 1992. *The Rhetoric of English India*. Chicago: University of Chicago Press.
Sunmonu, Yinka. 2003. *Cherish*. London: Mango.
Swales, Martin. 1978. *The German Bildungsroman from Wieland to Hesse*. Princeton, NJ: Princeton University Press.
Syal, Meera. 1996. *Anita and Me*. London: Flamingo.
Taylor, John Russell. 1998. "Dotting the Eyes." London *Times*, April 22, 31.
Theroux, Paul. 1998. *Sir Vidia's Shadow: A Friendship across Five Continents*. London: Hamish Hamilton.
Thieme, John. 1987. *The Web of Tradition: The Uses of Allusion in V. S. Naipaul's Fiction*. Hertford: Hansib.
———, ed. 1996. *The Arnold Anthology of Post-Colonial Literatures in English*. London: Arnold.
Thomas, Helen. 1999. "Black on White: Textual Spaces in Black Britain." *Wasafiri* 29: 5–7.

Tiffin, Helen. 1987. "Post-Colonial Literatures and Counter-Discourse." *Kunapipi* 9, no. 3: 17–34.
Tompkins, Jane. 1985. *Sensational Designs: The Cultural Work of American Fiction 1790–1860*. New York: Oxford University Press.
Traynor, Joanna. 1997. *Sister Josephine*. London: Bloomsbury.
———. 1998. *Divine*. London: Bloomsbury.
Unsworth, Barry. 1992. *Sacred Hunger*. London: Hamish Hamilton.
Vassanji, M. G. 1989. *The Gunny Sack*. London: Heinemann.
Veit-Wild, Flora. 1993. "'Dances with Bones': Hove's Romanticized Africa." *Research in African Literatures* 24, no. 3: 5–12.
Visram, Rozina. 1986. *Ayars, Lascars, and Princes: The Story of Indians in Britain, 1700–1947*. London: Pluto.
Viswanathan, Gauri. 1989. *Masks of Conquest: Literary Study and British Rule in India*. New York: Columbia University Press.
Walcott, Derek. 1986. *Collected Poems, 1948–1984*. New York: Farrar, Straus & Giroux.
Walmsley, Anne. 1992. *The Caribbean Artists Movement*. London: New Beacon.
Walsh, John. 1999. "Rail Firm Puts Poetry into Locomotion." London *Independent*, July 15, 1.
Walters, Vanessa. 1996. *Rude Girls*. London: Pan.
Wambu, Onyekachi, ed. 1998. *Empire Windrush: Fifty Years of Writing about Black Britain*. London: Gollancz.
Warner, Marina. 1992. *Indigo*. London: Vintage, 1993.
Waters, Chris. 1997. "'Dark Strangers' in Our Midst: Discourses of Race and Nation in Britain, 1947–1963." *Journal of British Studies* 36: 207–38.
Webb, Barbara J. 1992. *Myth and History in Caribbean Fiction: Alejo Carpentier, Wilson Harris, Edouard Glissant*. Amherst: University of Massachusetts Press.
Weber, Donald. 1997. "'No Secrets Were Safe from Me': Situating Hanif Kureishi." *Massachusetts Review* 38: 119–35.
Welsh, Sarah Lawson. 1997. "(Un)belonging Citizens, Unmapped Territory: Black Immigration and British Identity in the Post-1945 Period." In *Not on Any Map: Essays on Postcoloniality and Cultural Nationalism*, edited by Stuart Murray, 43–66. Exeter: University of Exeter Press.
West, Russ. 2002. "Middle Passages: Negotiating Black Identities in Contemporary British Fiction: Dabydeen's *The Intended*." *Arbeiten aus Anglistik und Amerikanistik* 50, no. 2: 166–78.
Williams, Raymond. 1973. *The Country and the City*. London: Hogarth Press, 1985.
———. 1976. *Keywords: A Vocabulary of Culture and Society*. Rev. ed. New York: Oxford University Press, 1985.
Wilson, Colin. 1956. *The Outsider*. London: Gollancz, 1990.
Wisker, Gina. 1993. *Black Women's Writing*. Houndmills: Macmillan.
Witte, W. 1979. "Alien Corn: The 'Bildungsroman': Not for Export?" *German Life and Letters* 33: 87–96.
Woodcock, Bruce. 1999. "'I'll Show You Something to Make You Change Your Mind': Post-Colonial Translations of the Streets of London." *Kunapipi* 21, no. 2: 57–65.
Woolf, Michael. "Negotiating the Self: Jewish Fiction in Britain since 1945." In Lee 1995a, 124–41.

Wylie, Dan. 1991. "Language Thieves: English-Language Strategies in Two Zimbabwean Novellas." *English in Africa* 18, no. 2: 39–62.
Wynne-Davies, Marion. 1995. *The Bloomsbury Dictionary of English Literature*. Rev. ed. London: Bloomsbury, 1997.
Young, Robert. 1990. *White Mythologies: Writing History and the West*. London: Routledge.
———. 1995. *Colonial Desire: Hybridity in Theory, Culture and Race*. London: Routledge.

Index

Abolitionist movement, 145, 148, 188, 195, 216n. 12
Abrams, M. H., 22, 23
Achebe, Chinua, 165, 166, 211n. 43
Adair, Gilbert, 136, 138
Adebayo, Diran, xv, 17, 100, 101–2, 104, 185; *Some Kind of Black,* 18–20, 29, 38–40, 44, 100, 204n. 34, 207n. 11
Adrus, Said, 108, 109, 142
affiliation, xv, 16, 25, 39, 65, 80, 93, 115–16, 121–22, 125–29, 142; defined, 6, 112–13
Agard, John, 58, 106, 107, 185, 194
Agbabi, Patience, 17
age, 6, 40, 98, 102, 109, 128, 131, 132, 134, 204n. 18; coming of, xiii, xvi, 36, 98
agency, xiii, 88, 94, 167, 171; textual, xiii, 36, 169
Ahmad, Aijaz, 207n. 13
Ahmad, Ali Nobil, 179, 215n. 8
Ahmad, Rukhsana, 15
Ahmed, Bashir, 211n. 1
Ahuja, Anjana, 206n. 6
Ali, Monica, 14, 170, 175, 180, 182
alienation, 25, 59, 65, 85, 93, 105, 106, 125, 158, 160, 205n. 41
Anti-Slavery Society, 195
Appadurai, Arjun, 178
appropriation, 27, 43, 104, 138
Araeen, Rasheed, 213n. 6
arranged marriage, 119, 120, 186
Ashcroft, Bill, 164, 201n. 5, 214nn. 20–21
Asian Women Writers' Collective, 15, 195, 204n. 22

Asian Women Writers' Workshop. *See* Asian Women Writers' Collective
Atwood, Margaret, 7
autobiography, 4, 5, 26, 27–28, 32, 132, 141, 188, 192, 195, 196

Back, Les, 19, 211n. 49, 216n. 7
Bakhtin, Mikhail, 215n. 26
Baldick, Chris, 22
Balibar, Etienne, 36
Ball, John Clement, 216n. 4
Bandele, Biyi, 186
Barthes, Roland, 163, 215n. 26
Baucom, Ian, 212n. 9
Benham, Mark, 213n. 5
Bhabha, Homi, 16, 53, 77, 149–50, 179
Bharucha, Nilufer E., 216n. 4
Bhatnagar, O. P., 204n. 26
Bidisha, 98, 135, 204n. 29, 205n. 40, 206n. 7
bildungsroman, xiii, 54, 67, 58, 150; African American, 28; anti-bildungsroman, 117, 211n. 5; and autobiography, 27, 28; bildungs-literature, 109; diasporic bildungsroman, xvii, 92, 94, 105, 171; dual, 26, 206n. 9; female, 26, 27, 204n. 35; multiple, 47, 150, 206n. 9. *See also* novel of transformation
Black Atlantic, xvi, 3, 85, 86, 211
black British literature, xii–xiv, xv–xvi, 7–9, 10–12, 14–16, 17–18, 20, 27; and landscape, 33, 45, 97; as national literature, 9–10; and post-colonial literature, xv–xvi, 9–10, 111, 115, 116,

237

118, 127, 131, 135, 144, 153, 156, 160–64, 171–75
black British, 8, 10–13, 14–16, 21–22, 171–75, 178–81, 202n. 6. *See also* British Asian
Blake, Ann, 200
Braithwaite, E. R., 31, 101
Brennan, Timothy, 199, 202n. 1, 212n. 9, 216n. 3
Briggs, Asa, 206n. 6
British Asian, xiv, xv, xvi, 8, 14, 15, 19, 20, 31, 58, 110, 116–22, 141, 171–75, 178–81, 202n. 6; characters in literature, 37, 40, 52, 119, 124, 131, 191; characters in films, 138–40. *See also* black British
Bromley, Roger, 200
Brontë, Charlotte, 23, 66
Brooke, Rupert, 99, 100
Brown, Stewart, 28, 81
Bryce, Jane, 199, 216n. 2
Brydon, Diana, 162
Buckley, Jerome Hamilton, 24, 25, 205nn. 38, 41
burden of representation, 30, 53, 105
Butcher, Maggie, 27, 199, 221
Byatt, A[ntonia] S., xvi

Caliban, 156, 158, 168
campus novel, 123
Caribbean Artists Movement (CAM), 12
Caribbean Voices (BBC), 92
Carr, Rocky, 204n. 34
Castles, Stephen, 207n. 3
Chaudhuri, Amit, 43, 44, 186, 206n. 4
Chrisman, Laura, 212n. 9
class, xiv, 10, 17, 37, 46, 47, 75, 98, 102, 112, 113, 115, 122, 125, 128, 129, 131, 133–35, 138, 160, 179, 204n. 18
Clifford, James, 65, 128
colonial subject, 32, 149, 168
colonialism, 42, 72, 115, 127, 201n. 5, 208n. 9; neo-, 110, 201n. 5
colonies, xii, xiii, xiv, 5, 43, 78, 83, 92, 93, 111, 144–45, 152, 160, 195, 203n. 8, 204n. 19, 213n. 2
Conrad, Joseph, 91, 149, 164, 165, 166, 214n. 22

consciousness, 54, 81, 93, 94, 104–5, 139, 142; double, 3, 97, 126; self-consciousness, 34, 83, 94; third-person, 50
contact zone, xv, 78, 133, 200
Corr, Christopher, 177, 178–90, 183
Couper, Alastair, 213n. 5
cultural change, xii, xvii, 13, 20, 21, 23, 42, 54, 64, 122
cultural diversity, xiii, 13, 14, 20, 38, 64, 106, 179, 183
cultural hybridity, xii, xv, 3, 20, 52, 59, 64, 112, 179, 204
cultural work, 88, 146, 147, 213n. 4

D'Aguiar, Fred, 61, 100; "Against Black British Literature," 10–12, 204n. 18
Dabydeen, David, 6, 100, 171, 187; *Disappearance*, 43, 153, 155, 157, 169; *A Harlot's Progress*, 187, 206n. 3; *The Intended*, xvii, 47, 149, 153–69, 171; interview with W. Binder, 151; "On Not Being Milton," 10–11; *A Reader's Guide*, 8, 199, 201n. 4; *Slave Song*, 153, 168, 208n. 7; *Turner*, 187, 213n. 13
Dahl, Mary Karen, 199, 216n. 5
Darko, Kari, 199, 216n. 2
Dawes, Kwame, 102, 103, 104, 105, 106, 213nn. 10–11, 13
defamiliarization, 119, 139
Dennis, Ferdinand, 199
Desai, Anita, 34
Desani, G. V., 171, 187
Dhondy, Farrukh, 44, 188
diaspora, 208n. 12; condition, 58, 63, 66, 94–95, 105; experience, 65, 95–96; and generation, 58, 63, 95, 171; and home, 62–63; identity, 64; Jewish, xi, 3, 42; literature, xvii, 58, 96; and memory, 62–67, 95; and return, 57–58, 63; South Asian, 15, 206n. 4; West Indian, 19; writer, 96. *See also* diasporization
diasporization, 11, 95, 96
Dickens, Charles, 23, 43, 53
Dilthey, Wilhelm, 23, 205n. 36
Dinkel, Ernest, 176, 178, 179
discrimination, 11, 52

displacement, xii, 59, 60, 62, 63, 106, 190; dislocation, 69, 85
Dodd, Philip, 114, 139
Donnell, Alison J., 199, 202n. 6
Döring, Tobias, 111, 201n. 5, 211n. 2, 214n. 17, 216n. 4
double consciousness. *See* consciousness
Douglass, Frederick, 27, 27
Dyer, Richard, 109–10, 121

Easton, Alison, 216n. 8
Edwards, Paul, 199
Emecheta, Buchi, 4, 16
Empire Windrush. *See* Windrush
Empire, British, xiv, 31, 42, 72, 73, 74, 79, 89, 98, 101, 114, 141, 144–47, 152, 154, 161, 169, 172, 174, 179; Empire Christmas Pudding, 143–45; Empire Marketing Board, 143–44, 213n. 2; "pornography of empire," 152, 154; "Visit the Empire" (Dinkel), 176, 178, 179. *See also* Windrush
Englishness, 13, 17, 32, 79, 83, 86, 100, 125, 133, 142, 157–58, 161, 172–73, 206n. 6, 209n. 20, 212n. 9
Equiano, Olaudah, xiii, 4, 22, 27, 28, 29, 101, 141, 171, 188, 189, 192, 203n. 11, 208n. 10, 216n. 12
essentialism, 8, 10, 14, 142
ethnicity, xvii, 13, 17, 39, 40, 54, 71, 107, 111–13, 114, 115, 116, 118, 121, 122, 125, 126, 128, 131, 134–35, 137–39, 141–42, 171, 174, 180, 183, 191. *See also* postethnic; posed ethnic
Evaristo, Bernardine, 100, 104, 106, 141; *The Emperor's Babe*, 189; *Lara*, 58, 80–96, 98, 101, 105, 172
exile, 12, 32, 34, 63, 93, 97, 98, 100, 107, 210n. 39

Fanon, Frantz, 50, 70, 80, 81, 168, 207n. 10
Feng, Pin-Chia, 204n. 35
Foucault, Michel, vii
Fryer, Peter, 4, 199, 201n. 2, 202n. 2, 203n. 8
Fuderer, Laura Sue, 204n. 35
fundamentalism, 16, 124, 127

Gang Starr, 7
Gee, Maggie, 174, 189
gender, 9, 17, 27, 40, 46, 59, 112, 128, 129, 132, 134, 157, 194, 195, 206n. 7
generation, xvii, 96–98, 171
George, Rosemary Marangoly, 62
Gerzina, Gretchen, 199
Ghose, Sudhindra Nath, 6, 31
Gibbons, Fiachra, 215nn. 2, 6
Gikandi, Simon, 151, 157, 200, 212n. 9
Gilroy, Beryl, 4, 6, 31, 101, 102
Gilroy, Paul, xvi, 3, 6, 7, 20, 63, 69, 179, 210n. 32
globalization, 21, 33
Goethe, Johann Wolfgang von, 23, 24, 28
Gohrisch, Jana, 216n. 3
Golding, William, 66
Goodness Gracious Me, 14, 198
Grass, Günter, 117
Grewal, Shabnam, 199, 203n. 17, 216n. 2
Griffiths, Gareth, 164, 214nn. 20–21
Guha, Ranajit, 210n. 33
Gupta, Rahila, 15
Guptara, Prahbu, xiv, 8, 29, 199
Gurnah, Abdulrazak, 4, 41–42, 189–90, 206n. 5

Hall, Stuart, xv, 11–13, 21, 49–50, 64, 145–46, 179
Hannerz, Ulf, 16, 204nn. 25–26
Harris, Wilson, 4, 90, 91, 152, 165, 171
Hashmi, Alamgir, 211n. 6
Head, Dominic, 180
Heath, Roy, 31
Hiro, Dilip, 31
historiography, 42, 60, 89, 143, 147, 210
Hollinger, David, 109, 112, 113
home, xii, 18, 21, 24, 32, 41, 58, 62–63, 69, 82, 84–87, 100
homophony, 173, 174, 183
hooks, bell, 211n. 6
Hosain, Attia, 4, 31,
Huggan, Graham, 111, 179, 182, 183, 212n. 19
Hughes, Peter, 216n. 3
Hunt, Marsha, 15
Hussein, Aamer, 216n. 4
Hutcheon, Linda, 214n. 21

Hutnyk, John, 14, 18, 216n. 7

identity, xii, 11, 13, 14, 17, 19, 21, 28, 30, 32–33, 40, 46, 52, 64–65, 67, 84, 86, 126, 151, 170, 180, 203n. 17, 204n. 24, 207n. 4, 210n. 37
Ilona, Anthony, 216n. 4
Immigration Act (1971), 5
Immigration. *See* migration
individualism, 124, 124, 129, 130, 212nn. 12–13
Innes, C. Lyn, xiv, 104, 120, 174, 200, 202n. 6, 202n. 2 (ch. 1)
intergenerational conflict, xvii, 29, 46, 58, 66, 96, 106, 171, 205n. 42
interpellation, 49, 58
intertextuality, xv, xvii, 7, 96, 127, 143, 156, 162, 164, 169, 214n. 17, 215n. 26. *See also* rewriting and writing back

Jacobs, Jürgen, 26
Jaggi, Maya, 180, 181, 204n. 31, 209n. 20, 215n. 9
Jamal, Mahmood, 211n. 6
James, C. L. R., 31, 202n. 7
James, Lawrence, 146, 147, 213n. 5
Jameson, Fredric, 53, 159, 166, 207n. 13
JanMohamed, Abdul R., 12, 118
Johnson, Joseph, 102–4, 106, 211n. 48
Journal of Commonwealth Literature (JCL), 200
Jusdanis, Gregory, 204n. 26

Kaleta, Kenneth C., 130, 216n. 3
Kapoor, Anish, 14, 109, 110
Kay, Jackie, 190
Kellaway, Kate, 15
Khan, Naseem, 199
Krause, Markus, 26
Kristeva, Julia, 215n. 26
The Kumars at No. 42, 14, 198
Kunapipi, 199, 200
Kunzru, Hari, 14, 170, 175, 180, 182, 190, 215nn. 5–6
Kureishi, Hanif, xv, 8, 100, 114, 137, 141, 173, 191, 199; *The Black Album*, 25, 26, 115, 116, 123–30, 131; *The Body*, 131, 212n. 14; *The Buddha of Suburbia* (novel), 47, 114, 116–21, 129, 135, 142, 163; *The Buddha of Suburbia* (TV), 138–39; *Gabriel's Gift*, 131; *Intimacy*, 116, 130–35, 137, 138, 204n. 29, 212n. 17; *London Kills Me*, 109, 136–42, 211n. 6; *Love in a Blue Time*, 135, 204n. 29, 211n. 7, 212nn. 7, 10, 12; *Midnight All Day*, 135; *My Beautiful Laundrette*, 115, 139; *My Son the Fanatic*, 124, 212n. 10

Lamming, George, 99, 100, 101, 191, 199, 210n. 39, 211n. 45, 216n. 3
Lane, Harriet, 181, 215n. 5, 216n. 9
Lane, Richard J., 200
Lawrence, Stephen, 203n. 15, 209n. 14
Lazarus, Neil, 207n. 13
Ledent, Bénédicte, 216n. 3
LeSeur, Geta, 27, 28, 29, 204n. 35
Levy, Andrea, 17, 45, 192; *Every Light*, 30, 45, 47, 171; *Fruit of the Lemon*, 58, 67, 68–80, 93–95, 98, 100; *Never Far*, 79, 192; *Small Island*, 192
Lima, Maria Helena, 54
Literary Review, 199
Lloyd, David, 12, 118
location, 10, 39, 59, 85, 168; of belonging, 63, 69, 75, 95; of residence, 63, 69, 95. *See also* displacement
logovorous reading, 156–58, 169, 171; defined, 156, 213n. 14

Macaulay, Thomas Babington, 210n. 41
Macherey, Pierre, 36
MacInnes, Colin, 174
Mahomet, Sake Dean, 29
Mahoney, D. F., 26
Malique, Jahanara A., 204n. 23
Mamdani, Mahmood, 31
Markandaya, Kamala, xiii, 4, 31
Marke, Ernest, 5
Martin, S. I., 103, 171, 192
Martini, Fritz, 205n. 36
McIntyre, Karen, 159
McLeod, John, 199
McWatt, Mark, 153, 214n. 24
memory, 18, 61, 66, 76, 81, 88–89, 91, 152; collective, 57, 58, 62–65, 67, 88, 91
Mercer, Kobena, 30, 53, 199, 213n. 6

Merritt, Stephanie, 215n. 5
Michel, Martina, 216n. 4
migrant writers, 6, 97, 202nn. 7, 4 (ch. 1)
migration, xi–xiv, 4–5, 48, 59–60, 82, 97–98, 112, 131, 203n. 9, 204n. 19, 206n. 4, 208n. 11, 210n. 39
Mihailovich-Dickman, Vera, 207n. 1
Miles, David H., 57, 210
Miller, Mark J., 207n. 3
Minden, Michael R., 204n. 35
Mirza, Heide Safia, vii, 202n. 6
Moore-Gilbert, Bart, 204n. 24, 216n. 3
Moretti, Franco, 204n. 35
Morgan, Ellen, 26, 27
Morrison, Toni, 204n. 35, 206n. 3, 208n. 7, 222
Moving Worlds, 200
multiculturalism, xii, xiv, 81, 109–13, 120, 139, 146, 179, 180, 183
Myers, Norma, 199

Nagra, Parminder, 14
Naipaul, V. S., xiii, xiv, 4, 6, 53, 102, 141, 171, 192–93, 199, 201n. 3, 212n. 19, 214n. 17, 216n. 3; *The Enigma of Arrival*, 32–35, 45, 141, 209n. 26; *The Mimic Men*, 193, 205n. 44; *Mr. Stone and the Knight's Companion*, 135
Nasta, Susheila, 120, 199, 200, 202n. 6
National Maritime Museum (NMM Greenwich), 143–48, 213n. 3
Nationality Act (1948), 5, 203n. 8
new ethnicities, 11, 12, 13
New Literatures in English, ix, 9
Newland, Courttia, xiv, 104, 193, 199
Newton, John, 148, 167, 168
Ng, Siu Won, 204n. 23
Nichols, Grace, 102, 185, 193; "epilogue," 58–62; 208n. 6; *The Fat Black Woman's Poems*, 208n. 6; *i is a long memoried woman*, 58, 68, 208n. 9; *Lazy Thoughts of a Lazy Woman*, 211n. 44
Niven, Alastair, 9, 10, 12, 175, 215n. 3
normalization, 49, 50, 51, 53, 216n. 13
novel of transformation, xiii, xvii, 3, 22–26, 27, 29–31, 96, 153, 171–73; diasporic, xvii, 92–96, 105; postethnic, 114–42; precursors to, 29, 31–35;
 and performative functions, 36–54, 65, 171, 173. *See also* bildungsroman
Nowak, Helge, 216n. 4
Nyatetu-Waigwa, Wangari Wa, 204n. 35

O'Regan, Nadine, 215nn. 1, 5
Ofili, Chris, 109–10, 121, 215n. 8
Okri, Ben, 100, 194
organicism, 5, 6, 16, 60, 62, 68, 75, 78, 91
othering, 50–51, 70
outsider within, xii–xiii, 36, 121, 133, 141
Owusu, Kwesi, 199, 202n. 6

Papastergiadis, Nikos, 62
Parameswaran, Uma, 216n. 3
parody, xvii, 38, 115, 119, 156, 164, 188
Parry, Benita, 201n. 5, 208n. 10, 214nn. 17, 24
passing, 47, 135, 141, 192, 193, 206nn. 4, 8
pastoral, 44, 78, 79
Patterson, Orlando, 209n. 21
people of color, 8. *See also* black British
performative function, xiii, xvi, 36, 42, 53, 65, 171, 173
Pettinger, Alasdair, 86, 207n. 2
phenotype, 11, 12, 47, 52, 154, 157, 210n. 29
Philip, Marlene Nourbese, 208n. 5
Phillips, Caryl, 58, 102, 105, 174, 193, 194, 200; *Cambridge*, 206n. 3; *Crossing the River*, 66–67, 90; "Following On," 96–98, 100; *The Nature of Blood*, 206n. 3
Phillips, Mike, 101, 202n. 3, 203n. 7
Phillips, Trevor, 202n. 3, 203n. 7
picaresque novel, 26, 28, 57, 94, 210n. 36
Pocock, Tom, 213n. 5
polyphony, 171, 173, 174, 183
Porée, Marc, 211n. 5, 212n. 13
pornography, 109, 152, 153, 154
posed-ethnic, 115, 116, 122, 142
post-colonial: Britain, 43, 65; criticism, xvii, 153, 160, 162, 163; literature, xv, xvi, 9, 10, 16, 53, 57, 111, 118, 131, 174, 182, 201n. 5; subject, 89; writing, 54, 111, 115, 120, 135, 144, 160–64, 165, 167, 169, 173, 175, 207n. 1. *See also* colonialism

postethnicity, 17, 112–13, 109; postethnic literature, 112–13, 109, 115, 116, 122, 125–29, 131, 134–40, 142, 171
Pouchet, Sandra Paquet, 216n. 3
Powell, Enoch, 8, 203n. 13
Pratt, Mary Louise, xv
Prince, Mary, 4, 29, 60, 123, 195
Procter, James, xiv, 170, 199, 200, 202n. 6, 203n. 16
public sphere, 30, 171, 178
Purves, Libby, 213n. 5

racism: critique of, 82, 105, 165; experience of, 12, 44, 70, 83–86, 157, 160; internalized, 70, 83, 125; institutional, 209; representation of, xii, 40, 44–45, 52–53, 67, 83, 93, 125, 165, 206n. 5; in society, xii, 3, 11–12
Rahila Gupta, 15
Ramchand, Kenneth, 31, 202n. 7
Ramdin, Ron, 199, 201n. 2
Ranasinha, Ruvani, 212nn. 12, 17, 216n. 3
Randhawa, Ravinder, 100, 119, 120, 195, 204n. 22
readership, xiv, 38, 102, 111, 118, 120–121, 142, 173, 207n. 11
readymades, 109, 110
Redfield, Marc, 23, 205n. 37
region, 9, 16, 128, 204n. 18, 206n. 7, 210n. 41
Reichl, Susanne, 133, 200, 212n. 15, 216n. 11
religion, xii, 54, 115, 128, 129
rewriting, 22, 28, 43, 45, 152, 156, 163, 164–66, 169, 171, 206n. 3. *See also* intertextuality and writing back
Rhys, Jean, 5
Riemenschneider, Dieter, 9
Riley, Joan, 195, 204n. 24, 216n. 3
Rose, Margaret, 214n. 21
Rushdie, Salman, xiv, 171, 172, 174, 175, 181–82, 188, 196, 199, 200, 201n. 3; *East, West*, 44, 178; *Imaginary Homelands*, 63, 214n. 23; *Midnight's Children*, 201n. 3, 212n. 8; *The Satanic Verses*, 44, 172; *Satanic Verses* affair, 123–24, 212nn. 8–9; *Shame*, 71, 85

Said, Edward, 6–7, 165
Sammons, Jeffrey L., 205nn. 37, 39
Sancho, Ignatius, 4, 29, 199, 203n. 11, 208n. 10
Sandhu, Sukhdev, 44, 200, 202nn. 6, 2 (ch. 1)
Savage, Jon, 191
Schoene-Harwood, Berthold, 52, 211n. 5
Seacole, Mary, 4, 29, 60, 196
Searle, Adrian, 110
Second Generation, 14
Selbmann, Rolf, 26, 205n. 36
Selvon, Samuel, 6, 16, 17, 31, 43, 44, 49, 97, 102, 197, 203n. 10; *The Lonely Londoners*, 31–34, 35, 48–49; "My Girl and the City," 22; *Ways of Sunlight*, 44
Sesay, Kadija xiv, 104, 199
Sewell, Tony, 202n. 3
sexuality, 39, 84, 123, 128, 130, 157, 191, 206n. 5, 211n. 3, 213n. 15, 214n. 22; homosexuality, 142, 207n. 11, 211n. 6; sex, 10, 204n. 18
Shakespeare, William, 164
Shamsie, Kamila, 44
Sharma, Ashwani, 14, 18, 216n. 7
Sharma, Sanjay, 14, 18, 216n. 7
Shohat, Ella, 201n. 5
Sivanandan, A., 4, 197, 203n. 17
slavery, 59, 61, 66, 72, 79, 80, 86, 87, 90, 92, 93, 145, 193, 195, 203n. 11, 208n. 9; slave trade, 90, 145, 148, 154, 194, 216n. 12
Smith, Ali., 181
Smith, Zadie, xi, xiv, xvii, 141, 170, 175, 180–83, 197–98, 215nn. 4, 5–6, 216n. 10
social mobility, 37, 47, 77, 113
sociolect, 46, 47, 74, 118, 160, 173
Sollors, Werner, 189
Sommer, Roy, 200
Soyinka, Wole, 4, 211n. 43
Spillers, Hortense J., 207n. 4
Spivak, Gayatri Chakravorty, 62, 201n. 5, 204n. 27, 208n. 10, 210n. 33, 216n. 6
Srivastava, Atima, 52, 67, 98, 198, 204n. 34, 206n. 7
Stone, Judy S. J., 216n. 5
stop and search, 82

Suleri, Sara, xvii, 116, 210n. 41
Sunmonu, Yinka, 212n. 11
Syal, Meera, xiv, 14, 25, 37, 38, 40, 46, 50, 51, 52, 69, 85, 99, 100, 171, 180, 198, 204n. 34, 211n. 5
syncretism, xv, 52, 112

testimonio, 26, 28, 53
Theroux, Paul, 141
Thieme, John, 16, 216n. 3
Third Text, 200
Thomas, Helen, 28, 208n. 10
Tiffin, Helen, 59, 164, 214nn. 20–21
Tompkins, Jane, 213n. 4
transracial adoption, 125, 212n. 11
Traynor, Joanna, 7, 210n. 30
Turner Prize, 109, 110

universalism, 10, 59, 107, 149, 160
Unsworth, Barry, 174

Vassa, Gustavus. *See* Olaudah Equiano
Vassanji, M. G., 73
Veit-Wild, Flora, 111
Visram, Rozina, 199
Viswanathan, Gauri, 211n. 41
voice, xvii, 30, 31, 81, 89, 135, 150, 160, 163, 167, 169, 171–74, 182, 183

Walcott, Derek, 10, 57, 88, 90, 203n. 14, 211n. 43

Walmsley, Anne, 12
Walsh, John, 106
Wambu, Onyekachi, 202n. 3, 207n. 2
Warner, Marina, 174
Wasafiri, 97, 102, 198, 202n. 6
Webb, Barbara J., 91
Wieland, Christoph Martin, 23
Williams, Raymond, 78
Wilson-Tagoe, Nana, 8, 199, 201n. 4
Wilson-Tagoe, Nana, *A Reader's Guide*, 8, 199, 201n. 4
Windrush (SS *Empire Windrush*), 4–5, 7, 48, 101, 106, 185, 192, 202n. 5; fiftieth anniversary, 101, 106, 185, 202n. 3; generation, 48, 49; writers, 6, 7, 17, 22, 32, 203n. 4
Winterson, Jeanette, 7
Wisker, Gina, 199, 216n. 2
Witte, W., 24
Wolfson Gallery of Trade and Empire, 144–47, 213n. 3
Woolf, Virginia, 7
writing back, 164, 214n. 23. *see also* intertextuality and rewriting
Wylie, Dan, 111
Wynne-Davies, Marion, 22

Young, Robert, 203n. 17

www.ingramcontent.com/pod-product-compliance
Lightning Source LLC
Chambersburg PA
CBHW020122240426
43673CB00038B/562